History Of Scandinavia: From The Early Times Of The Northmen And Vikings To The Present Day... - Primary Source Edition

Paul Christian Sinding

Nabu Public Domain Reprints:

You are holding a reproduction of an original work published before 1923 that is in the public domain in the United States of America, and possibly other countries. You may freely copy and distribute this work as no entity (individual or corporate) has a copyright on the body of the work. This book may contain prior copyright references, and library stamps (as most of these works were scanned from library copies). These have been scanned and retained as part of the historical artifact.

This book may have occasional imperfections such as missing or blurred pages, poor pictures, errant marks, etc. that were either part of the original artifact, or were introduced by the scanning process. We believe this work is culturally important, and despite the imperfections, have elected to bring it back into print as part of our continuing commitment to the preservation of printed works worldwide. We appreciate your understanding of the imperfections in the preservation process, and hope you enjoy this valuable book.

Hon:
 Charles Sumner,
the scholar and the statesman
with the deepest esteem
                    of the Author.

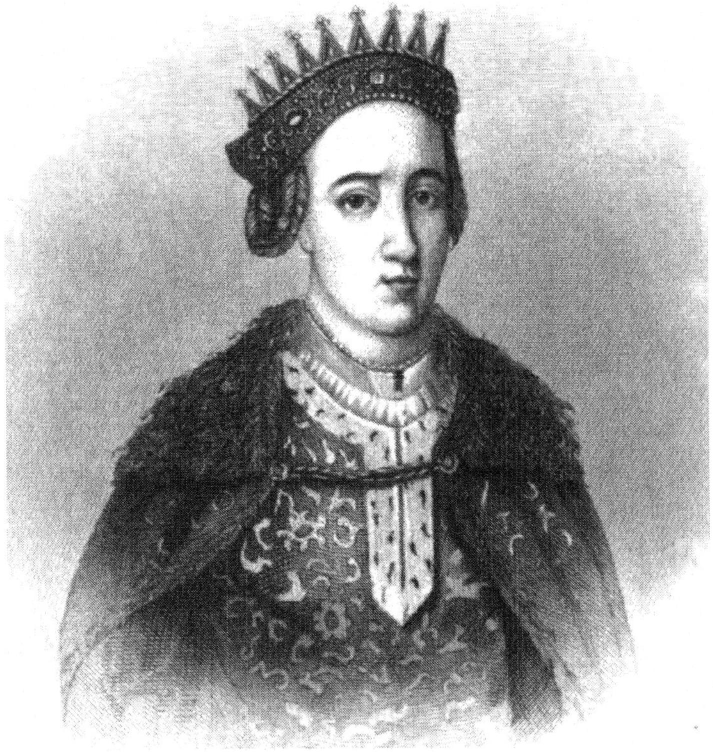

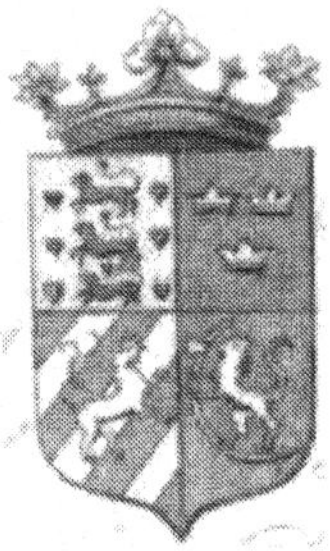

HISTORY OF SCANDINAVIA,

from the Early Times

OF THE

NORTHMEN AND VIKINGS

TO THE PRESENT DAY.

BY PROFESSOR PAUL C. SINDING, OF COPENHAGEN.

Professor of the Scandinavian Languages and Literature

IN THE UNIVERSITY OF THE CITY OF NEW YORK.

Non forte ac temere humana negotia aguntur atque volvuntur.—CURTIUS.

FOURTH EDITION.

PHILADELPHIA:
PUBLISHED BY E. H. BUTLER & CO.
1860.

Entered according to Act of Congress, in the year 1858,

BY PROFESSOR PAUL C. SINDING,

In the Clerk's Office of the District Court of the United States, for the Southern District of New-York

Philadelphia:
C. SHERMAN & SON, PRINTERS.

TO

JAMES LENOX, ESQ.,

OF THE CITY OF NEW-YORK,

The Man of Letters,

THE CHRISTIAN GENTLEMAN,

AND

THE STRANGER'S FRIEND,

THIS VOLUME IS

RESPECTFULLY INSCRIBED,

BY THE AUTHOR

PREFACE.

Although soon after my arrival in the city of New-York, about two years ago, learning by experience, what already long had been known to me, the great attention the enlightened population of the United States pay to science and the arts, and that they admit that unquestionable truth, that the very best blessings are the intellectual, I was, however, soon aware, that Scandinavian affairs were too little known in this country. Induced by that ardent patriotism peculiar to the Norsemen, I immediately resolved, as far as it lay in my power, to throw some light upon this, here, almost *terra incognita*, and compose a brief History of Scandinavia, which once was the arbiter of the European system, and by which America, in reality, had been discovered as much as upwards of five centuries before Columbus reached St. Salvador or Guanahany; without therefore saying that the few traditions about the Western hemisphere, very likely existing in the time of Columbus, have eclipsed that splendor which never will cease to invest the name of this unexampled discoverer.

The value of history being too generally appreciated to require any comment, I submit, to the forbearing criticism of the American public, this my essay of making the Scandinavian countries, especially Denmark, my fatherland, better known in the United States than before has been the case. Notwithstanding this composition has been a "labor of love," it has, on account of the want of sufficient literary sources, and of a thorough familiarity with the English language, for the stiffness of which I have to ask a kind forbearance, by no means been a short and facile undertaking, but has occupied my whole days and evenings for a long space of time. Nevertheless, should the present work, which I only offer as an introduction, be found calculated to promote even a little interest here for the valuable history of the North, my desire and purposes will be fully realized, and the great difficulties under which I have labored, richly rewarded.

May the Great Ruler of the Universe, who has borne me in safety across the ocean, abundantly pour blessings down upon each country that loves Him and the power of the atoning blood of His son; and allow me to express this wish especially for the kingdom of Denmark, where I have learned to prize knowledge above rubies, and left dear remembrances, never to be forgotten.

THE AUTHOR.

PROF. PAUL C. SINDING.

My Dear Sir:

The Scandinavian peninsulas—one hanging down from the mysterious North, the other jutting forth from the central mass of civilized Europe, to meet its comrade—are emblematic (in their geographical position) of the twofold *historic* interest with which they are clothed. While the legendary period of other peoples occupies a place subordinate to their clearer history, Scandinavia calls up before us, with equal power, the mist-robed Odin and the mail-clad Vasa. The strange adventures amid Northern seas, in a primitive age, are as prominent as the leadership of European politics in an age of remarkable light. We oddly mingle the old and the new, the dim and the bright, when we turn to Scandinavia, as we do with no other land. This double character naturally lends peculiar attraction to its history. Yet, with all this attraction, the history of no part of Europe is less familiar to the general mind; probably because the Scandinavian countries lie somewhat off from the world's great highways, and participate but moderately in the world's chief commerce. This should not be. The ignorance is a fault, especially among us of English descent, whose ancestral history is so intimately and variously associated with that of Denmark, Sweden, and Norway. The Norsemen have left the memorials of their habitation on the coasts and islands of Scotland, where Runic inscriptions tell the story of their prowess, while through much of England the familiar names of towns and hamlets are purely Norse. These are the fruits of the wild adventures of the Vikings. A Danish dynasty once ruled our fatherland, and the Conqueror who founded the present succession of British monarchs, was himself of Scandinavian blood, transplanted to a more southern clime. The stalwart men, who could venture upon unknown, cold, and stormy seas, in their small barks, on lengthy voyages, until, passing the new-found shores of Iceland, they landed among the green leaves of the Viinland coast, deserve to be known and saluted by every succeeding age.

And their posterity, still maintaining the best characteristics of the fathers, invite our regard and claim our encomiums. The names of Tegner, Hans Andersen, Fredericka Bremer, in literature; of Clausen, Madvig, and Rafn, in theological, philological, and archæological research; of Thorvaldsen in art, and of Ole Bull and Jenny Lind in music, are as household words in our American homes. Our merited regard for these well known worthies of our own day, must render keener our appetite for Scandinavian knowledge. This appetite amounts to a necessity, when we mark, that our ancestral history and mythology, and our composite philology, must be elucidated by the light of these chronicles and languages of the Norsemen.

It is, therefore, full time that our Universities should have their chairs of Scandinavian literature, as a needful part of the apparatus for a thorough English education, to render more complete the examination of the roots of our speech and race. While this want is felt, we may gladly hail any contribution to American literature, which tends to open this interesting field of research. In your volume, my dear sir, I recognize such a pioneer, and rejoice to give it welcome. In it may many laggards in this lore find an introduction to the old romantic legends of the Skalds, as well as to the more recent but no less romantic stories of the great and magnanimous Gustavus Vasa, Gustavus Adolphus, and the brilliant comets, Tordenskjold and Charles the Twelfth.

HOWARD CROSBY, A. M.,
Professor of Greek Language and Literature in the University of the City of New-York.

SUMMARY OF CONTENTS.

The Origin of the People—Mythology—Language—Skalds or Bards—Runes—The Warfaring Life—Piracy—Duels—Foster-brother Covenant—State and Condition of the Female Sex—Means of getting a Livelihood by—Victuals—Trade—Dwelling-places—Weapons—Funeral Solemnities—State Affairs—King—Peasants and Prefects—Slaves—Viking Expeditions—The Oldest Kings .... PAGE 19–49

First Period, from A. D. 811–1241.

1. Promulgation of the Gospel by Ansgarius—Gorm the Old and his Queen Thyra Dannebod—Harold Bluetooth—Christianity—Civil War—Palnatoke—Swen Splitbeard—Viking Association—Battle by Svolder—Conquest of England—Harold—Canute the Great—England and Denmark united—Pilgrimage to Rome—Battle by Helge-River—Ulf Jarl (Earl)—Conquest of Norway—The Discovery of America by the Northmen—The Union with England ceases 50–81
2. Magnus the Good—Swen Estrithson—Expedition to England—Ecclesiastical Affairs—Canute the Pious—New Expedition against England—Eric the Good—Expedition to Venden—Canonization of Canute the Pious—Canute Lavard—Nicholas—Civil War between Swen Grathe, Canute Magnusson, and Waldemar—Frederick Barbarossa—Battle on Grathe-heath in Jutland 82–103
3. Waldemar I. the Great—Absalon—Canute VI.—Bugislaw, of Pomerania—Waldemar II. the Conqueror—Conquests along the Baltic—Esthonia—The Captivity of the King—Science and the Arts 104–119

xii SUMMARY OF CONTENTS.

Second Period, from A. D. 1241-1536, the Introduction of the Reformation.

1. Eric Ploughpenning—Expedition to Esthonia—Abel—Christopher I.—Conflict with the Clergy—Archbishop Jacob Erlandson—Interdict—Eric Glipping—Battle on Loheath—War with Norway—Eric Menved—The Regicides—Archbishop John Grand—Peace with Norway—Expedition to Pomerania and Mecklenburg—The Hanseatic League 120–134

2. Christopher II.—Charter—War with Geert, Count of Holstein—Battle on Tapheath—Niels Ebbeson—Waldemar IV., Atterdag—Insurrection in Jutland—Magnus Smek of Sweden—War with the Hanseatic Towns—Rebellion—Waldemar leaves the country—Olaf—Queen Margarethe (the Semiramis of the North)—King Albrecht of Sweden—The Battle at Falköping in Sweden—The celebrated Union of Calmar 134–156

3. Queen Margarethe—Attempts to regain Schleswig—Eric of Pomerania—Dispute about Schleswig—War with the Hanseatic Towns—Rebellion in Sweden—Engelbrechtson—Charles Canutson—Dethronement of the King in Denmark and Sweden—Christopher of Bavaria acknowledged King of all three Kingdoms—Rebellion of the Peasantry 157–171

4. *The House of Oldenburg*—Christian I., the first King of the House of Oldenburg—Charles Canutson—Archbishop Jens Bengtson—Steno Sture, the Elder—Battle on Brunkehill—Pilgrimage to Rome—University of Copenhagen—The Charter of King Hans (John)—Division of the Duchies—Expedition to Ditmarsh—Rebellion in Sweden and Norway—War again with the Hanse Towns—*Christian II. the Tyrant*—Expedition against Sweden—Archbishop Gustav Trolle—The Slaughter of Stockholm—Sigbrit-Dyveke—Torben Oxe—The Beginning of the Reformation—Rebellion—The King flees—*Frederick I.*—Civil War—Rebellion in Skåne—Sören Norby—The Reformation spreads—John Tausen—Diet of Odensee—Diet of Copenhagen—The War of the Count—*Christian III.*—Shipper Clemens—Battle by Oxenhill—Literature and Language 172–225

Third Period, from A. D. 1536-1660; the acknowledgment of Lutheranism until the Introduction of Absolute Sovereignty.

1. *Christian III.*—Diet of Copenhagen—Charter—The Reformation introduced into Iceland—Intolerance—University and School

Affairs—Alliance with Sweden—New Division of the Duchies—Frederick II.—Conquest of Ditmarsh—Three Crowns—The Northern Seven Years' War—Daniel Ranzau—Peace in Stettin—Peter Oxen—Foundation of Kronborg—The Sound Dues—Lübeck—Hamburg—Science and Arts—Henrik Ranzau—Tycho Brahe—*Christian IV.*—The Queen-Dowager Sophia of Mecklenburg—Guardianship—Peasantry—Nobility 226–255

2. *Christian IV.*—Care and Interest for Norway—Variance with Sweden—Calmar War—Peace at Knœród—He encourages Science and the Arts—Commercial Affairs—Discoveries—Regulation of the Post Affairs—Manufactures—Buildings—Participation in the Thirty Years' War—Battle by Lutter, near the Barenberg—Peace of Lübeck—*Gustavus Adolphus* of Sweden plays a prominent part in the Thirty Years' War—Dissatisfaction amongst the Peasantry and Burgher Class with the Aristocracy—Dispute with Hamburg—Sound Dues at Elsenore—War with Sweden—Inroad of the Swedish General, Torstenson—Battle of Colberg by Femern—Danish National Song—Peace of Brómsebro—*Frederick III.*—Election of King—The Charter—Alliance with Holland—Corfitz Ulfeldt—Rupture with Sweden—Peace of Roeskilde—Renewal of the War—Siege of Copenhagen—The Dutch Admiral Opdam—Battle at Nyborg—Peace of Copenhagen 255–288

Fourth Period, from A. D. 1660–1852; (*from the introduction of the Absolute Sovereignty till the conclusion of the War with the rebellious Duchies.*)

1. *Frederick III.*—The Diet of Copenhagen—The Charter annihilated, and Absolute Sovereignty introduced—Kay Lykke—Corfitz Ulfeldt—Eleonora Christina—Dispute with Christian Albrecht of Gottorp—*Christian V.*—Acquisition of Oldenburg and Delmenhorst—War with Sweden and France—Admiral Niels Juel—Peace of Lund and Fontainebleau—Griffenfeldt—Ole Rómer—The Peasantry—Olaf Rosenkranz—Masius and Bagger—*Frederick IV.*—War with the Duke of Gottorp—Peace of Travendal—Eleven Years' War with Sweden—The Brilliant Comets *Charles XII.* of Sweden, and the Danish Admiral *Thundershield* (Tordenskjold)—Peace of Fredericksborg—Hostile Terms with Russia—Hans Egede christianizes Greenland—Science and the Arts—*Christian VI.*—The Peasantry—Ecclesiastical Affairs—School Affairs—Science and the Arts—The Navy—Count Danneskjold Samsó—

Frederick V.—Hostile Terms with Russia—Peter III. of Russia murdered—Manufactures—Commercial and Financial state—The Peasantry — Science and the Arts 289–369

2. *Christian VII.* — Alterations among the Higher Officers of State —Care for the Peasantry—The King's going abroad—Struensee and Brandt beheaded—The Queen banished—Ove Guldberg—The Queen-dowager Juliane Marie — Prince Frederick — Deed of Exchange with Russia—A. P. Bernstorff—The Armed Neutrality—The Finances—The Press—The Peasantry—Care for the Danish Language and Literature—The Charter of Naturalization—Crown Prince *Frederick*, afterwards *Frederick VI.*— A. P. Bernstorff—Henrik Stampe — Reventlow — C. Colbjórnson — Hostilities with Sweden—Neutrality during the French Revolutionary War—Independence of the United States acknowledged by Sweden and Denmark — Tripoli — Hostilities with England — Renewal of the Armed Neutrality—The Horrible Battle of the Baltic—Copenhagen cruelly bombarded, and the fleet carried away — War with Sweden—Peace of Jónkóping—Prince Christian August of Augustenburg — His Death — Charles John Bernadotte, Prince of Pontecorvo, elected Crown-prince of Sweden; later, King of Sweden—He dies—Oscar I. King of Sweden, died 1859, and Carl XV. ascends the Throne—War with Sweden, Russia, and Prussia —Alliance with France—Fierce Fight at Sehestedt in Schleswig—*Norway* granted a Free Constitution from the Danish Prince, Christian Frederick — Denmark loses Norway forever in the Peace of Kiel — Emancipation of the Peasantry from Feudal Bondage — Other important alterations in different branches of the Government—Care of the King for Public Instruction—University and School Affairs—Literature—Pecuniary Affairs—Representative Council given Denmark and the Duchies — *Christian VIII.* — School Affairs in Copenhagen and in the Country—Iceland—The Danish East India Possessions disposed of—Care for the Danish Language in the Northern part of Schleswig—Railroads—*Frederick VII.* — He gives Denmark a Free Constitution — Horrible War with the rebellious Duchies — Treaty in London 369–436

INTRODUCTORY REMARKS.

In the widest sense History must be considered the knowledge, the portraying, or the total sum of all that in nature, amongst men, and in the whole circle of experiences, there *is*, or *comes* to pass, *was*, or came to pass, and which accordingly only can be learnt through experience or instruction. History is, consequently, the opposite of Philosophy, which is the knowledge of all needful and universal truths, comprehensible only by the mere reason. But, nevertheless, if the cultivator of History is not guided by Philosophy, or the rules of reason, History will to him be only a barren act of memory, without life or nourishment for the understanding and heart; in short, History will not be a science to him; he will not clearly comprehend the consequences of events in their pragmatical connection. "It little concerns us to know," says Rollin, "that there were once such men as Dschengischan, Cæsar, Alexander, Gustavus Adolphus, Napoleon, Washington, and so on, and that they lived in this or that period, or died in this or that day; but it highly concerns us to know the steps by which they rose to the exalted pitch of grandeur we cannot but admire, what it was that constituted their glory and felicity, what were the causes of their declension and fall, and how in religious and moral respects they have influenced their own and after-ages; all of which we cannot obtain but by Philosophy, or more properly, by the Philosophy of History, through which we ascertain the causes of things or their phenomena. History itself is immense in reference to compass, circumference, and contents. A boundless ocean of facts and events lies behind us, while each day and each hour the stream of time is swelling in new and large billows of events, visions, and names; all of which, seen in the light of truth and pragmatical connection, are of exceeding interest and use. And of such great interest and use is the History of the Scandinavian Kingdoms, taken, as all History must be, in due connection with the contemporaneous History of other lands. This History is that of a brave and interesting people, which, on a large scale, has influenced the world, and is yet so little known to the United States, where I, however, rejoice at seeing so much interest paid to the culture of science. A talented young American wrote, last summer, an eloquent article in the *Journal of Commerce*, inscribed "Scandinavian History—a Work Wanted," wherein he says: "There is a nation, even now extant, possessing as brave a History as that of the Romans, as poetic as that of the Greeks; a nation that has controlled the World's History in many things, and at many times, and whose achievements in war and in letters, are worthy the most heroic age of Rome and the most finished period of Greece; a nation whose Philosophy outran their age, and anticipated results that have been slowly occurring ever since. This reference," he says, "can be true of but one people, and that people is the *Norsemen*, the dwellers in Scandinavia, who lived as heroes, lords, and conquerors; who, sailing out of the ice and desolation in which they were born and nurtured, conquered England, Scotland and Ireland; ravaged Brittany and Normandy; discovered and colonized Iceland and Greenland; and they can be said, with confidence, to have crossed the Atlantic in their crazy barks, and to have discovered this very continent, before Columbus, to have anchored in Vineyard Sound, and left a monument behind them; and wheresoever they went, they went as lords and rulers. And then their religion," he continues—"what a wild, massive, manly mythology! With nothing of the soft sentimentalities of more southern people, but continent of much that revelation has assured us to be true in doctrine—preaching ever the necessity of right, and doing right—of manliness, honesty and responsibility rewards and punishments." And he thus concludes: "Is there not some one who will plunge *in medias res*, and, bringing order out of confusion, give us this so greatly desiderated History of Scandinavia?"

These eloquent words, a correspondence with the talented writer, and later, an interview with him, have inspired me, a native Dane, having completed my theological studies at the University of Copenhagen, and penetrated with patriotic feelings, with a mind and courage to plunge *in medias res*, and to the best of my ability to do justice to that undeniably interesting subject. I dare not hope at all for such a success as has crowned a Bancroft, Irving, and Prescott; nevertheless I will plunge *in medias res*, and go fearlessly through all the difficulties which attend an explorer, flattering myself in hoping that the American public will bestow upon me their kind attention, and exercise forbearance with somewhat unidiomatic English. *Jacta est alea*, and I will commence by describing *the state and condition of Denmark, in the most ancient times, until the Provincial Territories were united, and Christianity began to be promulgated by Ansgarius, a learned and pious monk from Westphalia, in Germany.*

HISTORY OF SCANDINAVIA.

The Origin of the People—Mythology and Public Worship—Language—Skalds or Bards—Runes—The Warfaring Life of the People—Piracy—Duels—Foster-brother Covenant—State and Condition of the Female Sex—Means of getting a livelihood by—Victuals—Trade—Dwelling-places—Weapons—Funeral Solemnities—State Affairs—King—Peasants and Prefects—Slaves—Norse Expeditions—The Oldest Kings.

THE present inhabitants of Denmark, as well as of Norway and Sweden, are successors of the enormous *Gothic* tribe formerly dwelling round about the Black Sea and the Sea of Azov, to which district this tribe seems to have come from yet more eastern regions, afterwards wandering up to the northern coasts of the Baltic, whence the *one branch* of the Gothic tribe departed to the opposite tracts of Scandinavia, peopling and settling the southern part of Sweden, Skane, Halland, and Bleking, the Danish islands, together with the northern part of the Jutlandish peninsula, and likewise spreading itself over the greater part of Norway. *The other branch* of these ancient and distinguished Goths remained south of the Baltic, and oftentimes changing their dwellings, afterwards prevailed in Ger many, scattering under the great European emigration over a great part of southern Europe, Greece, Italy, Spain, Portugal and France, making considerable conquests, and even often exacting tribute. Divided here into Ostro and Visi-Goths, they erected, under their chief leader, *Theodorik*, the Ostrogothic kingdom in Italy, and the Visigothic in Spain under *Astulph*, and their influence and that of their descendants have since been permanent in Europe and the world. On the southern borders of Denmark, in the present Duchy of Holstein, dwelt the Saxons, belonging to the German Goths; higher up in Schleswig and in the southern and western part of Jutland dwelt the Angles and Jutlanders, forming, in a certain way, an intermediate line between the Scandinavian and German Goths. But as a great number of Angles, Saxons, and Jutlanders, in the middle of the fifth century, led by the brothers, *Hengist* and *Horst*, departed for England, founding there the Saxon Heptarchy, the more northern Goths settling in the regions which those had left, were afterwards the prevailing tribe in all Jutland and Schleswig. On the entrance of the Goths into Scandinavia, the land was inhabited by two reciprocally kindred nations, whose present names are *Laplanders* and *Finns*. Both of them had come from the east, but the Laplanders were forced by the Finns up to the remotest parts of

Norway and Sweden, where remnants of them are yet to be found. The Finns themselves were, after a valiant resistance, pressed back by the Goths, whose descendants at present live in Finland, which now belongs to the Russian Empire. It is also possible that some Celtic tribes, the primitive inhabitants of the south and west of Europe, have lived in the Scandinavian countries. The culture of the oldest dwellers of the north was at a very low ebb; they lived dispersed, rambling about the immense and impenetrable forests, and on the coasts adjacent to the ocean and the numerous lakes, many of which are now transformed into moors and marshy land, or dried up altogether. Game from the forests, and fish from the sea and lakes, supplied the inhabitants with nutriment and hides and furs to protect their bodies against the severe climate; and in such respects they were very well off, wanting nothing fortune could supply. Their weapons and hunting-tools were stones, but often made with curious and admirable workmanship—the use of metals being yet unknown.

Very interesting, deep, and instructive is the religion or the mythology of the Norsemen, wherein their character and peculiar views of life have received a proper embodiment, containing much of the spirit of obedience, for which St. Paul praises the heathens that are without the law, but do by nature the things contained in the law, showing the work of the law written in their hearts. Their religion, better, perhaps, called their mythology, announced also clearly the important doctrine of future responsibility—rewards and punishments. At all events, it was great, nervous, and poetic, and, in many respects, fit for facilitating the introduction of the higher light of Revelation, which first in the ninth century was brought to them. In the abyss of ages—thus read the old Sagas—all was without form and life, and darkness was upon the face of the deep, on which the warmth was continually operating, until *Ymer*, a giant sprang forth. But *Odin*, a Scandinavian Deity, yet supposed to be a historical person, having come from Asgard on the river Don (Tanais) in southern Russia, killed Ymer and his whole offspring; the bad and evil *Jetters* and *Thyrsers* (giants) were drowned in that stream of blood proceeding and flowing from Ymer's corpse, except one, who propagated the generation of Jetters or Thyrsers, and lived in continual enmity with gods and men. Of Ymer's body—thus read the old Sagas—Odin moulded and framed the ordained and settled world with mountains, rivers, lakes, trees, and clouds; and of the great ash-tree, *Yggdrasill*, whose topmost branches were said to dance eternally in the heavenly light, he moulded the first couple of men, *Askur* and *Embla*, who resided in *Midgard*. The gods themselves live in *Asgard*, close by Upsala, in Sweden. Odin, superior to all the other gods, is father of gods and men, and rules the whole world, which he,

B. C., 70.

by his wise and judicious eye, contemplates and views from his high *Hlidskjalf*, his heavenly seat, his royal palace. The peculiar God of War and Thunder is *Thor*, a son of Odin, most ardently worshipped by the warlike Norsemen, and kept long in memory even after the other gods were thrown into oblivion. He being considered the good principle, and chosen to bruise the head of all the evil principles, is incessantly fighting with the Jetters, slaying them with his hammer, the heavy *Mjólnir*. The brave having found an honorable death on the battle field were taken up to the mansion of the gods, and came to the splendid castle, *Valhalla*, radiating with shining shields and glittering swords, and where *Odin*, *Thor*, *Freia*, *Frigga*, and the *Nornas*, with their irrevocable decrees, were assembled. Odin's maidens, the *Valkyriers*, were continually rushing through the ether, seeking in all countries for the bravest heroes, whom they marked with their spearpoint, when the hour of death had come. The departed heroes, called *Einheriars*, pass their time in Valhalla, having every day the pleasure of arming themselves, marshaling themselves in military order, fighting and knocking down one another; but in the evening they get up again and return to Valhalla, where a festival meal is prepared for them, consisting of the flesh of a boar, called *Sahrimner*, which, though butchered every day, returns to life again, and the beautiful virgins, the Valkyriers, present to them the mead-horn, of which they drink till they are in a state of intoxication; but the pleasures of love do not enter at all into the joys of this extraordinary Paradise. Odin sits by himself at a particular table. A different lot or fate fell to the cowards who feared the battle and dangers of war, and allowed themselves to be cut off by disease. Cast down to *Helheim* (hell) they had to continue their life there, as silent, trembling shadows, without pleasure and exploits, and under the perpetual suffering of anguish, remorse, and famine. Odin himelf, Thor, and the keen Tyr, belonged to the *Asatribe;* while *Freia*, the goddess of love, together with *Njord* and *Frigga*, disposing of tranquil occupations, hunting, fishing, favorable winds on the ocean, and plenteous years, were ascribed to the gentle *Vane-tribe*.

Nevertheless, the dominion of the Valhalla gods was not to last forever, but the power to be given to another god, who should judge men conformably to a higher law, not as they were brave or cowardly, but as they were *good* or *evil*, for the Edda of Snorro says: "The world shall be judged in righteousness." The Valhalla gods, however, were safe as long as *Baldur*, the wisest and most righteous of all gods, and protector of innocence, was living. But the cunning and designing *Loke*, the evil deity and the father of treachery, by birth half related to the gods, half to the Jetters, and father of *Hela*, the *Fenriswolf*, and the dreadful *Midgards serpent*, smuggling himself into the fellowship of the gods, so prevailed, by his craftiness, upon Baldur's own brother, as to kill him. Now nothing can avert the declension of the gods and the perdition of the world. The sun becomes eclipsed, the ocean overflows, and the Midgards serpent rises from the deep. Loke and Jetters confederated with the burning and consuming *Surtur*, rush now upon Valhalla, which, together with *Niftheim* (Helheim) perish in *Ragnarok*, the twilight of the gods. All gods and Einheriars fall in the battle, and the whole world perishes. But a new earth rises from the ocean, and the Almighty God descends himself to judge men in righteousness. The honest and true get permission to enter into *Gimle* —Odin's gold-radiating palace—to live there in eternal joy with the Almighty, and in fellowship with the other gods, who had been purified through the flames. Gimle has no need of the sun, neither of the moon, for Odin gives it light himself. But the evil, perjurers, murderers, and seducers, could not enter into that society, but are cast down to *Nastrond*, the eternal fire, where they have to expiate their misdeeds crossing streams of yellow matter, and suffering great pain in the eternal flames prepared for them.

The gods were worshiped partly in the open air, in groves, or places encompassed by a circle of big stones, partly in wooden temples, among which that in Upsala (Sweden) was most famous. The public worship—the main point of which were sacrifices—was in general administered by the head of the family; at the temples priests were appointed—sometimes, also, priestesses. In order to honor the gods several great annual feasts were established, among which *Juel* (Christmas) was most remarkable as the most joyous and festival season to the Norsemen. From all quarters of the country men and women then resorted to the temples, making large offerings; friends and relatives presented one another with gifts, and many days were spent in feasts and gay compotations. In the spring there was a sacrificial offering, to ensure luck in war and in Viking expeditions (piracies) usually beginning at that season. With these barbarous people the number nine was supposed to have something in it of peculiar sanctity. Every ninth month, therefore, a sacrifice was offered up to the gods. The usual victims were horses, oxen, young swine, hawks, and cocks. From the entrails and the running blood the priests told the people their fortunes, and the flesh was prepared for a meal to the assembled sacrificers. Sometimes even men were offered—mostly slaves and prisoners of war—for the Norsemen, in their uncultivated state, were, to a certain extent, cannibals; to which *Dithmar*, a reliable historian of the eleventh century, bears witness, telling that before Odin's arrival the goddess *Hertha* was, in *Leira*, in the island of Sjelland, (Zeeland,) worshiped with great solemnity; and that every ninth year, in the month of January, the Danes offered up to her ninety-nine men, and the same number of horses, dogs, and cocks, in the firm assurance of thus obtaining her favor and protection.

The different classes of Norsemen, being of the same extraction, had also the same language, except some provincialisms, idioms, and differences in pronunciation, entirely inevitable where the same language is spoken over extensive tracts and territories. While thus the old Scandinavian language, in process of time, was undergoing several alterations, it was in the remote *Iceland* kept in its perfect purity, free from all foreign idioms. The general appellation of the common language was *Danish* tongue, the Danes being a long time considered the main people, and through several centuries playing the most important parts in the North. The language improved by discourses in public meetings, and by the songs of Skalds or Bards; and later, when the use of letters became customary, by a multitude of historical writings, particularly composed by the Icelanders skilled in old sayings, which were handed down to them from antiquity, a considerable number of which writings are yet left. The poets, generally called Skalds, who by their songs have immortalized ancestral achievements and exploits, were seldom missing in public meetings, drinking bouts, and other festival occasions. They stayed often at the royal courts and the manors of the Prefects, where they propagated, through their songs, achievements and exploits of Kings and Prefects to succeeding generations; and being often, not only eye-witnesses themselves, but even partakers of the achievements they have glorified in their songs. Their poetic productions, a great number of which have been preserved uncorrupted down to our very days, are of importance for History.

The Norsemen had some peculiar letters, consisting of sixteen marks or characters, called *Runes*, the origin of which ascends to the remotest antiquity. They were used not only by the Norsemen, but also by kindred tribes abroad. The signification of the word Rune (mystery) seems to allude to the fact that, originally, only a few have known the use of these marks, and that they mostly have been applied to secret tricks, witchcraft, and enchantments. There were both *plain* and *artificial* Runes, called *Lónrunes*, (the Scandinavian word Lón denoting secret,) with the latter of which a great superstition was connected, the priests believing, by aid of them, to be able to haunt a place, to dull weapons, to stop thunder and hurricanes, to cure or occasion diseases, and so on; and, when engraved on nails, wrists, rudders of ships, handles of swords, these Lónrunes were supposed able to bring a thing to a happy issue, or avert dangers. But the Runes were also used as communications in writing; for instance, on being engraved on thin wooden tablets, which were sent away as letters, or on being used to record a series of kings, genealogical tables, and the like. Worthy to be noted is also the use of Runes for inscriptions on stones, in order to preserve the remembrance of celebrated men and their achievements. To the most remarkable of such Rune-stones, to be found round about in the Scandinavian countries, belong the two *Jellingstones* in Southern Jutland, where it is supposed that the king, *Gorm the Old*, and his queen, *Thyra Dannebod*, have their sepulchre.

The warlike mind, so strongly and clearly expressed in the Northern mythology, appears in all parts of the popular life. Tranquil occupations did not enjoy any reputation among the ancient Norsemen, while war and fighting were a sure way of acquiring an eminent name with contemporaries, glorious fame with succeeding generations, and means and riches in abundance. To eat bread in the sweat of the brow was considered inglorious. Life was of little value, and had to be risked at any cost for honor; and an old warrior, when unable to wield his sword, often caused one of his friends to kill him, to avoid a natural death, which was an exclusion from the privileges of Valhalla. But, although frequent wars and mutual challenges were carried on in Scandinavia, the Norsemen often sailed to far-off regions to win honor and renown. Yet, however, not only desire for warfare allured the Norsemen from home, but much more, the necessity of procuring such necessaries of life and such enjoyments as they could not have in their own countries. In the spring, great crowds of new-raised men, fit to bear arms, usually went away from home, mercilessly plundering coasts and lands, wherever they made their appearance, and in the fall returning with rich spoil and prisoners of war, who thereupon became slaves. Such expeditions were called *Vikingefarter*, and the partakers *Vikings*. Some made even such a life a business, and spent nearly all their time on the ocean as pirates, despising the easier country life, and speaking disdainfully of sleeping under a sooty ceiling, or sitting round a warm stove with old women. According to the character of the Norsemen, their disputes were nearly always settled by arms. "It was more honorable for men," say the old Sagas, "to fight by sword than to quarrel by tongue;" and when, therefore, a quarrel arose, either on account of personal offences, or concerning inheritance and borders, then the sword was usually the judge. After challenging one another to a duel, they met on a place surrounded by a circle of big stones, or hedged in by wicker-work, or also on a small island, and if the challenged did not punctually make his appearance, he lost his reputation; nobody would keep company with him, and sometimes even a high pole was erected, on which Runes were engraved, announcing his name and infamy. The challenged, however, was permitted to prevail upon another to fight instead of himself; but, in general, they were loth to do so, as it always set the principal in an unfavorable light. One murder became generally the cause of another; for, although fines could be paid as atonement for a murder committed in an open and honest duel, the near relatives often required blood for blood; a manner of thinking which a father, being offered money for a murder committed on his only son, properly expressed in answering: "I will not carry the corpse of my dearly beloved son in my pocket-book." And if a murder was committed cunningly and treacherously, then vengeance of blood was an unavoidable obligation, from which the surviving relatives could not withdraw without total loss of their reputation. Revengeful and inexorable as the Norsemen were in their enmity, so faithful and self-denying they proved themselves in their friendship. Warriors valuing one another highly, often made a contract called *Foster-brother Covenant*, by which they, under the observance of different solemn ceremonies, mixed blood together, swearing allegiance, and binding themselves by a fearful oath to avenge the death of one another, by inflicting severe punishment upon the murderer. This covenant was now and then extended even so far as to promise not to outlive one another; and the ancient History of Scandinavia sets forth many beautiful examples of such faithfulness and self-denying love. Though bloody and implacable in war, they were not strangers to the virtues of peace; hospitality and kindness to strangers, which are the common virtues of rude nations, the dwellers of Scandinavia possessed in a very high degree, and appreciated highly, and they entertained for each other the most kindly feelings of regard. Every traveler was received kindly, and the person of the guest considered holy; and when a man entered into the house of his enemy, with whom he everywhere else would have to abide the issue of a bloody fight, he was, as long as he was his guest, safe from any outrage or mischief. On the whole, it was as if the Apostle's words had been known to the ancient Norsemen: "Be not forgetful to entertain strangers, for thereby some have entertained angels unawares." It is, therefore, very wrong, when some partial historians, as for instance Voltaire, set forth a few instances of brutality and barbarism among the Norsemen as characteristic of the manners and genius of the whole race.

The respect, likewise, which the dwellers of Scandinavia entertained for the female sex, was a striking feature in their character, and could not fail to humanize their dispositions. The state and condition of the female sex in society at large, was better in the north than in most other countries where Christianity had not produced a salutary revolution. The daughters, brought up in their paternal home, and taught occupations pertaining to females, were permitted to partake in social enjoyments and public meetings. Even the females appreciated bravery and a manly mind; the want of which with the males, was, in their opinion, not reparable from other excellencies. The father or guardian disposed, according to custom, of the hand of the unmarried girl, but in reality she was, however, at her own disposal, being very seldom given in marriage against her own option. The wedding ceremony, performed under the observance of religious ceremonies, was attended with festivities during several days, whereafter the husband guided his wife to her new home, handing her the *bunch of keys* (Nógleknippet) as a sign of her duties as the mistress of the house. Monogamy was customary; nevertheless the husband cohabited now and then with concubines,—a cause of frequent divorces and bloody fights. As for chastity and pure manners, the old sayings report well, and speak in high terms of the women of the north. They were true to their country, their husbands, their friends and their home, and their love did not cease on this side the grave. The science of healing, imperfect as it might be at that time, was mostly practiced by women, to whom, also, the peculiar gift to interpret dreams was ascribed; which gift, according to the old sayings, Odin had sent down to all women from his splendid Hlidskjalf.

The business of the Norsemen was hunting, fishing, and breeding of cattle, also a little agriculture. *Pytheas*, a merchant from Marseilles, in Southern France, who, about three hundred years before Christ, arrived in a country which he calls *Thule*, generally considered to have been Southern Norway, tells that the inhabitants understood how to till barley, and prepare a drink of honey, and that they did not, as in Southern Europe, thresh their grain in the open air, but binding it up into sheaves, carried it into large barns to be threshed. The most common food of the Norsemen was the flesh of wild and domestic animals, fish, and vegetables; horse and swine flesh were considered the finest dishes; beer and mead were their drinks. Trade was exercised by the keen northern navigators on far-off coasts, but their traffic was often turned into piracy, and the sword was substituted for gold and silver. Grain, honey, flour, salt and cloth were brought from England. Oriental commodities came by land to Russia, from whence the Norsemen imported them, and the harbors of Northern Germany drew together commercial connections with Middle Europe. Scandinavia herself had only very few wares to export; nearly none but fish, fur, and amber, which was found on the shores of the Baltic and on the western coast of Jutland. Coins were unknown, and payment was, therefore, made by pieces of gold and silver, or wares exchanged for wares. Of mechanical arts there were in ancient times only very few. Nevertheless, the art of ship-building, and dexterity in hammering arms and ornaments were highly valued and exercised by free-born men, while plainer works and domestic services were made by slaves. The women were very skillful in weaving tapestry, and interweaving figures of men, animals, and landscapes

The dwellings of the Scandinavian people were made of timber, and the construction was plain, one room being both kitchen, bed-chamber, and sitting-room. In the middle of the room were the stove and the chimney, and to let out the smoke an opening was made in the ceiling, which also let in light to the room; for windows were unknown. Nevertheless the rich and prominent families had more convenient dwellings: kitchen, parlor, bed-chamber, bathing-room, and often a handsome hall.

The Norseman's dearest and most important property were his arms. In ancient times they were plain and artless, and, like other implements, made of stones; later, of copper; for it was a long time before the Norsemen learnt how to forge iron. Their aggressive weapons, frequently mentioned in the old sayings, were clubs, stones, swords, battle-axes, slings, bows, arrows, and spears; their defensive were shirts of mail, helms, and shields, adorned with figures of animals, as armorial ensigns, and so highly appreciated as to be hereditary. On the whole, for the young Norseman, whose education was, like the ancient Spartan's, exclusively calculated for a military life, the practice in using arms was necessary to make his body pliable and hardy; by the early and frequent exercises of which they also acquired an almost incomprehensible dexterity and muscular strength in using and wielding the sword. Braver men never lived; truer men never drew the bow. They had courage, fortitude, sagacity, bodily strength, and perseverance;

they shrunk from no dangers, and they feared no hardships. "Odin is for us—who can be against us?" was their watchword; and the old Sagas say: "Here it was beautiful to live, heavy to die." Penetrated with a lively desire for acquiring honor and renown, the ancient Norsemen employed all their efforts to keep their famous ancestors in an unshaken memory; and when an eminent chief had died, his relatives and friends decreed solemn funeral honors, called *Gravól*, (parentations,) by which a glorious mention was made of the actions of the deceased, and drinking cups of beer emptied in his honor, the present guests obliging themselves to honor his glorious and sacred memory by promising to perform some distinguished deed. To make such a vow, and empty such a cup of memory, which was called the *Minnicup*, was a duty indispensably incumbent on the son, before he could place himself in the chair of state of his celebrated father.

In remotest antiquity the corpses were buried in the earth; later, burnt, the ashes being stored up in urns—a custom ascribed to Odin. At a later period it became again customary to bury the corpses, and heap up gigantic hills, many of which are yet to be found. The corpses of more distinguished persons were, however, seldom buried in the bare earth, but in a vault (mausoleum) surrounded with big stones; and upon the vault was generally laid a tall stone, with an inscription—(Rune-stone.) According to the general opinion, that in the life to come the deceased would have to acquit himself of the same office as here, the best decorations, and things which had belonged to his situation and office, were laid down in the sepulchre; wherefore, also, in said sepulchres, frequently are found swords and other arms, different implements, finger-rings, bracelets, necklaces of pearl and amber, and mosaic work, and the like ornaments.

Denmark, Norway, and Sweden were, in ancient times, divided into small portions, districts and provinces, (Herreder, Sysler,) more of which by degrees were so united as to form small states, until at last all these single provinces made up three kingdoms, which for many centuries had mostly only one king. These ancient kings of Scandinavia were—thus record the old sayings—beloved and honored by their people, as fathers and friends. They did not expect their subjects to kneel to them when they came to ask a favor or advice, nor did their subjects ever prostrate themselves, like those of great monarchs of Asia or Egypt. Their power was limited, and their function, as written laws had not yet existed, was to settle disputes which might arise among the selfish and ignorant, to make laws and alter the old ones, by which the people and the influential men consented to be governed, and to lead their subjects in war. To offer sacrifices, and take a leading part in divine worship, was also often the king's business. For this the subjects gave their king large farms and lordships, a considerable part of the spoils of war, and the highest places at all feasts, and in the public deliberations—that is, in the assemblies or assizes (Thinge)—where they consulted together concerning public affairs; and they always addressed him with respect. Moreover, forests and untilled tracts of land, and ornaments found in the earth, belonged to the king. When a king died, the people convened to elect his successor; but, though heirship was not fully entitled to ascend the throne, the eldest son of the deceased king was generally chosen, in order to avoid disputes. Upon the failure of the blood royal, the election was entirely free. The government seems, on the whole, to have been almost an absolute monarchy, of a mixed, hereditary, and elective nature.

The peasantry was, in this early age, almost the only corporation of Scandinavia. By a peasant was understood, not alone a husbandman, an agricultor, but every free-born person who was possessed of real estates, with whatever office he else might be invested. Thus the peasantry constituted the people. But above the peasants ranked the *chiefs* or *leaders*, not on account of peculiar privileges, but of the greater credit and influence they enjoyed, because they were in possession of larger property, and descended from distinguished families. From among such families the kings in general took earls (Jarler) to rule the conquered provinces, and all the warriors and officers who constituted their court (Hird). The peasants and the chiefs constituted the Diet, and met at the assize (Thing), a place selected for this very purpose, and surrounded with holy ash trees or with a circle of stones. Here they consulted concerning war and peace; here the kings were elected; here the laws were passed or annulled, and lawsuits decided; and without the consent of the Diet the king could not decide upon anything of consequence. The laws were few and simple, consisting mostly in customs; the punishments were mild, and most crimes could be atoned for by paying a fine; yet assassination, high-treason, arson, and burglary, were now and then punished, either by slavery, outlawry, or forfeiture of life. The slaves were divided into native Scandinavians and foreigners. In the many wars which the Norsemen waged with southern Europe, they made prisoners, who became slaves, if their relatives or friends could not pay for their liberation. Also, many slaves were made by trade. Their condition was miserable. The ancient Norsemen hardly acknowledged slaves to be men. A slave might be beaten, starved, and otherwise tormented, or be killed by his master's order, and the abuser might go unpunished. They could not buy, sell, nor inherit—not take oath, not marry—but were sold and bought as other wares. Slaves never carried arms, except when expressly armed for military service. One of the most toilsome but necessary labors of slaves, was the preparation of corn or wheat. In those ages there were neither wind nor water mills, corn being beaten by slaves, or pounded, or ground in a hand-mill. There were, however, many slaveholders who never practised these cruelties, and the slaves of Scandinavia were, on the whole, treated with more humanity than in other parts of Europe. Slaves were even sometimes let out to serve other citizens, and in that case they were permitted to have a part of their wages, and the money thus earned was often saved to purchase the liberty of the slaves. A kind master granted, sometimes, a faithful slave his liberty, whose children then could become citizens, and enjoy all civil privileges. Of course, the introduction of Christianity put a stop to many abuses of slavery, and the first Scandinavian Christians treated their slaves kindly, approving of St. Paul's words to the Athenians: "God made of one blood all nations of the earth, bond and free."

Upon the whole, nothing is more horrible and affecting than such debasement of a fellow creature. The Greek poet, Homer, who lived about twelve hundred years before Christ, says truly: "Whatever day makes man a slave takes half his worth away."

Of the great European Emigration the Norsemen were, properly speaking, not partakers, except as far as Jutlanders, Angles and Saxons, at about the same time, under the command of the two brothers, Hengist and Horst, set out for and conquered England, and erected the Saxon Heptarchy, the history of which is very obscure. The duration of the several kingdoms,

A. D., 449.

till their union under Egbert, is almost all that A. D., can be noted with any approach to historical 827. certainty. But it is beyond all question, that the Cimbri and Teutons, and later, the Goths and Longobeards, and the other people mentioned, have emigrated from Scandinavia, except, perhaps, that some single crowds from the north might have joined the kindred tribes south of the Baltic. But after that great agitation, called the European Emigration, had subsided, an emigration from Scandinavia commenced in the seventh and eighth centuries, breaking out violently in the ninth and tenth centuries. The *Normans* (the Danes, Norwegians, and Swedes, commonly styled so in southern Europe,) had undoubtedly formerly made frequent expeditions (Vikingefarter) to near and far-off regions; but now their expeditions began to be made in greater numbers, intending not only to obtain booty, but even possessions and dwellings abroad. The union of the provincial territories under one king, both in Denmark and Norway, and the introduction of Christianity, and the change of manners and customs connected therewith, had made many dissatisfied with their native country. This, together with a strong desire for a warfaring life, induced numerous crowds from all regions of the North to go away to seek a new home; and the southern lands, which by the dissolution of Charlemagne's A. D., empire, were enervated and entirely defenceless, 843. were a tempting bait for the Normans. Their expeditions extended from the Baltic straight down to the coasts of Africa, and to the innermost parts of the Mediterranean sea, which had so often formerly resounded with the strife of Latin arms. Nor were their enterprises confined to these coasts. They descended all along the shores of Portugal and Western France, and thereafter along the largest rivers of Europe—Elbe, Rhine, Scheldt, Seine, Loire, Garonne, and Rhone. They dared, on their small flat-bottomed vessels, to make irruption into the inland parts of the countries, spreading terror and causing the most terrible havoc wheresoever they went. The flourishing cities of Holland and Germany, Nimvegen, Liege, Bonn, Cologne, and Aachen, were consumed by their fire, and they went over the entire dreadful drama of warlike glory. Finally Arnulf, the German Emperor, put a stop to their invasions and cruelties, after having completely defeated them near *Lóven*, in Belgium.

A. D., 891.

To France was the cruel Danish Viking, Hastings, a horrible scourge. He marched twice to the gates of Paris, plundered, and exacted tribute. The third time Paris was saved by the bravery of Count Odo, afterwards King of France. Then he prepared to set out for Rome, resolving to give full way to his natural desire for conquest; but mistaking the city Luna for Rome, he attacked and obtained it. Yet no rest for France, until Charles the Foolish, King of France, gave up to Rollo, or Rolf

A. D., 886.

A. D., 911.

Gange, a Norwegian chief, a whole province, which was now called Normandy. Alfred the Great, of England, had, in resisting the cruel Hastings, to withstand a skillful veteran. For three years he had, undismayed, contended against Alfred, till he at last had to yield indignantly to that noble King of England. Hastings had marked his course with blood; but whatever was done by him, fell short of the merciless ferocity of other Danes, who, about the same time, laid England waste. Scotland, the Hebrides, and Ireland were thrown into the most extreme desolation by the Danes and Norwegians, who in Ireland were called *Ostmen* (men of the east.) The exclamation of a monk of Worcester is forcible: "*O quam crebris vexationibus, quam gravibus laboribus, quam diris et lamentabilibus modis, non solum a Danis, verum etiam ab filiis satanicis Hastingii, tota vexata est Anglia.*" Not till the Norsemen had won pleasant dwellings, and states by them were founded in France, Italy, Ostangel, Northumberland, on the Island of Man, and the Orkney Isles, as also in Russia, where they were called *Vareger*, did the tumult gradually subside; while, at the same time, the fierce passions of the Norsemen were in some degree moderated by the mild precepts of the Gospel.

A. D., 897.

The oldest events in Scandinavia are only known from the old sayings or traditions, which first, at a later period, have been written down, and therefore do not give the events back in their true form, but are mixed up with fiction, which has given rise to an insuperable chronological difficulty. The traditions are so varied, that it is often impossible to discover the truth of any of the circumstances. The materials from which these traditions are compiled, are in Scandinavia, as in Rome, and Greece, the legendary ballads, which are in every country the first records of warlike exploits. Of consequence are also the calendars and annals kept by the priests, and the genealogical tables kept by the earls and other distinguished families. But poetic historians have afterwards mingled so much fiction with truth, that often only few of their assertions can be deemed authentic. The history, therefore, of Scandinavia, through the first eight centuries after Christ, until King Gorm the Old, is properly and correctly called the *Fabulous Age*, because deprived of the nature of historical evidence, and often involved in impenetrable obscurity, and accordingly, full of the greatest improbabilities; while the period before Christ, destitute of all light, is called the *Obscure Age*. Odin, supposed to have arrived in Scandinavia about seventy years *before* Christ, and, according to the religious ideas of the Norsemen, considered the Supreme God, is by some historians described as a real historical person—a mighty king—who has ruled the northern countries. Several sons are ascribed to him, who, after his death, divided Scandinavia into equal parts. *Heimdal* is said to have reigned in Skane, *Niord* in Sweden, *Seming*

A. D., 883.

in Norway, *Balder* in Angel, (Schleswig,) and *Skjold* in Sjelland (Zealand) and Jutland; the latter being the head of an illustrious generation of kings, called *Skjoldunger*, who are said to have resided in *Leire*, (Lethra,) twenty English miles from Copenhagen. In Christ's time *Frode Fredegod* (Pacific) is said to have been King of Denmark. The rulers at that time were not called kings, but *Drots*, and *Rig*, ruler of Skane, adopted first the title of king. A new generation begins with *Dan Mykillati* (The Splendid). A. D., 250. Almost all historians agree that he was the founder of the country called Denmark. Some have from him derived the name Denmark; but it is more probable that it has originated from the word *Dan*, denoting *low* or *flat*, and from *Mark*, denoting *overgrown with wood;* the name Denmark thus denoting a flat land, overgrown with wood. After a reign of forty years, with the utmost justice and reputation—thus record the old sayings—he died greatly lamented by his subjects. He ordered his courtiers to bury him solemnly, and in full equipage, in a hill; and because it from his time became customary to bury the kings in such hills, the following age is called the *Hill Age*. At a subsequent time *Rolf Krake* was king. The graces of his person are said to have equaled those of his mind; and his stature and strength to have been so extraordinary, that he was surnamed Krake, an old Danish word expressive of those qualities. He has become famous for his bravery and martial spirit, and for the twelve giants (Berserkers) he kept at his court; among whom *Bjarke, Hjelte,* and *Wiggo* ought to be named. Berserker is a word of frequent occurrence in the Sagas, and denotes giants or warriors. They were often seized with a kind of frenzy, either arising from an excited imagination, or from the use of stimulating liquors—committing then the wildest extravagances, and striking indiscriminately at friends and foes. Rolf Krake was killed by the base perfidiousness of his own sister, Skulda, married to Hjartvar, Rolf's viceroy in Skane, whom he had distinguished by numberless instances of his favor, and even exempted him from paying taxes for three years. Meanwhile Hjartvar, prompted by his wife, buckled for war; making haste, at the time expired, to Leire, where he in the night assaulted the sleeping king and his Berserkers, who had intoxicated themselves at a banquet Rolf had given in honor of his sister's arrival. Rolf and all his Berserkers were put to the sword, except Wiggo, who promised to avenge the death of the king. He kept his promise, and pierced Hjartvar with seven dagger-stabs.

A. D., 600.

In the middle of the seventh century the brothers *Rerek* and *Helge,* thus sing the old Sagas, reigned jointly in Leire, at the same time as *Ivar Vidfadme* (*i. e.*, who surpasses his bounds,) made himself ruler over a great part of the North, besides Sweden, which he already ruled. To enter into possession of Sjelland, he gave his daughter, Audur, in marriage to Rerek, though she herself preferred the more warlike Helge. After that, he kindled variance between the brothers, so that Rerek, in a fit of jealousy, killed his brother, whereafter Ivar Vidfadme succeeded in conquering Rerek and becoming master of Sjelland. But some time after, Ivar lost his life on an expedition to Russia (Garderige), whither his widowed daughter had fled for refuge. About this time Hamlet, a Danish prince, whom Shakspeare has immortalized, is said to have enjoyed for a great number of years the Danish throne. It is, however, doubtful, in spite of assertions to the contrary, whether Hamlet ever was king of Denmark, all the best critics affirming that he was killed in a battle, just as he was endeavoring by force to succeed to the crown; and even Saxo Grammaticus does not place him among the Danish monarchs. *Harald Hildetand*, a son of Rerek and Audur, now brought under subjection all the countries his grandfather, Ivar Vidfadme, had ruled, and became a mighty and sovereign king. But, after bearing sway a long time in peace, *Sigurd Ring*, his nephew, and viceroy in Sweden, raised a sedition against him. The memorable battle was fought at *Bravallahede*, in Smaland, Sweden, where the most noble heroes and giants of the whole North encountered; amongst whom was the notable *Stærkodder*, whose bravery and gigantic size have been so much praised in the heroic songs. But

A. D., 700.

A. D., 730.

Harald Hildetand fell in the battle, Sigurd Ring gaining the victory; whose reign, however, is not worthy of much notice. He is said to have founded the city of Ringsted, in Sjelland, called after him. The more remarkable has his son, *Regner Lodbrok*, become, of whose exploits and enterprises of hazard the old sayings record so much. Perpetually roving in defiance and war, partly on the southern and eastern coasts of the Baltic, partly in Flanders, partly in Scotland, Ireland, and England, and being lord and ruler wheresoever he went, he was, at last, captured by King Ella, of Northumberland, who, so say the English historians, threw him, bound, into a dungeon filled with snakes, vipers, and poisonous animals; thus ingloriously putting an end to a life grown old in glory and victory.

A. D., 794.

The great Danish historians, Saxo Grammaticus, Pontanus, and Meursius, correspond with the English in this circumstance. His four sons avenging his death, divided now the wide-spread realm which Ivar Vidfadme, Harald Hildetand, and Sigurd Ring had gathered together. *Björn Jernside* obtained Sweden, *Hvidsærk* Jutland and Wenden, *Ivar Beenlós* Northumberland, and *Sigurd Snake-eye* Denmark, Skane, Halland and Southern Norway. The historian, Meursius, speaks in high terms of Sigurd Snake-eye. "God," says he, "enabled him to complete a reign as pregnant with real felicity as any which the annals of Denmark can show." A grandson of his was *Gorm the Old*, who collected the separate Danish provinces into one aggregate body.

Thus has been traced the History of Scandinavia, from the fabulous age down to the period of historical evidence; on the accounts of which we accordingly could bestow an implicit credit. Christianity, also, now commenced to be preached; paganism at length entirely disappeared, and the influence of a purer faith became discernible in the lives and actions of the old Norsemen

FIRST PERIOD.

FROM THE COLLECTION OF THE SEPARATE PROVINCES INTO ONE BODY, AND FROM THE FIRST ENDEAVORS TO INTRODUCE CHRISTIANITY, UNTIL THE DEATH OF VALDEMAR VICTOR, AND THE ISSUING OF THE JUTLANDISH LAW, 1241.

I.

From the Foundation of the Danish Kingdom till A. D. 1042.

Promulgation of the Gospel by Ansgarius—Gorm the Old and his Queen, Thyra Dannebod—Harald Bluetooth—Christianity—Civil War—Palnatoke—Svend Splitbeard—Viking Association—Battle by Svolder—Conquest of England—Harald—Canute the Great—England and Denmark united—Pilgrimage to Rome—Battle by Helge-River—Ulf Jarl—Conquest of Norway—The union with England ceases.

A FEW years before Gorm's accession to the Danish throne, the promulgation of Christianity was commenced, but met with great opposition from the warlike mind and rude manners of the people. The humble and self-denying spirit taught by Christianity was in no accordance with the stubborn mind of the ancient Norsemen. The Christian idea of the life to come, as a spiritual union with God and the Saviour, was very much opposed to the hope of the northern pagans for

Valhalla, and the sensual enjoyments expected there. The doctrine of fasting, abstemiousness, and chastening the body, displeased the Norsemen, who wished to enjoy the pleasures which this life offered them, and appreciated a strong and vigorous body. A long time, therefore, passed away, till Christianity as an active principle entered their hearts; but it is to be observed, that the victory was gained, not, as in many adjacent countries, by violence and compulsion, but by the intrinsic power of the Gospel itself. Several points, also, of the heathen doctrine facilitated the introduction of Christianity. The doctrine of the pious Balder, of the destruction of the gods, after which a holy and righteous God was to rule, paved the way for the Christian ideas. The heathens' Loke, Gimle, and Nastrond, became easily the Christians' devil, kingdom of heaven, and hell; as also the outward pomp and splendor of the Catholic divine service influenced the tractable mind of the ancient Norsemen. The Frankish emperors (the Franks were some petty German tribes, who in the fifth century had established themselves as a nation in the provinces lying between the Rhine, the Weser, the Maine and the Elbe, including the greater part of Holland and Westphalia,) endeavored to spread Christianity among the Norsemen, in order thereby to bridle these troublesome neighbors. Charlemagne had with violence compelled the Saxons to embrace Christianity, and thus deprived the people of its independence. But the daring and efficient *Godfred*,

King of Jutland, apprehending his designs, protected the Saxons, and commenced war. Making large progress, and even threatening to visit Charlemagne in his residence, Aachen, the emperor was happy enough to get rid of that intelligent and brave enemy, Godfred unfortunately being treacherously killed by one of his own people. His successor, *Hemming*, made peace A. D., with Charlemagne, by which the river Eider was 811. appointed the limit between Denmark and Germany. Louis the Pious, a son of Charlemagne, not so able as his father, but of a more pious mind, concerned himself very much in spreading Christianity in Denmark, sending thither the Archbishop *Ebbe*, of Rheims, who, nevertheless, did not perform anything of consequence. But a Jutlandish sub-king, *Harald Klak*, who had been banished from the country, fled to the emperor for refuge, hoping by his aid to regain the kingdom. While staying there, Harald was baptized in Ingelheim, by Mainz, the emperor himself being sponsor at the christening, and putting on him the white baptismal robe. It was after his return from Germany that we may date the era of Christianity in Denmark. *Ansgarius*, called the Northern Apostle, a learned and pious monk in the cloister of Corvey, Westphalia, was the happy instrument of spreading Christianity in the North. The emperor was looking for a man who could guide Harald Klak home, strengthen his faith, and spread the Christian doctrine amongst his people. Ansgarius undertook this bold and difficult enterprise; and, attended by another energetic monk, Autbert, arrived in Denmark, A. D. 827. where he first resided in Hedeby (now the city of Schleswig), at that time a flourishing commercial city, and erected a missionary school, preaching the Kingdom of God, and teaching those things which concern the Lord Jesus Christ. Such was the force of truth—or such, perhaps, the inconstancy of human nature, always eager after novelty—that Christianity spread with amazing rapidity, and was greatly aided in its progress by the zeal and piety of the king. After some years' preaching and baptizing in Denmark, he went, advised by the emperor, to Sweden, preaching Christianity there for a year and a half. The emperor, learning what rapid progress the new doctrine had made in Scandinavia, purposed now, in order to promote it A. D. 834. still further, to erect an archbishopric in Hamburg; and Ansgarius, with whose Christian zeal he was highly pleased, was accordingly appointed Archbishop. Autbert, his faithful and pious attender, was already dead, deeply bewailed by Ansgarius. But the Northern Vikings (freebooters) some time after attacking and ravaging Hamburg, put unfortunately a considerable stop to the missionary undertaking of Ansgarius. Through several years he had to ramble about, helpless and forsaken; while the disturbances, which broke out at the soon ensuing death of the emperor, could but withdraw attention from the advancement of

Christianity in the North. Finally, Louis the German, interesting himself in the subject, united the bishopric of Bremen with the archbishopric of Hamburg, and took care of Ansgarius, who anew commenced to preach, set the school of Hedeby again on foot, and, because of the favor he enjoyed with the Jutlandish sub-king, *Erik*, was permitted to build in this city the first church—the very first—in Denmark But upon returning from another journey in Sweden, he found King Erik dead, and Christianity under persecution of the new king, who put several of the most devout and zealous Christians to death, who had refused to abjure their religion. Others he forced or bribed into a compliance with his will. He leveled all the churches with the ground, and sent an army to ravage Saxony, chiefly because the people of that country had received the light of the Gospel. But Ansgarius spoke so convincingly to the king, that he not only withdrew his resentment, which had grievously oppressed the Christians, but published entire liberty of conscience, and embraced the true faith. He erected, at his own expense, a magnificent church at Ripen, in Southern Jutland, ordered the pagan temples to be razed, and now became as zealous a Christian as a little before he had been a bigoted heathen. Upon the recommendation of Ansgarius, he appointed persons properly qualified for teaching the Gospel in every corner of his dominions, allowed them handsome salaries, and took Ansgarius for

A. D., 845.

his counselor, not only in spirituals but in temporals likewise. He died the proselyte and chief support of that religion which, only a few years before, he had persecuted with such cruelty and bitterness. Of the new church erected by him at Ripen, *Rembert*, a disciple of Ansgarius, was appointed minister. At sixty-four years of age Ansgarius died in Bremen, after a powerful and self-denying endeavor for spreading the Gospel in Scandinavia. Rembert, above mentioned, succeeded him in the archbishopric, acting with the same apostolic zeal as his great teacher, whose biography he has written and published in Latin. A following king of Denmark, by the name of Frotho, prepared, the better to propagate the faith, an embassy to Pope Sergius III., to acknowledge his supremacy in spirituals, and to request that he would send some persons perfectly qualified to teach the Gospel in Denmark, when death claimed him, and deprived his people of an excellent prince. The spread of Christianity in Scandinavia gave additional vigor to the papal power, for the Norsemen, with all the zeal of new converts, became eager to prove their sincerity by some enterprise in support of the pontiff, whom they regarded as the great director of their faith and hope. Contemporaneously with Rembert's efforts for preaching and spreading Christianity, *Gorm the Old* was king of Denmark. He is chiefly to be remembered for collecting all the small provinces into one body. At that time the Danish kingdom comprised Sjelland, with the adjacent islands, Jutland and South Jutland (now Schleswig), where the Eider river was the limit towards the south, and Skane, Halland, and Bleking, in Southern Sweden. But, though these parts were now thus united, they preserved for a long space of time their popular peculiarities, each part having its own laws, and the king receiving his homage separately in each province. We are not able to detail many facts of the reign of Gorm the Old, but we know, however, that he was a bitter enemy to the Christians, whom he persecuted in every quarter, demolishing their churches and banishing their clergy. Amongst other sacred buildings, he totally destroyed the famous cathedral in Schleswig, and ordered the pagan idols to be erected wherever they had formerly stood. While his two sons, Canute and Harald—twins by birth, and rivals in glory—were gathering laurels abroad, Gorm took arms against the Saxons, with a view to oblige them to renounce Christianity, but the emperor, *Henry the Fowler*, soon came to the relief of the Saxons, defeated Gorm, and forced him to permit Christianity to be preached in Denmark. [A. D. 920.] Gorm's queen, generally called *Thyra Dannebod* (the ornament or solace of the Danes), has rendered herself distinguished by founding *Dannevirke* (a great wall of earth and stones across Schleswig, strongly fortified by moats and tower bastions), to protect the country against inroads of the Germans. Already Godfred, before mentioned, had erected a like fortification, called *Kurvirke*, but the irruption of Henry the Fowler had proved that the country needed a stronger bulwark, wherefore the queen founded that famous Dannevirke, remnants of which are yet to be seen. Gorm, loving his son *Canute*, generally called Canute Danaast (the Splendor of the Danes), more than Harald, declared, dreading the death of his dearly beloved son, of whom he for a great while had received no intelligence, that whosoever might tell him of his son's death should lose his life. Finally, notice was given of his death on a Viking expedition in England. The queen, not risking to tell it to the king, made the courtiers observe an unusual silence at the table, and had the apartment covered with black cloth. Guessing the reason, Gorm cried out: "Surely Canute, my dear son, is dead, for all Denmark is mourning!" "*Thou* sayest so, not *I*," answered the queen; upon which the king sickened with grief, and died in a good old age.

A. D., 941.

Harald Bluetooth, his son, was immediately elected king, but he refused to accept the crown until he had first performed his father's obsequies with all the magnificence becoming his high rank. About the same time Hakon Adelstan was King of Norway, who had to fight with his nephews, sons of King Erik Bloodaxe; of all of whom, Harald Greyskin, countenanced and supported by the Danish king, succeeded, after the death of Hakon Adelstan, in ascending the throne of Norway. But, as he did not pay the tribute promised the Danish king for his support, hostility broke out, and Hakon Jarl, whose father, Sigurd, had been killed by Harald Greyskin, now found refuge in Denmark, inflaming the enmity between the kings to an extreme degree. At the same time *Gold Harald*, a son of Canute Danaast, above mentioned, and consequently a nephew of Harald Bluetooth, had come back from his piracies, and claimed now, by virtue of supposed right, a share of the Danish Kingdom. Hakon Jarl advised the king to kill Harald Greyskin, and then, to gratify his nephew's wish to a certain extent, to let him have Norway; of which advice the king approved. Accordingly, Harald Greyskin was now, under pretence of friendship, allured down from Norway, and killed by the Lymfiord (a river running through the northern part of Jutland), by Gold Harald; who was, however, soon after insidiously murdered by Hakon Jarl, who had made the king believe that Gold Harald hardly could bear so great honor. This heinous action done, Harald Bluetooth sailed with wind upon the beam to Norway, which he easily conquered, and divided between Hakon Jarl and Harald Grænske, a Norwegian prince; after whose death, soon ensuing, Hakon Jarl became ruler of all Norway; under oath, however, of allegiance to Harald Bluetooth. Thus Norway became a province to Denmark. After Harald Bluetooth had settled this affair, he sailed against the Venders, who committed horrid depredations on all the coasts of the Baltic, but

he attacked them with such vigor, that he reduced and plundered all their strongholds, and, among the rest, the rich and important city of Wollin, built on an island of the same name, which is formed by two branches of the river Oder. But he had scarce rid his hands of this war when his aid and protection were solicited by Styrbear, King of Sweden, who was driven out of his own dominions by Erik Victor. To enforce his request Styrbear had brought along with him *Gyntha*, his sister, a lady of admirable beauty. The stratagem had the intended effect; Harald Bluetooth became enamored of her, married her, and promised the brother all the assist-
A. D. 983. ance in his power. Nevertheless Styrbear was defeated by Erik Victor, at Fyriswall, near Upsala.

The progress of Christianity, which Gorm the Old had resisted and disregarded, began now to attract the notice of the ruling power, and was, during the whole reign of Harald Bluetooth, vigorously promoted by *Adeldag*, who now was invested with the archiepiscopal see of Hamburg. Besides the two churches in Schleswig and Ripen, above mentioned, a third was built in *Aarhuus*, situated on the eastern coast of Jutland, and bishoprics were established in said cities. But, although in favor of the
A. D. 955. new doctrine, the king would not comply with the exorbitant and undue claims which the German emperor, Otho I., arrogated to himself. The German kings claimed, by virtue of their dignity as Roman empe-

rors, to be acknowledged the secular head of the whole Christian world, as the Pope was the ecclesiastical; which claim Otho I. realized by giving to those bishoprics above mentioned, immunity and real estates in Denmark. His successor, Otho II., claiming the same, excited the resentment of Harald Bluetooth, who collected all his forces, and pitched his camp on the narrow neck of land at Schleswig, to intercept Otho, but was defeated, the mighty emperor demolishing the famous fortification, Dannevirke, and making his way through the country right up to the Lymfiord. A treaty of peace was made, and the king received baptism by Bishop Popo—Otho, the emperor, being sponsor—and the same ceremony was performed on his son, *Swen*. Bishoprics were now also established in Odensee and in Roeskilde, where Harald Bluetooth erected a splendid church. *Odinkar Hvide*, a native Dane, commenced now to preach Christianity, and annihilate the pagan worship; all of which excited the resentment of the heathen party, in front of which went the king's own son, Swen, and his master-in-arms. *Palnatoke*, a mighty chief from the Danish island Fjunen, who from the depth of his heart was addicted to heathenism, and besides that, believed to have several personal offences to be avenged upon the king. Harald Bluetooth, however, determined not to be wanting in his duty, raised an army and gave battle to his son, who aspired to his father's crown. But the king was defeat-

A. D., 974.

A. D., 991.

ed, and shot by the hand of Palnatoke, while he was walking in a grove near his camp. Before leaving Harald Bluetooth, it ought to be noticed that he removed the royal residence from Leire (Lethra) to Roeskilde, where the Danish kings resided for about five centuries, till Copenhagen, during the reign of Christopher of Bavaria, was made the capital.

Harald Bluetooth was succeeded by his son Swen, generally called *Swen Splitbeard*, from some peculiarity observed about his beard. He is also sometimes called Swen Otho, in compliment to his godfather, the emperor. Nearly all his time was spent in making expeditions to Norway, Germany, and England. Notwithstanding Swen Splitbeard and the mighty chief, Palnatoke, above mentioned, had been on a very intimate footing, their good understanding soon ceased; for the murder committed by Palnatoke on his father, Harald Bluetooth, required vengeance of blood. Palnatoke resorted to Jomsburg, a fortress on the Island of Rügen, on the coast of Pomerania, founded by Harald Bluetooth to maintain the Danish dominion in these regions. Here Palnatoke established a band of northern Vikings, who, by severe laws, preserved the ancient warfaring life and manners, and by the name of *Jomsvikings*, for a long time struck the whole North with fear. Palnatoke's institutions tended to instil into his Vikings the contempt of life. "A man," says the chronicle of Iceland, "in order to acquire glory for bravery, should attack a single

A. D., 991–1014.

enemy, defend himself against two, and not yield to three, but might, without disgrace, fly from four;" and it was, on the whole, glorious to seek every opportunity of encountering death. Some instances of their savage heroism are recorded which almost exceed belief. In an irruption made by the Jomsburgers into Norway, the invaders were defeated, and a few were taken prisoners. They were sentenced to be beheaded, and this intelligence they received with every demonstration of joy. One said: "I suffer death with the greatest pleasure; I only request that you will cut off my head as quickly as possible. We have often disputed," said he, "at Jomsburg, whether life remained for any time after the head was cut off: now I shall decide the question. But remember, if so, I shall aim a blow at you with this knife which I hold in my hand. Dispatch," said he, "but do not abuse my long hair, for it is very beautiful." Not till the eleventh century was this piratical stronghold destroyed by Magnus the Good. The following chief of Jomsburg, the designing *Sigvald*, by stratagem made Swen Splitbeard, who had taken up arms against him, a prisoner, and compelled him to acknowledge the independence of Jomsburg and Venden (all the provinces along the Baltic); and Swen was first set at liberty on promising to pay a ransom of twice his own weight, when full armed, in pure gold. The ransom was settled at three payments, but the king's person was confined till the last payment was made, which was raised by the generosity of the Danish ladies, who sold their jewels for this purpose. Upon his return he, therefore, ordained that the women should inherit the half of all estates, real and personal; although it seems more probable that such an act of benevolence and kindness is to be ascribed to the mild influence of the Gospel, that offers the same rights to both sexes. Swen Splitbeard, thirsting for vengeance, induced Sigvald, at a wassail-bout, to undertake a very hazardous expedition against the mighty Hakon Jarl, in Norway, who had shown the same unwillingness to pay tribute to Denmark as his predecessor, Harald Greyskin; Swen himself making a vow to wage war against England, which had for some years thrown off her subjection to the throne of Denmark. The elsewhere almost indomitable Jomsvikings were totally defeated at Hjórringebay; Sigvald himself had to make his escape, and Norway was not subdued. Swen Splitbeard was more successful in his expedition against England. The impotent Anglo-Saxon king, *Ethelred II.*, also called Ethelred the Irresolute, held at this time the supreme authority in that kingdom. Putting all to the fire and sword, wherever he went, and treating England with the utmost severity, Swen obliged the English king to acknowledge his superiority, and to get rid of the Danes by paying a large sum of money, called *Danegeld*. But an important event took place now in the North. The Norwegian prince, *Olaf Trygveson*, who had been allied to

A. D., 994.

Swen in England, left him treacherously for Norway, the throne of which he ascended, after the death of Hakon Jarl, without taking any oath of allegiance to Swen, who from his ancestors had inherited the sovereignty over Norway; and the misunderstanding increased when Olaf, without Swen's consent, married his sister Thyra, who had fled from her husband, King Burislaw, of Venden. Add to this, that *Sigrid Storraade*, Swen Splitbeard's queen, before married to Erik Victor, of Sweden, had been greatly provoked to wrath against Olaf Trygveson, who, when he some years ago had courted her, but without success, had beaten her with a stick, and called her an old hag of threescore and a pagan bitch. She, of course, now urged both her husband and her son, Olaf Skótkonung, of Sweden, to vengeance. Swen Splitbeard, Olaf Skótkonung, and Erik Jarl, a Norwegian prince, who lived at the Danish court, attacked Olaf Trygveson, who with his fleet had gone through Earsound (Oeresund, the small sound between Denmark and Sweden), to Venden, where his wife was lawfully possessed of some real estates. A very bloody sea-battle was fought by *Swolder*, on the Pomeranian coast. Seldom a more memorable naval engagement has been fought, whether we regard the kings that contended, or the whole kingdom that was in dispute. Olaf Trygveson was, after a most heroic resistance, defeated, and his fleet totally dispersed. Escaping out of the battle with a few ships, he was so

9th Sept. A. D., 1000.

closely pursued, that, to avoid the disgrace of being taken prisoner, he precipitated himself into the sea and was drowned. The most renowned heroes of Norway shared in this battle, and the heroic songs of Einar Tambeskjelver, the great archer, Ulf the Red, and Thorgeir, who all fought as madmen, resound yet among the rocks of old Norway, which was now divided between the three victors, and had to submit to the conditions which they dictated. But while Swen was taken up with settling the affairs of Norway, Ethelred II. had taken advantage of Swen's absence to perform a dreadful carnage among the Danes in England. Informed of it, Swen immediately appeared in England with a powerful army of the most valiant soldiers, came off victor everywhere, turned Ethelred out, who had to flee to Normandy; and Swen Splitbeard was at his death an undisputed sovereign of the whole of England. In the beginning of his reign, he persecuted the Christian doctrine; but, before he expired, he began to perceive the folly he had committed in persecuting the faith in which he had been baptized and instructed. Afterwards, in prevailing upon the people to receive the light of the Gospel, he was aided by *Popo*, a German bishop of great piety and eloquence, who, by dint of example and persuasion, brought about what the king's authority could not effect. Several miracles are related of this prelate; and, indeed, he was possessed of the happy talent of impressing the people with whatever

A. D., 1002.

A. D., 1014.

notions he thought fit; in which alone, of course, consisted his supernatural powers. A see was given to Popo, with power to preside over the Danish clergy; while at the same time he was suffragan of Adeldag, Archbishop of Hamburg.

Swen Splitbeard had two sons, *Harald* and *Canute;* and the Danish historian, Meursius, says, "that Harald, by right of primogeniture, succeeded his father to the throne of Denmark, while Canute, who at Swen's death lived in England, was elected King of the Danes there." But the Englishmen, taking advantage of Canute's youth, threw off the subjection they had promised his father, Swen Splitbeard, and called the fugitive Ethelred II. back from Normandy, and a general insurrection broke out. After having ordered the tongues and ears of the English hostages to be cut off, and, on the whole, shown an inflexible severity, Canute repaired to Denmark, where he brought together a numerous host of brave soldiers, and a well-manned fleet, with which he went back to England, accompanied by Erik Jarl, from Norway, Thorkel the High, and Ulf Jarl, who afterwards married Canute's sister, Estrith. He met with the English fleet, commanded by King Ethelred in person, whom he defeated after a sharp engagement. The valiant *Edmund Ironside,* who had succeeded his father Ethelred on the throne of England, was forced to yield the half of England to Canute. But a month after, Edmund Ironside was treacherously killed

A. D., 1017.

by his brother-in-law, Edrik Streon, whereupon Canute was acknowledged king of the whole of England. The first measure of Canute was now to seize Edmund's two sons, whom he sent to his ally, the King of Sweden, Anund Jacob, with the request that they might be put to death. Humanity, however, induced the Swedish monarch to spare their lives and send them into Hungary. Canute, now ruler of England, tried to make himself both beloved and esteemed there; he reigned with great judiciousness, paid respect to the privileges of the native people, and raised them to the highest offices; advanced commerce and literature, and courted, in a particular manner, the favor of the Church, by munificent donations, and by presenting monasteries with rich gifts; and he has, indeed, much better title to saintship than many of those who adorn the Roman calendar. To make himself yet more popular, he wisely married the virtuous *Emma* of Normandy, the queen-dowager of Ethelred, whom the English people loved dearly. But while he thus tried to make himself popular, and provide for the welfare of the State, his despotism and cruelty were often insupportable, and those whose influence seemed pernicious to him, he was not scrupulous in putting out of the way. Thus he caused Edrik Streon and Thorkel the High to be killed; the first of whom was invested with Mercia, the latter with East Anglia, as absolute fiefs. To confirm his power, and perform the conquests he had in view, he established a standing army, called the *Thingmannalid*, consisting of the most famous warriors; and, on account of the sumptuous armor they had to wear, containing only the richest and most conspicuous. To this army he gave a peculiar law, called the *Vitherlagslaw*, which for a long time enjoyed a great credit in Europe.

His brother Harald, King of Denmark, died after a reign of four years. Weak from his infancy, he was little able to rule, and his profligacy, entire contempt of decency and morality, rendered him odious to his subjects. Nothing need be said of him but that he reigned four years; whereupon Canute, generally called *Canute the Great*, was unanimously chosen to succeed him on the Danish throne, which thus, after an interval of only four years, was reunited with England; which, superior to Denmark in refinement, arts, trade, and agriculture, long exercised a beneficial influence upon the Danish kingdom. To Canute the Great has Denmark to ascribe the *complete introduction of Christianity;* for under him the last vestiges of the pagan worship were destroyed, its idols overthrown, its altars demolished, and its temples closed; and Christianity has since prevailed in Denmark, and formed the great bond of the social happiness, and the great source of the intellectual eminence which this remote quarter of the globe now so richly enjoys. Many English clergymen migrated in this period to Denmark. English clergymen were mostly invested with the Danish bishoprics;

and, on the whole, Canute considered England the main realm, and resided there. But he deserved well, also, of Denmark, by bringing a great portion of Venden under subjection, and subduing the formidable Vendish pirates. About the same time Christianity was introduced into Sweden, under *Olaf Skótkonung*, who was baptized by an English clergyman, Sigfrid; and into Norway, under *Olaf the Pious*, who, with three hundred brave men, traveled round and destroyed the heathen idols.

Before relating Canute's last expedition to Norway, his exploits there, and his end, it may be noticed that he, like most royal persons in the period under consideration, made a pilgrimage to Rome, to pay, in that sacred city, his devotion to the relics of some deceased saint, and obtain from the Pope remission of his sins. While in Rome he established, by assent of the Pope, a caravansary for Scandinavian pilgrims; procuring his subjects, also, on the same occasion, several commercial privileges. Upon his journey to Rome he chanced to meet with the German Emperor, Conrad II., whom he induced to renounce his claims to the Margraviate of Schleswig, founded by Henry the Fowler, and a marriage was stipulated between Canute's daughter, *Gunhilda*, and Conrad's son, *Henry*.

A. D., 1026.

About this time, or a little before, the Scandinavians began to make discoveries in the North and West. The Faroe islands had been discovered at the latter end of the ninth century, by some Scandinavian pirates, and soon after this, Iceland was colonized by the Norwegians. The Icelandic chronicles also relate, that the Norsemen discovered a great country to the West of Ireland; and it seems, indeed, very clear that they made their way to Greenland, in the end of the tenth century—and they are thus the very first discoverers of America. The settlement made in Greenland, though comprising only a small population, seems to have been very prosperous in mercantile affairs. They had bishops and priests from Europe, and paid the Pope, as an annual tribute, 2,600 pounds of walrus teeth as tithe and Peter's pence. But the art of navigation must have been at a very low pitch, for the voyage from Greenland to Iceland and Norway, and back again, consumed five years; and upon one occasion, the Government of Norway did not hear of the death of the Bishop of Greenland until six years after it had occurred. Unfortunately, the Norsemen forgot too soon the navigation thither; and their discoveries have, therefore, not derogated from that immortal renown, which Columbus, five centuries later, acquired.

But the discovery of America by the Northmen, in the tenth and eleventh centuries, is of so great interest and importance to American antiquity, that I must dwell a little upon this subject. The great antiquarian of Copenhagen, Prof. C. Rafn, has investigated deeply upon the subject, and his facts and assumptions rest mainly on the authority of ancient Icelandic manuscripts, which doubtless are authentic. Iceland was discovered in 863, by the Dane *Garder*, who was of Swedish extraction. Only a few out places of this distant island had been visited previously by Irish hermits. Eleven years subsequently, thus relates Rafn, a Norwegian, *Ingolf*, began the colonization of the island; the colonists established in Iceland a flourishing republic, where the Old-Danish, or Old-Northern language was preserved unchanged for centuries, and Iceland became the cradle of a Northern historical literature, of immense value. The location of this remarkable island compelled its inhabitants to exercise and develop their hereditary maritime skill, and thirst for new discoveries across the vast ocean. The talented American, W. Gilmore Simms, of South Carolina, rightfully remarks, that it is in favor of the Icelandic Sagas, that they do not seem to have been written to assert any claim of discovery. The very first of these old documents, to which I will request the reader's attention, is the Saga of *Bjarne Herjulfson*. This bold navigator was preceded by *Erik the Red*, by whom *Greenland* was discovered in 983, and who, three years afterwards, by means of Icelandic emigrants, established the first colony on its southwestern shore, where, in 1124, the Bishop's see of *Gardar* was founded, which subsisted for more than 300 years. The head firths or bays were named after the chiefs of the expedition. *Erik the Red* settled in

Ericksfirth, *Einar*, *Rafn*, and *Ketil* in the firths called after them, and *Herjulf* on Herjulfness. On a voyage from Iceland to Greenland, this same year (986), *Bjarne Herjulfson*, a son of Herjulf, was driven far out to sea, towards the southwest, and for the first time beheld the coasts of the American lands, afterwards visited and named by his countrymen. In order to examine these countries more narrowly, *Leif the Fortunate*, son of Erik the Red, undertook a voyage thither in the year 1000, from which his father was discouraged by an omen. His son, Leif, however, was not discouraged. With thirty-five hardy men, he landed on the shores described by Bjarne, detailed the character of these lands more exactly, and named them according to their appearance *Helluland* (Newfoundland) was so called from its flat stones, Hella signifying a flat stone; *Markland* (Nova Scotia), from its woods; Markland, that is woodland, and *Vineland* (New England) from its vines. It is therefore wrong, when some historians tell, that Greenland was called Vineland by the Northmen, hardly any vines being found there. Here in Vineland (New England), Leif the Fortunate remained for some time, and constructed large houses, called after him Leifbudis (Leif's booths). A German, named *Tyrker*, who accompanied Leif on this voyage was the man who found the wild vines, which he recognized from having seen them in his own land, and he gave the country its name from this circumstance. He departed then in the spring for his native country, where the intelligence of his discovery created great sensation. Two years afterwards, Leif's brother, *Thorwald*, pursued the adventure thither, and in 1103, caused an expedition to be undertaken to the South, along the shore, but was killed, in the summer of 1004, on a voyage northwards, in an encounter with the natives.

But among the most interesting of the Sagas at this period, is that of *Thorfinn Karlsefne*. The word Karlsefne signifies "a man destined to become great." He is the most distinguished of all the first American discoverers. He was an Icelandic merchant, whose genealogy is carried back in the Old-Northern annals to Danish, Norwegian, Scottish, and Irish ancestors, some of them even of royal blood. In 1006, this chief, on a merchant voyage, visited Greenland, and married there *Gudrid*, the widow of Thorstein (a third son of Erik the Red), who had died the year before, in an unsuccessful expedition thither. Accompanied by his wife, and by a crew of 160 men, on board three vessels, he repaired in the spring of 1007 to Vineland, where he remained for three years, and had many communications with the aborigines. Here his wife Gudrid bore him a son, called *Snorre*, who was the very first child of European parents born in America, and became the founder of an illustrious family in Iceland, which gave that island several of its first Bishops. But the birth of this child is remarkable for another reason, for up to this child the great Danish sculptor, *Albert Thorwaldsen*, traces his lineage, along with that of many other eminent Scandinavians.

The notices given by this illustrious navigator, Thorfinn Karlsefne, and, on the whole, by the old Icelandic voyager chroniclers respecting the climate, the soil, and the productions of this new country, are very characteristic, and correspond with the language of less questionable narrators, five hundred years later. Nay, we have even a statement of this kind as old as the eleventh century from a writer, not a Northman, *Adam of Bremen*, who states, on the authority of the learned king of Denmark, Svén Estridson, a nephew of Canute the Great, that the country got its name from the vine growing wild there; and it is a remarkable coincidence in this respect, that its English re-discoverers, from the same reason' name the large island, which is close off the coast, *Martha's Vineyard*. Spontaneously growing wheat (maize or Indian corn) was also found there.

Upon the whole, it is the total result of the nautical, geographical, and astronomical evidences, in the original documents, which places the location of the countries discovered, beyond all doubt. The number of days' sail between the several newly-found lands, the striking description of the coasts, especially the white sand-banks of Nova Scotia, and the long beaches and downs of a peculiar appearance on Cape Cod, are not to be mistaken, and cannot but open our eyes with interest. In addition hereto we have the astronomical remark that the shortest day in Vineland (New England) was nine hours long, which fixes the latitude of 41° 24′ 10″, or just that of the promontories, which limit the entrances to Mount Hope Bay, where Leif's booths, above mentioned, were built, and in the district around where the old Northmen had their head establishment, which was named by them *Hóp*.

The Northmen were, also, according to Prof. Rafn, acquainted with American land still farther to the South, called by them *Hvitramannaland* (the land of the White Men) or *Irland it Mikla* (Great Ireland). The exact location of this country has not been stated; it was probably, says Rafn, North and South Carolina, Georgia and Florida. In 1266, some priests at Gardar, in Greenland, did also set on foot a voyage of discovery to the arctic regions of America, and an astronomical observation proves, that this took place through Lancaster Sound and Barrow's Strait, to the latitude of Wellington's channel. The last memorandum supplied by the old Icelandic records, is a voyage from Greenland to Markland (Nova Scotia) in 1347.

Thus the claim that the Northmen were the very first discoverers of America, seems to be placed on good foundation, and it is embodied in the able and elaborate work of Professor C. Rafn, of the Royal Danish Society of Northern Antiquities. However, this does not, I may be allowed to repeat it, lessen the great merits of Columbus, nor have I referred to it for this purpose; but we ought, nevertheless, not to forget, that Columbus visited the Danish island, Iceland, in 1477, had access to the archives there, and must, doubtless, have heard of the former discoveries of its roving sea-chiefs. Be, therefore, not ashamed, Americans, of claiming the old Northmen, who sailed forth in swarms from their northern hives, as your earliest ancestors. Your lineage is, in the main, Anglo-Saxon, with a large infusion of Scandinavian blood. And permit me to say, that when you trace your parent stock, through the kindred tribes of Angles, Saxons, Normans, and Danes, up to those hardy mariners, whose prows first saluted the American shores, you may boast of an exalted and heroic lineage. And I still dare to pit that race, both here and in England, for all that constitutes individual and national prowess, against any other on God's green earth. Try them yet, man to man, on sea or shore, in peace or war, and they will work out an ultimate and lasting triumph. They are not laggards in peace, not dastards in war.

But also with the east had the Northmen connection. The same age which saw the bearded Vikings, the Grim-visaged Sea-Kings of the North discovering Iceland and America in the far West, beheld them also in the East, and with extraordinary energy. Summoned thither from the Scandinavian North, the old Russian historian, *Nestor*, assures us, that under the name of Variago-Russians they established the Russian Empire in 862, and for more than a century exercised great influence on its affairs, both internal and external. The correctness of this statement by Nestor, and the important part played by the Scandinavian Russians, in the first period of that power, becomes evident at once from the names borne by the historical actors themselves, almost all of which belong to the Old-Danish or Old-Northern language, and are recognized in the Northern Sagas and Runographic monuments. The men "of the Russian nation" sent by *Oleg* in 907 and 911, as embassadors to Constantinople, were all Northmen; and *Liutprand*, Bishop of Cremona, who, in 968, visited Constantinople, expressly asserts that the people whom the Greeks called Russians, were the same nation as those named Northmen. These Northmen, Danes, Swedes, Norwegians, and some English, flocked, usually, there by land, through the Russian territory, and took service in Constantinople in the Imperial life-guard, under the name of Varangers.

A remarkable confirmation of the statement made by Nestor, would be afforded, if we could, says Prof. Rafn, venture to assume that the name *Igvar*, occurring on several Swedish Runic stones, is the Russian crown-prince *Igor*. Sixty Runic monuments have been carefully examined; twelve of these inscriptions speak of an Igvar, and are carved in memory of men who had taken part in his expedition (*i faru med Igvari*), some of them even as ship-commanders.

To return to Canute the Great. While he tarried in Rome, *Olaf the Pious*, of Norway, and *Anund Jacob*, of

Sweden, availed themselves of Canute's absence to fall upon Denmark, both of them fearing his increasing power, and being angry because Norwegian mutineers had found an asylum at the Danish Court. The united kings making great progress, *Ulf Jarl*, who was married to Estrith, a sister to Canute, and appointed lieutenant-governor under the king's absence, deemed it necessary for the country to have a head, and prevailed upon the people to elect the crown prince, *Hardi Canute*, king. Canute informed of this, in his opinion, arbitrary conduct, hastened home, but though highly angered with Ulf, he delayed his vengeance till the enemies were driven away. A battle was fought by *Helgebrook* in Skane, where Canute himself would have perished, had it not been for Ulf's aid. But even this could not appease the exasperated king, who, under pretence of friendship, invited him to a drinking-bout in Roeskilde. They played at chess together. The king making a wrong move, would undo it, but Ulf Jarl being angry, upset the chess-board, and left. "Dost thou now fly, thou cowardly Ulf?" cried the king. "Thou didst not call me cowardly," answered Ulf, "when the Danes, by Helgebrook, like dogs, betook to their heels, and I saved thy life." The king, yet more irritated at this answer, caused Ulf to be killed in the cathedral of Roeskilde, to which he thereafter gave a whole county as a propitiatory sacrifice for his crime. Canute now put himself at the head of a brave body of

A. D., 1027.

men, sailed with a mighty fleet to Norway, and compelled Olaf the Pious to fly to Garderige (Russia). Olaf, however, shortly after reappearing, attempted to regain his kingdom, but fell in the battle at *Stiklestad*, close by Trondhjem. Canute the Great was now the most formidable potentate perhaps in Europe. Denmark, England, Norway, South Scotland, and a great part of Venden were tributary to him, and his alliance was courted by the greatest monarchs. Canute, who had three sons, now appointed his son Swen viceroy of Norway, but he despised the Norwegians to such a degree, that they dethroned him, and placed Magnus the Good, a son of Olaf the Pious, upon his father's throne. Thus Canute's mighty realm began already to be dissolved, when death suddenly terminated his, in many respects, so glorious life. History has surnamed him the Great. He was successful in his wars, and bore the sceptre with prudence and judiciousness, but not always with justice. He was very much dazzled by ambition, vanity being his besetting sin, so that he even threatened a Skald with death for not having magnified him sufficiently in a poem. The poor Skald had to compose another one, in which he then told that Canute ruled the world with the same omnipotence as God does heaven, and with this flattery he was pleased.

A. D., 1030.

A. D., 1035.

All eyes of the Danish people were now bent upon *Hardi-Canute*, the eldest son of Canute the Great, and

the crown was placed on his head, while *Harold Hare-foot* (nimble-footed as a hare) ascended the throne of England. Hardi-Canute has obtained the appellation *Hardy*, from the valorous actions he performed in Russia, when his father sent him thither in pursuit of Olaf, king of Norway. After his accession to the Danish throne, he immediately prepared to regain Norway, and met Magnus the Good by Góta-Elf, where
A. D., both armies were ready for battle, when the dif-
1038. ference unexpectedly was composed by a compact, that each should keep his kingdom until his death, but the survivor inherit both kingdoms. After a short reign, died Harold Harefoot, and Hardi-Canute, by his mother Emma acquainted with his brother's death, now united England with Denmark without any oppo-
A. D., sition. After a violent administration of three
1042. years he died, to the great comfort of his English subjects, who now seized the opportunity of entirely shaking off the Danish yoke. The union of Denmark and England was broken, England electing *Edward Confessor*, son of Ethelred, as king, and the Danes making no attempt to resist the voice of the nation. Since that time the kings of Denmark have never ruled England, although several attempts were afterwards made.

4*

II.

1042—1157.

Magnus the Good—Swen Estrithson—Expedition to England—Ecclesiastical Affairs—*Canute the Pious*—Expedition again against England—*Eric the Good*—Expedition to Venden—Canonization of Canute the Pious—*Canute Lavard—Nicholas*—Civil war between Swen Grathe, Canute Magnusson and Waldemar—Frederick Barbarossa—Battle on Grathe-heath, in Jutland.

On the death of Hardi-Canute, Denmark and Norway were, according to the agreement of Góta-Elf, united under *Magnus the Good*. The male lineage of the royal family of Denmark was extinct, but a descendant in the female line, Swen Estrithson, a son of Ulf Jarl and Estrith, sister to Canute the Great, was yet alive. He put in his claim to the throne, and had the address to gain over a great number of the Danish nobility to his interest. The Danes, who lately had ruled so many people, would reluctantly be subject to Norway, and Swen Estrithson, therefore, found no difficulty in being elected king of Denmark, and consequently a war broke out between him and Magnus the Good. Swen equipped a fleet in Jutland, gave battle to Magnus, but was routed, being forced to take shelter in the island of Fjunen. Here he refitted, and ventured upon another engagement, which terminated as unsuccessfully as the former. His whole fleet was dispersed, and he himself obliged to flee to Anund Jacob, of Sweden, for refuge. Of these disburbances the Venders took advantage, making desolating invasions, overrunning the coasts of Jutland, and laying waste all the country through which they passed. But Magnus, neither wearied nor daunted, raised an army, gave them battle by *Lyrskow*, in Schleswig, and conquered these barbarians, though superior in numbers. After this memorable combat, the war between Magnus and Swen was renewed, and the latter was about to give up all hope of the crown of Denmark, just as Magnus the Good died. The Norwegians separated now from Denmark, electing *Harald the Hardy*, a half-brother of Olaf the Pious, their king; and the Danes called *Swen Estrithson* to the Danish throne, to which he by blood was the nearest heir. Upon the whole, highly beloved for his pleasing address, and captivating manners, and very much esteemed for his learning, his re-appearance in Denmark was hailed with general joy. But, far from finding the throne a bed of roses, he had for seventeen years to stand up for his kingdom against the warlike Norwegian king, *Harald the Hardy*, who had lived a great number of years in exile, been hardened by military service in Constantinople, and was of a most invincible courage. He now laid claim to Denmark. *Swen Estrithson*, though often totally defeated, and even, in the bloody battle at *Nisaa*, in Halland, in danger of life, kept up an unshaken spirit, and when he had no reason to expect it, Providence wrought a happy change in his situation. The civil divisions in

England had roused Harald the Hardy's ambition to extend his conquests and influence, and he resolved upon an expedition to England in order to assist Toste against his brother Harald Godvinson, who had ascended the throne of England, by the title of Harold II. A battle was fought at *Standford-bridge*, where both Toste and the Norwegian king, Harald the Hardy, were killed, by which means Swen Estrithson recovered the peaceable possession of all his Danish dominions. But the death of Harold II., of England, who was A. D., slain in the memorable battle at Hastings, fought 1066. with William of Normandy, called the Conqueror, furnished Swen Estrithson with an opportunity of putting in his claim to the crown of England, as the only remaining descendant of Canute the Great. He made two expeditions to England, but both of them fell short of success, and William the Conqueror brought all England under his control.

Besides his many excellent qualities, which entitled him to honor, Swen Estrithson merits, particularly by his care for ecclesiastical affairs, the greatest gratitude of the whole Danish nation. To the five bishoprics already established, he added four: Wiborg and Bórglum in Jutland, and Lund and Dalby in Skane, in order the more easily to prevail upon the Pope to erect an archbishopric in Denmark, and thus make the northern church free from any dependence on the foreign archbishopric of Hamburg, the pressure of which Swen himself had felt to such a degree, that the Hamburgish archbishop, *Adelbert*, under the menace of excommunication, constrained him to part with his queen, Jutta, because she was a step-daughter to his first wife. Negotiating with several Popes concerning this important matter, he died before it was settled. The number of churches was, under his reign, considerably increased. There were three hundred in Skane, one hundred and fifty in Sjelland, and one hundred in Fjunen. The authority of the Church, to which the king in the case above mentioned had to submit, was, however, often of great weight in restraining rudeness, cruelty and transgression of law. Thus, for instance, when the king had ordered some of his guests, who at a merry compotation had used abusive language about him, to be killed the next morning in the cathedral of Roeskilde, and he thereafter would enter the church to attend his devotion, the entrance was forbidden him by Bishop William, who excommunicated him, (the very first case of ban in the North); and after he had first, as a contrite sinner, put on sack-cloth and asked remission of his crime, the absolution was pronounced by the bishop. A few years before Swen Estrithson's death, the Venders occupying the coast of the Baltic right from Denmark up to the Gulf of Finland, called *Vagrers* in Holstein, *Obotriters* in Mecklenburg, *Wilzers* as far as Oder River, Curlanders, Liflanders and Esthonians, had again revolted, leveled all the churches with the ground, pillaged the City of Schleswig, and, in derision, broken the crucifixes which mistaken piety had erected. But the greatest insult to the king was the manner in which they treated his sister, *Syrith*, whom they stripped naked, and in that condition sent to Denmark. He immediately raised an army to revenge these injuries, but had to drop his resolution, the Venders being too superior in numbers; and for upwards of one hundred and fifty years the desolating piracies of these barbarians continued, till at length the great Waldemar learned how to bring them under due subjection.

Swen Estrithson was a man of letters; he loved the cultivation of the mind and the conversation of the wise, and corresponded in Latin with the enlightened Pope Gregorius VII. (Hildebrand); and he was so well versed in the history of the North, as to be able to communicate to the learned *Adam of Bremen* important information, which he used in his description of Denmark. (Descriptio Adami Bremensis.) The clergy, in whom Swen Estrithson had taken so great interest, have extolled the character of the king as the most pious and merciful monarch that ever filled the throne of Denmark, although his incontinence was so great, that of thirteen sons he left behind him not one was legitimate, and, what is more, he had polluted the house of God by the cruel murder of several of his nobility. On his death, in Jutland, his son, Canute, was employed in quelling a rebellion, which appeared in Es- A. D., 1076.

thonia, while *Harald Hein,* his eldest son, was elected king, after warm disputes about the succession. The election of the king always took place, at that time, at a general diet (Danehof), usually held in Sjelland by Iise Fjord, or in Wiborg in Jutland. The king elected here traveled thereafter round to receive a special homage in the provincial courts, in Skane on *Sliparehog* near Lund, in Jutland close by *Wiborg,* in Sjelland by *Ringsted,* and in South Jutland (Schleswig) on *Urnehead.* Five of Swen Estrithson's children successively arrived at the dignity of the crown: an instance, perhaps, not to be equaled in history. Harald Hein, the eldest one, reigned with clemency, unengaged in any hostilities; but being somewhat unprincipled and weak, he was surnamed *Hein* (*i. e.,* a soft stone). His short reign, however, is remarkable in reference to an important alteration in the legal procedure. Formerly, persons who were accused of crime had to prove their innocence either by *duel* or *fire ordeal,* the latter of which being considered an immediate judgment from God, and consisting in that he who was charged with a crime had to take in his hand a piece of red-hot iron, or to walk barefoot and blindfold over nine red-hot plowshares. If the person escaped unhurt, he was declared innocent, otherwise he was condemned as guilty. But Harald Hein passed a law, by which criminals, where positive evidence was wanting, should be allowed to clear themselves by an oath, when certain impartial persons, called arbitrators, swore that they felt convinced that the accused had told the truth. This law was received with universal approbation.

On the death of Harald Hein, *Canute the Pious*, his brother, was recalled from Esthonia, and appointed his successor. He was, at this time of ignorance and selfishness, highly eminent for the honesty and glory of his actions; pious in peace, brave in battle, an able ruler, and above the usual temptations of lust, luxury, and avarice, except the thirst of sovereign power and of extending his territories; which, after he had quelled the rebellion in Esthonia, led him to embark once more in war, and attempt the recovery of England, the great jewel in the eyes of the Danish kings. Taking measures to ingratiate himself with his father-in-law, *Robert*, Earl of Flanders, and with his brother-in-law, *Olaf Kyrre*, King of Norway, he equipped by their aid a great fleet of a thousand ships in the Lymfiord, and raised an army with all possible expedition. But while the fleet and army were waiting at the appointed rendezvous, until Canute had appointed regents to govern the kingdom in his absence, William the Conqueror, anxious to turn off this imminent danger, had bribed the commanders-in-chief, and Olaf, the king's own brother, joined the bribery. The fleet separated, and Canute the Pious had to postpone his expedition to England. Olaf was brought, bound in chains, to the king. Canute, not wishing to pollute his

A. D., 1080.

hand with his brother's blood, sent him to his father-in-law, the Earl of Flanders, requesting him to watch Olaf so narrowly as to prevent his return to Denmark. On the bribed commanders-in-chief heavy penalties were inflicted; which, however, being called in too arbitrarily and despotically, occasioned a sedition in *Vendsyssel* (a county in Northern Jutland), which soon spread over the whole of Jutland. Canute the Pious, who, moreover, from the time he had granted the tithe to the clergy, had wholly alienated the minds of the people from him, had to escape to the Island of Fjunen, whither the rebels pursued him, and killed him in St. Alban's church of Odensee, while kneeling before the altar. His queen, *Edela*, fled with her little son, Charles, afterwards called Charles the Dane, to her father, in Flanders (Belgium). Both he and his grandfather were concerned in the great Crusades.

A. D., 1086.

Canute the Pious was not only pious, but also keen and active, and a grave and vigorous king. He punished with inflexible severity, and without respect of persons, every transgression of law, and employed all his efforts to root out all residue of rudeness of antiquity, especially the horrible piracy. *Egil Ragnarson*, a chief on Bornholm, an island in the Baltic, who was found guilty of this crime, was hung without mercy. To promote the culture of the country, he showed foreigners who settled in Denmark all possible benevolence and protection. He took a particular care to diminish the vast gulf that hitherto had existed between freemen and slaves, and aided the clergy in their efforts for this important matter. Nevertheless, it took a long time before the spirit of Christianity could master this evil, traces of it being found even up to the fourteenth century. The wealth, privileges, and possessions of the clergy, had so efficient a promoter in Canute the Pious, that the clergymen could place themselves on terms of equality with the freeholders of land. He made the clergy the most eminent order of the kingdom, placed the bishops in the same rank with princes and dukes, and liberated the clergy from subjection to the general tribunal, establishing a special court, consisting only of clergymen. He also granted, as above mentioned, the Danish clergy tithe, which Charlemagne already, in the year 812, had introduced into Germany. This tithe, however, was not paid during the reign of Canute the Pious, the people regarding it as the very worst kind of servitude.

Canute's death was no sooner known than a sum of money was raised by the friends of Olaf for his ransom; and his brother Nicholas sent to the Earl of Flanders to conduct him to Denmark, where he was raised to the throne. The glory that Canute the Pious, in many respects, had shed upon the country, was soon obscured by his brother and successor, *Olaf the Hungry*, a surname given him on account of a dreadful famine which, in consequence of a bad harvest, prevailed so much under his reign, that the richest people in Denmark were forced to supply the want of bread with roots and other vegetables, while the poor perished in the streets and highways. It had long been customary with the nobility to dine with the king on Christmas Day, and they were accordingly invited. When dinner was served up, the king called for bread, but was told that there was not a morsel in the whole kingdom. The clergy declared that it was a punishment sent by heaven for the murder committed on Canute the Pious, and the Bishop of Roeskilde made a pilgrimage to the Holy Land, thereby to appease the Almighty, and atone for the crimes of the people. After an inglorious reign of nine years, Olaf the Hungry expired, and the crown was transferred to his noble brother, Erik, who deservedly has been called *Erik the Good*. Under this excellent prince Denmark began to retrieve her ancient power. He was brave, humane, and kind, liberal to the distressed and poor, eloquent and public spirited; and he preferred the arts of peaceful industry to destructive wars, wherefore he by right has got his fair surname. Nevertheless he could not avoid making several expeditions to Venden, to protect his country against those cruel pirates, whom he pursued into all the different parts of the Baltic, and punished severely those who fell into his hands, in order to terrify others by these examples. A dispute with *Liemar*, the Archbishop of Bremen, concerning some temporalities, in-

A. D., 1095.

duced him to renew his father's efforts to procure for the North an archbishopric; he also wished to get his murdered brother, Canute the Pious, canonized, or enrolled in the calendar of saints. To supplicate the Pope, *Urbanus II.*, for it, he went in person to Rome. His petition was willingly granted by his Holiness. After the king's return from Rome, Canute the Pious was accordingly taken up from the grave, and with great solemnity enshrined in the splendid St. Canute's Church of Odensee. By this Denmark got a *national* saint; to whose grave pilgrims traveled for many centuries, from all northern lands, in order to pay their devotion to his remains, hoping aid thereby for spiritual and bodily affliction. Some time after he vowed a pilgrimage to the Holy Land, to do penance and expiate a murder he, most likely in a state of intoxication, had committed. His people, who loved him dearly, unanimously remonstrated against his design; they embraced his feet, and bathed them with their tears, begging that he would stay at home and rule his kingdom, and not expose to danger a life upon which depended the felicity of a whole kingdom, and laid it before him that it was more acceptable in the sight of God to remain and discharge his royal duties. But a mighty enthusiasm had taken possession of his mind, and crying out, "It is the will of God!" he accordingly set out. Passing through Greece, the king was magnificently entertained in Constantinople by *Alexius Commenus*, where he spoke with the Varangers, the imperial life-guard, consisting of northern people, chiefly of Danes. From thence he took ship for Cyprus, an island in the Mediterranean, where shortly after his arrival he died, without reaching the sepulchre of the Redeemer; but *Bothildis*, his devout queen, and faithful companion of his pilgrimage, reached Jerusalem, where she died and lies buried.

A. D., 1103.

The canonization of Canute the Pious, which had been granted by the Pope, became of so great consequence that in his honor several clubs or *fraternities* (Danish, *Gilder*), were instituted, the object of which was mutual protection against violence and outrage, and mutual aid in case of sickness, shipwreck, fire, and other calamities. When a member of such a fraternity was charged with any crime, the others were bound to assist him by oath and witness. Likewise, when a member had been murdered, the others should gather the fine, or if refused to be paid, demand vengeance of blood on the slayer. These fraternities had, like all institutions in the Middle Age, an ecclesiastical stamp. They were dedicated to some saint, whose name they adopted. Donations were given to the church and the poor, and requiems sung for the dead. Some fraternities, that enjoyed a greater reputation than others, were called *royal*, because dedicated to Canute the Pious, Canute Lavard and Erik Ploughpence. Others were established by merchants and mechanics. But when, in course of time, the laws and institutions of the State obtained more solidity and strength, such private associations became superfluous, ceasing, at length, altogether, by the introduction of the Reformation. By means of these fraternities, which promoted harmony, fellowship and industry among the inhabitants of the same city, the power and importance of the burgher class were considerably raised and extended, commerce developed, and prosperity produced, while, on the other hand, the peasantry remained in a state of deep dependence.

Not till the spring of next year the intelligence of the death of Erick the Good reached Denmark, where now *Nicholas*, his brother, was elected king by the people, and their choice confirmed by the Diet. They were urged the more to do this by the severity of *Harald Kesia*, a son of Erik the Good, who had ruled the kingdom during the absence of his father, and who they foresaw would render them unhappy if they raised him to the throne. The Papal bull respecting the erection of a national archbishopric did not arrive in Denmark till after Erik's departure for Palestine, and the first archbishop in the North, *Adzer*, who resided in Lund, in Skane, was, therefore, not appointed before the beginning of the reign of King Nicholas, when a Papal legate was sent for that purpose. By this alteration the Church, the power of which Canute the Great and Swen Estrithson had founded, and Canute the Pious widely extended, obtained internal strength and position, while the State was yet too weak to maintain the civil affairs. But frequent collisions arose hereby between the Lords spiritual and temporal; and the archbishops of Lund, on account of their large real estates and great revenues, often made head against the kings, and raised seditions and civil wars, in which the kings very often got the worst, till at length the civil government obtained sufficient moral strength, and the power of the Church had to yield to that of the State. The separation of the Church from the State was consummated by introducing celibacy, the first papal bull ordering which was issued to the Danish church shortly after the creation of the Lundish archbishopric, but met with a long and obstinate opposition from the Danish clergy, and a hundred years after two hundred priests in Jutland protested decidedly against it. But in vain. The unmarried life became a rule for the clergy in the North as well as in other Christian countries, and had there, as everywhere, the corruptive consequence, that the priests cohabited with concubines, and what is worse, often gave loose to appetites, that not only were sordid, but inhuman.

A. D., 1123.

At first, King Nicholas wielded his sceptre with great applause, but falling off in his character, he fell into the utmost contempt, and involved himself and his country in a variety of misfortunes. The breach of the public tranquillity took its rise from the Vendish prince *Henry*. Entering into an alliance with the Nordalbingi, properly the Holsteiners, he soon subdued the whole country between the Elbe and Schleswig. Nicholas gave battle to Henry, whose horse broke through and put in confusion the Danish cavalry. Nicholas was defeated, and forced to retreat with precipitation into Denmark. The peace of the interior parts of the country was disturbed by the two turbulent sons of Erik the Good — Harald Kesia and Erik Emun — who had a bloody dispute over their patrimony. Fortunately for the country, *Canute Lavard*, their brother, was a prince of a noble mind, and inspired with patriotic feelings and love of freedom, which somehow supplied the king's inability. Constraining his brothers to keep quiet, chastising the rapacious Venders, and perceiving the misery to which the Duchy of Schleswig was reduced by the Venders and Obotriters, he requested the government of Schleswig, which he at length obtained. His first measure was to subdue the haughty Vendish prince, Henry, above mentioned. With a body of troops he marched in the middle of the night directly to a castle on the frontiers of Schleswig, where Henry kept his head-quarters, and was fortunate enough to surround the place, before the Vendish prince received any intimation of his approach. In this situation, Henry, perceiving that resistance would be fruitless, mounted his horse and escaped, after which he sued for peace, promising to submit to any terms which the conqueror should think fit to impose. Thus the valor of Canute

Lavard not only secured the Duchy of Schleswig to the crown of Denmark, but procured to himself the dignity of a Duke. After the Obotritish royal family was extinct, he became, through the instrumentality of his admirer, *Lothar of Saxony*, (German Emperor,) King of the Obotriters. He encouraged agriculture, planted new kinds of corn, built mills, invited German mechanics to settle in Roeskilde and Schleswig, and accustomed the warlike people to the arts of peace. But the great esteem he enjoyed, and the kindness and predilection the people bestowed upon him, procured him enemies, who increased in proportion to his virtue. They easily found means to persuade the weak King, Nicholas, and his son Magnus, who was very envious of Canute, that ambition was the spring of all Canute's actions; that, far from being satisfied with the crown he wore and with the Duchy of Schleswig, he aspired at a still higher dignity, and that his popularity was paving an easy way for his ascending the throne of Denmark. The plot was ready to break out, when a sudden revolt in Pomerania and Mecklenburg (Obotrit) called him to his own country, and for a time postponed his fate. He quickly subdued the rebels, and returned to Denmark. Having no suspicion of treachery, he was attacked in a little wood close by Ringsted, in the island of Sjelland, by *Magnus* and *Henry Skate*, his cousins, and slain. Thus fell the generous, the great Canute Lavard, the ornament and support of Denmark,

A. D., 1131.

and the greatest hero of his age in the North. But he lives still in the legends and heroic songs. He was privately interred in the church of Ringsted, without any other monument than what he had established in the hearts of the Danes, who to this very day adore his memory. The news of his death soon reached Roeskilde, the residence of the court, and the king himself could not help shedding tears at the loss of this great man, though he was privy to the plot. The murder committed on Canute Lavard was about to raise a sedition, which was only prevented by King Nicholas sentencing his son, Magnus, to perpetual banishment, who went to Sweden, where he was elected king of the Vestrigoths. But, however, he soon returned. Upon the news of his return, Erik Emun, a brother of Canute Lavard, took up arms to avenge his memory. Both parties now prepared for war, and king Nicholas drew to his side all the bishops of Jutland, and several of the principal nobility of the kingdom, besides the conspirators in the murder of Canute Lavard, who were all strongly attached to the interest of the king and his son Magnus. An obstinate battle was fought by *Fodevig*, in Skane, where the mean Magnus fell, A. D., together with five bishops and sixty priests, and 1134. king Nicholas escaped by an ignominious flight to the city of Schleswig, where the members of the fraternity of St. Canute, the surveyor of which Canute Lavard had been, assassinated him and his train, dispatching the king with twenty stabs. Such was the merited death of king Nicholas, after a miserable reign of thirty years. When his friends represented to him the danger of his fleeing to Schleswig, so strongly attached to Canute, he told them that majesty had nothing to fear from shoemakers and tailors. Nevertheless, he fell by the hands of those very citizens he affected to despise. With Nicholas ended the reign of Swen Estrithson's fifth son, according to the promise Swen had on his death-bed exacted from the nobility.

Agreeably to a former election in a full assembly of the nobility and commons of Sjelland and Skane, *Erik Emun* was now proclaimed king, and administered the government for three years, but in a very miserable and wicked way, his capricious cruelty reigning uncontrolled. He caused his brother, Harald Kesia, and his nine sons to be put to death, without remorse or pity, believing, as he said, that neither his own authority nor the public tranquillity could be sufficiently established while his brother and nephews lived. As for the youngest son of Harald Kesia, he made his escape in a peasant's dress to Sweden. Meanwhile the Venders made a sudden irruption into Holstein, and laid waste with terrible desolation every place through which they passed. To repress their insolence, Erik Emun assembled a fleet, embarking in each vessel four horsemen, (the very first time that cavalry was carried over the sea,) besides foot, with which armament he passed over into their country, and soon reduced it. From thence he went to the Isle of Rygen to punish the inhabitants, who had not only assisted the Venders, but exercised the most desperate piracy on the high sea. Having subdued them, he compelled the whole island to swear allegiance to the crown of Denmark. They did not, however, long continue in this state of submission, for no sooner had Erik Emun returned to Denmark, than they revolted again, and assisted the Venders. Some disturbances arose now in Norway between Harald Gille and Magnus Sigurdson. Harald solicited Erik Emun's aid, who made no scruple of promising it as soon as he had put an end to the affairs in which the revolt of the Isle of Rygen and its capital, Arcona, now involved him.

Against these islanders he set out a second time, and so totally subjected them that he apprehended no other rebellion. He thereafter applied himself to the performance of his promise to Harald Gille, passed over to Norway with his army, and, in a decisive action with Magnus, defeated him and took him prisoner. His victory he disgraced by his cruelty; for, to prevent all attempts to reinstate the unfortunate king, he put out his eyes, emasculated him, and enclosed him for life in a monastery, raising Harald Gille to the throne of Norway. While his mind was thus cruelly employed, an unfortunate dispute arose among the bishops about the archbishopric of Lund, then vacant. *Eskild*, bishop of

Roeskilde, supported by the people, raised an army and obliged the cruel king to retire to Jutland, where his people, weary of bearing his cruelty, caused *Black-plogus*, a nobleman, to kill him, while administering justice in full court. As none of the three princes, who because of their birth were most entitled to the crown, to wit: *Swen*, son of Erik Emun, *Waldemar*, son of Canute Lavard, and *Canute*, son of Nicholas, had yet reached the maturity of age, *Erik Lamb*, a nephew of Erik the Good, surnamed the Lamb, from the mildness of his disposition, was chosen king. He had scarce ascended the throne when the divisions among the clergy broke out afresh. Eskild went over to Skane, and assumed the title and authority of primate, without obtaining, or indeed asking, the permission of the new king, who, observing the obstinacy with which the whole province of Skane espoused his cause, had to drop all resistance. The dispute about this archbishopric of Lund, was the first occasion the kings of Denmark had to repent of their having invested their prelates with temporal authority, and elevated them to such a pitch of power as rendered them dangerous to their sovereigns. Erik Lamb also made an expedition against the Venders, who had resumed their old trade of piracy, but he came off unsuccessfully; after which he fell into an inactivity and indolence that greatly impaired his reputation, and at length he embraced the resolution of renouncing his throne, and of passing the remainder of

A. D. 1137.

his days in quiet retirement and monastic penance, in the convent of St. Canute, in Odensee, where he lived a short time, busied with the practices of religion and pious contemplation. A. D., 1147

Upon the death of Erik Lamb, a *civil war* of ten years broke out between the three princes above mentioned, and the frequent and destructive invasions of the Venders reduced Denmark to great straits. An agreement was, however, made between the three pretenders, who shared the countries of Denmark with one another; but the agreement was not sincerely meant, for Swend and Waldemar soon after turned Canute out of the country, who had to flee to the German emperor, *Frederick Barbarossa*, for refuge. The emperor, anxious to get a proper opportunity to renew the old pretension to superiority over Denmark, was fain to meddle with this affair, and invited Swen and Waldemar to the Diet of Merseburg, where Swen had to acknowledge himself a vassal of the emperor, and grant Canute a share of Denmark. After returning, he would not, however, acknowledge his vassalage; and by assuming German manners and customs, he lost the love of his people. An insurrection broke out in Skane, and he maintained only a few years a precarious power, though assisted by the treacherous archbishop Eskild, of Lund, and by German auxiliaries from Henry Lion, of Saxony, and at length he had to share the realm with his competitors. Swen now mused on treason, A. D., 1153.

and he and Eskild agreed to kill Canute and Waldemar, who were treacherously invited to a drinking-bout in Roeskilde. Canute was murdered, but Waldemar put out the candles, and perceiving the door standing ajar, he pushed it open and escaped to Jutland, where he met his friend, the martial Absalon, afterward bishop of Roeskilde and archbishop of Lund, who also had fled away from the slaughter. A battle was fought on *Gratheheath* by Wiborg, where Swen, later called *Swen Grathe*, lost battle and life, his corpse being cast into a stone-quarry. Thus ended all the plots and machinations of the treacherous Swen. Seldom were victorious news more joyfully received than the tidings of the victory over Swen. The people cried out for a ruler to lead the troops to conquest and reinforce the whole army; and the Danish crown devolved now on Waldemar, the glorious son of Canute Lavard, for many years a model for kings.

A. D., 1157.

III.

1157—1241.

Waldemar I. the Great—Absalon—Canute VI—Bugislaw, of Pomerania—Waldemar II. the Conqueror—Conquests along the Baltic—Esthonia—The Captivity of the King—Science and the Arts.

WALDEMAR I. was joyfully received as king, and began his reign with the practice of every virtue that became a sovereign. He owed much of his success to his manners as well as to the uncommon energy of his mind. His composure of countenance and firmness of manner, says Saxo Grammaticus, were so great, that whatever resolution he had formed, he would adhere to. His first step towards gaining the esteem and affection of his subjects, was the conquering of the lands along the Baltic, and the putting a stop to the destructive piracies of the Venders. He made, therefore, several expeditions; but Henry Lion, of Saxony, above named, also keeping a strict eye upon Venden, and having already subdued several of these lands, endeavored to enlarge his dominion over the whole. Waldemar, therefore, judged it wise to be on friendly terms with the emperor Frederick Barbarossa. To obtain his alliance was not difficult for Waldemar, the more as the emperor considered the power of the Danish king a useful bulwark against the ambitious Henry Lion, who continually went too far. By his affability and eloquence, he won the emperor's affection and confi- A. D., 1162 dence so much as to promise Denmark energetic assistance to conquer Venden. Waldemar the Great, brave himself, and skilled in war, and assisted by such a hero as bishop *Absalon* (also called Axel), continued indefatigably his endeavors for subduing Venden, to which he made twenty expeditions. Absalon fitted out a large fleet and army, which, cruising round the Vendish coasts, landed at various places, plundered the towns, which were unprotected by the inhabitants, conquered Arcona, the fortified capital of the island of Rygen, and destroyed their idol, *Svantevit*, on which they firmly relied, the pagan priests telling that this idol every night rode a white horse and persecuted the foes of the Venders. This horse, therefore, was every morning exposed, covered with sweat, to the view of the people, to confirm their belief, and consequently they were astonished at seeing Svantevit, without any resistance, dashed to pieces by the Danes. The feeling between Waldemar and Henry Lion, varied very often, but was never very good, though a marriage was agreed upon between Gertrude, the duke's daughter, and Canute, the king's son. While all this was passing, an embassy came from Norway, requesting Waldemar to assist the Norwegian king, Erling Skakke, and his son Magnus Erlingsen, against Sverre, a competitor for the crown. Crossing over with an army, he was joyfully received, the campaign resulting in the Norwegian province Vigen's yielding to Waldemar. Having thus rendered himself master of the whole of Venden, converted the inhabitants to Christianity, and conquered a part of Norway, Waldemar had duties, in his opinion, paramount to all other considerations, namely, to preserve his kingdom from civil war. He caused therefore, his son, Canute, to be elected his successor, anointed and crowned. But the many princes aspiring to the crown, were very much displeased with this action of Waldemar, one of whom, *Buris*, a nephew of Swen Estrithson, mused upon treason, but was caught, maimed, and incarcerated. The archbishop Eskild, of Lund, who already, as bishop of Rocskilde, had stirred up a sedition against Erik Emun, and shared in the civil war after the death of Erik Lamb, dared also to defy Waldemar; but the king's rapid progress obliged the proud Eskild to ask peace in the most submissive terms, and to restore to the king all the possessions which the former kings had given to the see of Lund. Eskild was so chagrined with this humiliation, that he resigned his mitre and retired to a private convent in France, where he stayed for seven years. But after his return to Denmark, his position became yet more slippery, his two nephews engaging themselves in a conspiracy against the king. Suspected and hated, A. D., 1177. he soon after repaired to Paris, where he died. Absalon was elected his successor to the archbishopric of Lund. It was shortly before these affairs with the rebellious Eskild that Waldemar laid the foundation of the city of *Dantzic*, in Western Prussia, so famed for its trade and opulence. At first it was composed of the huts of poor fishermen, but Waldemar conferring upon the inhabitants certain privileges and immunities, it soon became a flourishing place of commerce. Thereafter he founded in Denmark the cities of Nyborg, Corsór, and Callundborg. About the same time Absalon built the castle of Stegelburg, afterwards called *Axelhusia*, then Hafnia, and now the celebrated port and city of Copenhagen. The intention of this castle was to overawe the pirates, and afford a safe protection to the Danish merchantmen.

Towards the close of Waldemar's life a revolt happened in Skane, to appease which the king immediately dispatched Absalon. The inhabitants, displeased with the oppressions of the royal bailiffs, and with the institution of tithe allotted to the clergy for their support, raised a great sedition, refused to pay the usual taxes, and particularly the bishop's tithe, and restored to the inferior clergy their ancient privilege of marriage. They insisted that the superior clergy were an unnecessary load upon the people, fattening upon the spoils of the land, while their flocks were left to find heaven in their own way. Waldemar, however, being more favored by the peasantry than Absalon, was prosperous in quelling this sedition by fair means; but when the imperious Absalon would by no means desist from claiming his tithe, which circumstance contributed in no slight degree to heighten their animosity, they rebelled anew, but were totally defeated by Absalon at *Dysiaa*, in Skane, and reduced to the necessity of yielding to the terms of the king. Soon after Waldemar the Great expired, after a glorious reign of twenty-five years. The respect in which he was held was strikingly exhibited at his death. A. D., 1181. A. D., 1182. The peasants drew the hearse, and his remains were interred in the church of Ringsted, and it was ordained by the citizens that his memory should be held in reverence. *Canute VI.*, his son, already chosen to succeed him to the throne, began his reign with pursuing the same course as his great father, guided and assisted by the same faithful counselors and brave warriors, archbishop *Absalon* and his brother, *Esbern Snare*, to whom was soon added the king's own brother, the victorious *Waldemar*. His reign was universally acceptable to the people, as he appeared equally remarkable for his firmness, clemency, liberality, activity, and justice. The first business he was engaged in, after his ascending the throne, was to answer the German emperor, Frederick Barbarossa, who, through an embassy sent to Denmark, had enjoined on the young king the duty of acknowledging himself a vassal of the Roman empire. His answer, in this emergency, shows the energy of Canute's character. "Please to inform your emperor," he said, "that the king of Denmark is just as independent in his kingdom as the German or Roman emperor in his empire, and that it were better for me to resign my crown, than to submit myself to him, even if he should declare war against me for rejecting his impudent enjoinment. I am ready to put my army in motion, and thus decide the fate of my kingdom." This answer highly exasperated the haughty emperor, who now stimulated *Bugislaw*, Duke of Pomerania, to attack Denmark. The Duke prepared himself to attack the isle of Rygen with five hundred men of war, but Absalon, informed of it, and seeing that no moment was to be lost, fitted out a fleet and overtook the surprised Venders, who lost four hundred and sixty-five ships, threw down their arms and sued for quarter, and the proud spirit of the duke began to give way. After this glorious victory, Pomerania and the Obotritic Venden had to submit to Denmark, Canute VI. now taking the title, *King of the Slavi and Venders*. Afterwards Canute made several expeditions to the eastern coasts of the Baltic, made conquests in Esthonia, and forced the inhabitants to embrace Christianity, but the Danes no sooner left, than they returned to heathenism and piracy. The war being ended between Denmark and Venden, a profound peace ensued for some years; the Danes thus having an opportunity of turning to the arts of peace. But while they were thus cultivating peaceful occupations, the vigilant king was not unmindful of making fresh preparations for war, well knowing that these intervals of ease would not fail to give his enemies fresh vigor for new designs. *Adolph*, Count

A. D., 1184.

of Holstein, *the archbishop* of Bremen, the *Margrave* of Brandenburg, and several princes of Northern Germany, happened to make depredations on the Danish coasts, wishing to arrest the strongly rising power of Denmark. This mighty alliance became the more dangerous, as bishop *Waldemar*, of Schleswig, an illegitimate son of Canute Magnusson, above mentioned, was meditating treacherous plans, and intended to take part with the German enemies of Denmark, and with king Sverre of Norway. But nothing was capable of subduing the courage of the king and of his undaunted brother, *Waldemar*, Duke of Schleswig, who captured and imprisoned the rebellious bishop, and defeated the other foes. The bishop was put into a gloomy prison, where he was compelled to pine for many years. Adolph had to yield himself prisoner of war; Holstein, Lübeck, Hamburg, and Lauenburg to submit to Denmark, and the Count of Schwerin to acknowledge himself a vassal of the Danish king; Denmark thus now being invested with a greater power than ever before. But towards the close of the reign of Canute VI., a marriage between *Ingeborg*, a sister to Canute, and *Philip Augustus* of France, occasioned a vehement dispute, Philip repudiating the princess, and not till a papal edict from Innocent III. had compelled him to join her again, was the dispute abated, and a threatening war avoided. After an active reign of twenty years, Canute VI. died, A. D., universally lamented. A year before, Absalon, 1202.

his friend and wise counselor, had been stricken by the hand of death. This extraordinary man—the greatest man the North had produced in the Middle Ages—was possessed of the greatest courage in opposing danger, and the greatest presence of mind in retiring from it. No fatigue was able to subdue his body, nor any misfortune to break his spirit; and moreover, he was a wise counselor in public and ecclesiastical concerns, and a great friend of science and the arts. Under the powerful direction of such influential archbishops as Eskild, Absalon, and his successor, Andrew Suneson, the ecclesiastical affairs gained a firm footing, Eskild composing a *canon law* for Skane, and Absalon one for Denmark; both of which were admitted of by the people and confirmed by the king. But, unfortunately, the power of the clergy was now increasing too much. In exclusive possession of the learning of the time, and from the Pope invested with the power of deciding the salvation of men's souls, the clergy acquired very easily a vast authority over the illiterate people of the Middle Ages; and the superior clergy, besides their ecclesiastical dignities, were frequently in possession of the most influential and lucrative offices of the state, and the archbishoprics, bishoprics, and abbacies, gradually obtained great possessions, so as to be nearly raised to an equality with principalities. The archbishops and bishops had fortified castles, kept soldiers, and were ready at a moment's notice, to make head against the kings. As the church increased in intrinsic strength, so she grew in riches and external power. Both kings and private people endowed her with an immense deal of real estates; and by the immunity conferred by the kings upon the church, she attained a degree of opulence and splendor nearly unrivaled, unless in Italy, during the Middle Ages; while unfortunately the augmentation of the wealth of the church brought with it a detrimental appetite for expensive and demoralizing pleasures amongst the clergy. At the period under consideration, the *nobility*, equal in rank to the clergy, but above the burgher class and the peasantry, commenced to be a peculiar class, with peculiar privileges; the whole population of Denmark thus being divided into nobility, clergy, burghers, and peasantry. The nobles possessed considerable estates in land, and were distinguished from the rest of the people, not by knowledge and cultivation of mind, but only by their superior luxury, and they often ruled the public affairs by the weight of an authority gained from riches and mercenary dependents. In short, the kingdom came now for many centuries under the tyranny of a hateful aristocracy, which the kings themselves often could hardly master, afterwards bitterly repenting of having raised such dregs of society. At first the nobility was only *personal*, but became in the period following *hereditary*, the obligations being few, but the prerogatives and privileges not to be numbered

Canute VI. being childless, his brother, Waldemar II., the Conqueror, ascended the throne, receiving in Lübeck homage from the subjugated lands and princes. Holstein, which Count Adolph, to regain his liberty, resigned, was given to Waldemar's nephew, Albert of Orlamünde. Waldemar II. prosecuted the conquests of his father and grandfather. The affairs in Germany were very favorable for Waldemar in carrying out his designs. Philip of Schwaben, Otto IV. a son of Henry Lion of Saxony, and Frederick II. of Hohenstaufen, who disputed for the dominion, all attempted to gain the friendship and protection of Waldemar II. Waldemar resolved to assist Frederick II., who returned to the Danish king, as a sign of gratitude, an imperial letter of confirmation in his German and Vendish conquests. Saxony, Bremen, Brandenburg, and several countries in Northern Germany joined together to oppose this monarch's power and progress, and raised a strong army, ready to act wherever its services should be required, which was, however, too weak to resist his victorious arms. Waldemar had long been bent upon humbling the rebellious bishop Waldemar of Schleswig, who, after being set at liberty, had again taken part with the enemies of his fatherland, and got himself appointed archbishop of Bremen. But Waldemar the Conqueror understood how to teach him obedience, and at length he was obliged to have recourse to a cloister, where, showing a very bad moral

A. D., 1214.

conduct, and sinking even to the level of vulgar men, he terminated his dishonorable life. No sooner had the German affairs permitted Waldemar to breathe a little freely, than he undertook several expeditions to the remoter coasts of the Baltic, conquering considerable tracts of Prussia; but most remarkable is his great expedition to Esthonia (called the Northern Crusade) under the command of the archbishop Andrew Suneson. Neither Denmark nor the other Scandinavian countries having taken any share in the great European crusades for the recovery of the Holy Land, Waldemar the Conqueror considered himself greatly indebted to the Christian Church. He went, therefore, to Esthonia, to christen the heathen inhabitants. The Esthlanders, at first pretending subjection, fell suddenly upon the Danish army, near to *Reval*, and a great confusion ensued; but the archbishop inspired the Danes with courage, persuading them that a flag, with a white cross interwoven on a red ground (later called Dannebrog), which the Pope had sent, had fallen down from heaven; to which statement, and the effect produced by it, the successful issue of the battle, and the conquest of the whole of Esthonia, are chiefly to be ascribed. The kingdom of Denmark now included Denmark, Holstein, Ditmarsh, Lauenburg, Schwerin, Mecklenburg, Rygen, Pomerania, Esthonia, Oesel (an island close by Russia), and several tracts of Prussia and Curland. But Waldemar the Conqueror was form-

A. D., 1219.

ing still more gigantic plans, love of dominion being the chief passion of his heart, when one disastrous night annihilated the fruits of the toils of three kings and of the victories of sixty years. Whilst engaged in the chase on a little island, Lyò, by Fjunen, the king and his son fell into the power of Count Henry, of Schwerin, were gagged, put on board a ship and carried to Germany, where they were kept prisoners for three years in the castle of Daneberg. A general confusion arose, the princes who were his vassals revolted from him, Hamburg and Lübeck fell away and became free cities, establishing, in conjunction with other maritime towns, a mighty alliance, called the *Hanseatic League*, and the emperor, Frederick II. of Hohenstaufen, formerly Waldemar's confederate, rejoiced now at seeing his disaster and calamity. Under such circumstances Waldemar had to subscribe to the hard conditions his enemies exacted for his release. The terms were severe, but were the best that could be procured. He should lay down to Count Henry forty-five thousand ounces of silver, resign Holstein to Count Adolph, quit his other German and Vendish possessions, except Esthonia and Rygen, and never make war again. Promising inviolably to observe these severe conditions, he came back to his kingdom on Christmas-eve, disconsolate and enraged, but more than ever beloved by his subjects, who now be-

A. D., 1223.

A. D., 1226.

came better acquainted with the sublimity of his virtues by this trial of adversity.

But Waldemar's patriotism, swallowed up in one great ruling affection, the love of his country, could not allow him to keep his promise. He applied to the Pope, was absolved from his engagements, made preparations for war, raised at length a great army, and entered Holstein, with all the resentment of a prince highly injured. Multitudes were flocking to his standard, and in the beginning, he was crowned with success. But leading his army back from Itzeho, which he had conquered, he was met by the bishop of Lübeck, the archbishop of Bremen, the duke of Saxony, the duke of Holstein, the Ditmarshers, the earls of Schwerin, Oldenburg and Mecklenburg, at the head of a prodigious army. A battle was fought at *Bornhòved* in A. D., Holstein, with incredible fury on both sides; but 1227. here Waldemar was totally defeated, and lost one eye. Being very much blamed for the perfidious breaking of his promise, he answered that a dispensation given him from the Pope, Honorius III., should be a sufficient excuse. After this transaction the king had the soul-rending misfortune to lose his eldest son, Waldemar, who was shot accidentally at a hunting-party, and from that time Waldemar the Conqueror dropped all intention of pursuing revenge. " Now," he said, " if God continues life and health, I will have nothing more to do with warfaring life, but for the remainder of my days employ all my efforts to promote the internal welfare of my kingdom." And so he did. His very first care was to give wise and beneficial laws, amongst which were the *Skanish* and the *Jutlandish* law, which he, shortly before his death, laid before the people, at a diet in Vordingborg, the Jutlandish law, even to this day, being valid in Schleswig, and not before 1685 abrogated in Denmark.

Waldemar the Conqueror was twice married: first to the Bohemian princess, *Dagmar*, and next to *Berengaria*, from Portugal, who became mother to *Erik*, *Abel*, and *Christopher*, one by one succeeding to the throne. Dagmar was highly beloved, but Berengaria much hated on account of her pride; and it became a proverb among the peasantry: " Blessed be Dagmar, cursed be Berengaria the old hag, the Lord be with the king." Waldemar had now attained to an advanced age. He had seen his kingdom raised to the highest pitch of glory and power, he had seen it sink A. D., into the deepest distress, and now he saw it 1241. again restored to peace and felicity, when death claimed him.

The means by which the inhabitants got their livelihood in this period were, agriculture, breeding of cattle, fishing and commerce, but all as yet on a small scale. The fishing was an important means of subsistence, and the Lymfjord and Earsound (Oeresund) were known for their abundant herring grounds. The trade was driven with Northern Germany and England; and between Jutland and Norway was a lively intercourse. Fish, cattle and horses were the most important articles of exportation. The most ancient coins of the North are from the time of Swen Splitbeard. Not only the kings, but also the bishops were permitted to coin.

Learned literature was cultivated exclusively by the clergy. Nevertheless the arts of poetry passed at an early period into the hands of the nobles, chiefly because love (*minne*) and devotion to the ladies were the soul and essence of the latter. In general they were called *Minnesongers*, or the *Nightingales* of the Middle Ages, considering the whole female sex as a sacred virgin. But on the whole, neither science nor the arts had reached a very high point, and young people being desirous of a deeper knowledge than they could acquire at home, had to go to the celebrated University of Paris, and at the close of the twelfth century a special college for Danish students was founded in Paris. Here, for instance, Absalon and Andrew Suneson completed their studies. Absalon, a man of letters himself, favored learned literature, and encouraged the renowned *Saxo Grammaticas* to compose a history of Scandinavia, which he did, in elegant Latin, he, therefore, being surnamed Grammaticus. Cotemporaneously with Saxo, the Icelandic writer, *Snorre Sturlason*, lived: a man of rare talents, who has made himself famous by composing *Heimskringla*, or "The Sagas of the Norwegian Kings," down to Magnus Erlingson, A. D. 1162. At the age of sixty-three this eminent man was assassinated by his own relatives on his manor, Reykiaholt, in Iceland. The celebrated work called the *Edda*, where we see, amidst many absurdities, the traces of a luminous and rational system of religion, and which therefore long was considered the sacred book of the Scandinavians, is often ascribed to Snorre Sturlason, while it more probably was composed by *Saemund*, a clergyman in Iceland, who died A. D. 1133. The whole doctrines of the ancient religion and mythology are unfolded in this celebrated specimen of national poetry.

A. D., 1241.

SECOND PERIOD.

FROM THE DEATH OF WALDEMAR THE CONQUEROR, AND THE BEGINNING OF THE DISPUTES ABOUT SCHLESWIG, UNTIL THE INTRODUCTION OF THE REFORMATION, 1241—1536.

I.

1241—1319.

Erik Ploughpenning—Expedition to Esthonia—Abel—Christopher I.—Conflict with the Clergy—Archbishop Jacob Erlandson—Interdict—*Erik Glipping*—Battle on Loheath—War with Norway—*Erik Menved*—The Regicides—John Grand—Peace with Norway—Expedition to Pomerania and Mecklenburg—The Hanseatic League.

ERIK, later surnamed Ploughpenning, some years before chosen successor, took upon him the title of king after the death of Waldemar the Conqueror, his father. A great error ascribed to him is the dividing of the kingdom among his brothers: Schleswig was given to *Abel*, and Laaland and Falster to *Christopher*. This division contributed very much to the declension of the kingdom, and to the diminishing of the royal power; and especially in reference to Schleswig, this system of division had ruinous consequences; for Abel and his successors tried now to make Schleswig an hereditary and independent possession in their family, all of which resulted in a series of destructive internal wars, Schleswig thereby more and more being alienated from the kingdom. Under these circumstances, Abel soon assumed a hostile position towards Erik, the more as he claimed the Duchy of Schleswig as an independent sovereignty. A war broke out, in which, however, the king got the better, Abel being obliged to submit. Next year a Diet was held in Roeskilde, in which the king expressed his eager desire to reclaim all the former possessions of Esthonia and Livonia, which had been lost amidst the late civil commotions. The Diet giving its assent to his proposal of undertaking an expedition thither, he then laid before them the necessity of raising the proper supplies by an additional tax of a certain sum to be paid by each plough, under the name of *ploughpenning*, by which term the king was afterwards surnamed. After returning from Esthonia, the king marched his army against the counts of Holstein, who had laid siege to the fortress of Rendsburg. On his arrival at the Danevirke, that strong wall above mentioned, he bethought him of a visit to his brother Abel in Schleswig, who had taken no part in this quarrel. He entered, however, into an altercation with Abel, who caused the king to be killed in a boat, and his body thrown into the river Sley. Abel endeavored to screen his shocking crime by promulgating a report, that the king had perished in the river by the boat's foundering, but shortly after all was discovered by the mangled body of the king, which was thrown by the waves on the shore, and taken up by some monks.

Erik Ploughpenning falling without male issue, the states, though they detested *Abel*, on account of the unnatural crime he had committed, chose him king to avoid a civil war, which would certainly have ensued on setting him aside. By these means they also indisputably re-united the duchy of Schleswig to the crown. After a reign of two years, neither active nor useful, he was killed in an expedition he undertook against the Friesers, leaving the state in a most declining condition. A. D., 1252. If the royalty had remained in Abel's family, Schleswig would have been re-united with the kingdom, and all future contests prevented; but *Christopher I.*, the third son of Waldemar the Conqueror, was happy enough immediately to be acknowledged king, although the throne was promised to Abel's sons, Waldemar and Erik. Both parties exerted all their power to gain the ascendancy. The king encompassed Schleswig with his army, and claimed, as uncle, the guardianship of Abel's children, but these were supported by the counts of Holstein. Seasonably for the king, some of the German princes offered their mediation, and a peace was concluded on these terms: that Christopher should have the guardianship, but restore the duchy of Schleswig as a fief to Waldemar, the eldest son of Abel, when he had attained to his majority. About the same time Christopher was entangled in a sharp contest with the clergy. The imperious *Jacob Erlandson*, without the king's consent or knowledge, was chosen archbishop of Lund. Descended from a conspicuous family, and very well versed in the ecclesiastical laws, he was, on account of his long stay in foreign lands, strictly acquainted with the condition of the Church everywhere. Secure of the Pope's protection, he not only disregarded all forms, but totally changed the ecclesiastical laws and statutes of Skane, and took the liberty, of his own accord, to substitute some new ones of his own. He consecrated other bishops without asking the royal consent, brought secular affairs under the ecclesiastical jurisdiction, and usurped fines and other perquisites belonging only to the king. He forbade the peasantry of his archbishopric to perform military service; and when the king had summoned a diet of the people at Nyborg, the archbishop, as a mark of disrespect, convoked at the same time a synod at Weile, Jutland, called the *Weile Constitution;* where it was decided that, when a bishop was imprisoned, or in any way molested by the king, an interdict should be laid upon the kingdom, and all divine service cease. Christopher I., highly incensed at this haughty conduct, would now confiscate all the fiefs formerly given to the archbishopric of Lund, but a violent riot arose amongst the archiepiscopal peasants, who ravaged

A. D., 1256.

the country with unheard-of cruelty; and as now the archbishop also declined crowning Erik, the king's son, and threatened to ban the bishops who might do so, the king caused him to be imprisoned. Agreeably to the resolution of the synod of Weile, the whole kingdom was immediately interdicted. The king now wrote to the Pope, representing to him the haughty conduct of the archbishop, the injustice and absurdity of a prelate's assuming to himself a share in the royal prerogative, and the hardship, that he should have it in his power to lay a whole people under interdiction. These remonstrances were no sooner dispatched to Rome, than the Pope commanded that the ban should be intermitted, and all the priests within the kingdom should administer the communion, under the penalty of losing their tithes and stipends. At the same time the king fell a victim to the plot of a canon by the name of *Arnfast*, who poisoned him, and as a reward, was promoted by the rebellious archbishop to the bishopric of Aarhuus, in Jutland. Christopher I. had found the treasury exhausted on his accession; at his death he left things in much the same situation—the treasury exhausted, and the nation split into two powerful factions. In the doubt and dismay which followed the death of Christopher I., a few voices saluted his son, *Erik Glipping*, with the title of king, but the majority would not ratify the choice, as he had not yet attained to full age, and the queen dowager, the manly *Marga-*

A. D., 1259.

rethe of Pomerania, called *Sorte Grethe* (Black Grethe) on account of her dark complexion, had to assume the reins of government. She commenced her guardianship with a signal instance of clemency, on pardoning the haughty Jacob Erlandsen; who, nevertheless, after being set at liberty, treacherously joined the duke of Schleswig, avowing his intention to dethrone the king and replace the duke. Shortly after a new faction arose, headed by count *Jarimar*, of Rygen, who, gathering multitudes of robbers and murderers, and making an inroad into Sjelland, defeated, at *Nestved* in Sjelland, the peasantry, which the queen dowager had raised, where ten thousand peasants lost their lives. Thereupon Jarimar went to Skane, where he, fortunately for Denmark, was killed by a country-woman. The country was soon after alarmed by a dangerous irruption of *Erik*, a son of Abel, who, because the queen dowager would not comply with giving him Schleswig as an *hereditary* fief, but only as a *personal*, joined the counts of Holstein, and commenced a war, in which the royal troops were totally defeated at *Loheath*, close by the city of Schleswig. The queen dowager and her son, the minor king, were taken prisoners, she being sent to Hamburg, and he closely confined on Alsen, an island in the Baltic. The queen dowager was, however, soon released, but the young king not till the expiration of three years, during which time the queen dowager governed the kingdom, assisted by the duke *Albert of*

A. D., 1261.

Brunswick, to whom the prefectship had been entrusted. The young king, now past minority, was scarcely settled on the throne, when his kingdom was again alarmed by the rebellious Jacob Erlandson rejecting repeated proposals of agreement, and even bidding defiance to the commands of the Pope; and not till the queen dowager herself determined on going to Rome, was a reconciliation made, according to which the king had to pay the archbishop the sum of fifteen thousand ounces of silver, and replace him in his ecclesiastical dignities. When Jacob Erlandson was returning home from Rome, he died by the way before reaching Denmark, the king rejoicing very much at having got rid of this spiritual tyrant. But, unfortunately, the king had, both within his own land and abroad, other foes not less to be feared. With Magnus Lagabœter, King of Norway, married to Ingeborg, a daughter of Erik Ploughpenning, a dispute arose, Erik Glipping, in the confused condition of the kingdom, not being capable of paying the dowry. The Norwegian king arriving with a great fleet in Skane, was, however, defeated by the Danish army; but under the sons of Magnus a destructive war commenced, during the course of which the defenceless Danish coasts and maritime towns were grievously vexed by the piracies and formidable pillages of the Norwegians. Nevertheless, Erik Glipping engaged himself in the civil disturbances of Sweden, where the brothers *Waldemar* and *Magnus Ladelaas* were

A. D., 1274.

disputing for the throne; but he reaped neither honor nor profit by his interference, and the power of the state began to decline. Magnus defeated Waldemar at *Hove*, A. D., in Westrigothland, and was acknowledged King 1275. of Sweden, the agriculture of which he vigorously promoted; the peasantry, therefore, surnaming him Ladelaas, *i. e.* the protector of the barns. With these disturbances in Sweden, in which Erik Glipping involved himself, came a war with *Erik*, Duke of Schleswig, who continued to sow the seeds of dissension; but the king entering the duchy with a powerful army, and seizing upon the fortress of Tónder, which he razed, the duke was constrained to submit, and lost his duchy a short time before his death; after which Schleswig, for thirteen years, remained united with the kingdom, until unfortunately again Waldemar, called Duke Waldemar IV., a son of Erik, above named, was invested with Schleswig as a fief. But not content with it, he now also laid claim to Aró, Alsen, and Femern, three islands in the Baltic. He fell, however, into the hands of the king, had humbly to throw himself at his feet, resign his claim, and make a confession in writing of his want of loyalty to his sovereign. Besides these incessant contests and disputes, Erik Glipping was frequently at variance with the noblemen, because of his A. D., violence and want of candor, and he was, at a 1282. diet of *Nyborg*, compelled to promise, in writing, to rule more justly, and in accordance with the laws of the state. The same year a pestilential disease occurred, by which great numbers of men and cattle were swept off; terrible fires also happened in different parts of the kingdom; and, to crown the misfortunes of this year, Margarethe, the queen dowager, died, after having, with great discretion and policy, governed the kingdom and her son for the space of twenty-three years. Erik Glipping now comforted himself with the pleasing hope of enjoying the remainder of his life in tranquillity, but his subjects growing more and more weary of him and his transgressing the limits of his authority, and disgusted at his debauching several wives and daughters of the nobility, formed a conspiracy against the king, privy to which were *James*, count of Halland, and *Stig Anderson*, who ran him through the body with a sword He fell beneath the blow at *Finderup*, by Wiborg, in Jutland, where he was diverting himself with hunting for a few days. Thus, in less than fifty years, four Danish kings were dispatched by assassination. A.D., 1286.

These events having occurred, the situation of the kingdom became yet more gloomy, *Erik Menved*, likewise surnamed *the Pious*, being only twelve years of age at his father's death. In want of a leader, the affairs of government fell into the hands of the queen-dowager, *Agnes of Brandenburg*, whose respectable qualities were universally esteemed. Being, however, without that firmness of mind which perseveres in difficult times and cases, she imprudently made duke Waldemar IV. of Schleswig, joint guardian, even resigning to him the disputed islands, Aró, Alsen, and Femern, so that he acquired a power in the state which properly belonged to better men. A formal sentence of death was pronounced against the regicides, who, escaping to Norway, appealed to the king, *Erik Præstehader* (i. e., the hater of the priests), to whom they swore allegiance, and received from him the fortress of Kongshel, strong by nature and art. Besides that, they brought into their occupancy several fortified places of the Danish coasts and islands, whence they, for a space of nine years, ravaged their native country with fire and sword, breathing vengeance wherever they went, and seeming to threaten to depopulate the kingdom by a continual drain of its forces. One of the conspirators, however, was, some years after, taken in Roeskilde, and broken upon the wheel. About the same time a new contest with the clergy ensued. *John Grand*, a kinsman of Jacob Erlandson, and related to the regicides, had been appointed archbishop of Lund, although highly against the consent of the king and the queen-dowager. No sooner had he reached this dignity, than he joined the regicides and the Norwegians, doing all within his power to injure the king and blast his credit. But at last the king caused him to be apprehended and imprisoned in *Sòborg*, a castle in North Sjelland, where he was placed in a subterranean dungeon and treated with the utmost severity. He was, however, fortunate enough to escape to Bornholm, a remote island in the Baltic, from whence he repaired to Rome, to appeal to the Pope himself, at that time the imperious and domineering *Bonifacius VIII.* By his coloring the facts, he incensed his Holiness violently against the king, and was acquitted of all guilt, while a penalty of forty-nine thousand ounces of silver was inflicted upon the king, which he, however, decidedly declined paying. Erik Menved, rightly imagining the Pope had been deceived by a false representation of the nature of the dispute, remitted to Rome an appeal, and heavy complaints of the archbishop. But without avail. The whole kingdom was, by the papal legate, *Isarnus*, laid under a new interdict of five years. After a lapse of some years the king, in order to be reconciled with the Pope, sent a most supplicating letter, entreating that he would be pleased to remove the heavy curse, and receive himself and his subjects again into the bosom of the church. His Holiness granted the request; the interdict was taken off, the payment of forty-nine thousand ounces of silver reduced to ten thousand, and John Grand was transferred to an archbishopric in France. A. D., 1298.

The duke of Schleswig, Waldemar IV., sided for a while with Norway and the regicides, but being totally defeated in *Greensound*, he was obliged to conclude peace, and give back Arò, Alsen and Femern. With

A. D. 1309. Norway, the long war was finished by the treaty of Copenhagen, by which the province of Halland was ceded to the Norwegian king, Hakon V., and made over to him in perpetuity. But it was only a short time that Denmark enjoyed the blessings of peace, which were soon interrupted by her restless Swedish neighbors. The dukes Waldemar and Erik, brothers to *Birger*, king of Sweden, occasioned great disturbances. Erik, a crafty and ambitious young prince, who, on account of his being married to Ingeborg, a daughter of Hakon V., had expectations of ascending the throne of Norway, was anxious to dethrone Birger, and thus also become king of Sweden. Erik Menved, the Danish king, married to a sister of king Birger, took part in the Swedish disturbances, and made several expensive expeditions to Sweden, to defend his brother-in-law and preserve to him his throne. The rebellious dukes had surprised Birger in his castle *Hatuna*, and imprisoned him. Erik Menved raised an army, and led his troops to the frontiers of West Gothland, where he was met by the enemy. Both armies encamped within sight of

A. D. 1310. each other for some days, and at length a peace was agreed to, in Helsingborg, in consequence of which king Birger was restored to a part of his dominions, and the dukes received the remainder, on oath of fidelity and homage, as vassals of the crown. But Birger, breathing vengeance, invited his brothers to a drinking-bout in *Nykòping*. After having treated them with magnificence, he suddenly ordered his people to break into their apartments while they were asleep, to seize them, to strip them, and fetter their necks and heels with iron chains. They were thrown into a dark dungeon, where they died of hunger. But a sedition now arose against Birger, who had to flee from his kingdom, and died a fugitive in Denmark. A. D., 1317.

To regain the great territories in Germany which Waldemar I. and Waldemar the Conqueror had conquered, was a favorite thought of Erik Menved; wherefore he, through a series of years, made frequent expeditions to bring the cities and princes of Pomerania and Mecklenburg under subjection, but without avail. Towards the close of his reign, he had a new dispute with the clergy, in which, however, he got the better, the rebellious archbishop of Lund, *Esger Juel*, being compelled to refrain from war and leave the country But soon the kingdom was distracted with internal dissensions, which had broken out amongst the stirring noblemen, who formed a conspiracy against the king's life, and caused a great insurrection in North Jutland, where the people refused payment of the taxes imposed by the king and the diet, of which *Christopher*, the king's own brother, dishonoring himself by treacherous connections with the insurgents, was the ringleader. Not being capable of realizing what he had expected, he went over to Sweden, where he lived in exile till the year 1318, A. D. Upon his death-bed the king wished, however, to be reconciled to his brother, and accordingly granted him a free pardon, without stipulating any terms. Though having fourteen children by his queen, Ingeborg, Erik Menved died childless, after a reign of thirty-three years, leaving his kingdom in a most declining condition, on account of the many external and internal wars, and of the general abandonment of all the virtues by which, under the two great Waldemars, it had risen to power and greatness. To procure money to defray the charges of these wars, a great deal of the royal fiefs and other revenues had been mortgaged to native and foreign magnates, by all of which the kingdom had become weakened. Contemporaneously with this, a mighty league was formed in the northern part of Germany, called the *German League of the Hanse-towns*, which, in process of time, became extremely dangerous to the northern countries. It arose in the middle of the thirteenth century, when several seaport towns joined together to defend their mercantile neutrality. By degrees this league increased its military resources, and after the middle of the fourteenth century it comes clearly into view as a domineering policy in the North, acquiring a great superiority in the Baltic, and gaining a permanent footing in Denmark, Norway, Sweden, and Russia, where the league, comprising the important commercial cities, Hamburg, Lübeck, Bremen, Rostock, Wismar, Stralsund, and Novgorod, mastered all mercantile affairs; and their power increased so rapidly, that five hundred men-of-war could soon be mustered from these cities; and the imprudent Danish kings, Abel, Erik Glipping and Erik Menved, during whose internal and external wars the star of the League was in the ascendant, had often to have recourse to the assistance of the Hanseatic towns, which understood how to fish in foul water. Upon the whole, the superiority of the Hanse-league was the chief cause that Denmark's cities and burgher class in the Middle Ages never rose to any power or importance, the German merchants importing almost all articles manufactured.

II.

1319—1397.

Christopher II.—Charter—War with Geert, Count of Holstein—Battle on Tapheath—Niels Ebbeson—*Waldemar IV., Atterdag*—Insurrection in Jutland—Magnus Smek of Sweden—War with the Hanseatic-towns—Rebellion—Waldemar leaves the country—*Olaf*—*Queen Margarethe* (the Semiramis of the North)—King Albrecht of Sweden—The Battle at Falköping—*The Union of Calmar.*

Upon the death of Erik Menved, *Christopher II.*, his brother, was elected and declared king, although Erik, even while lying in his last gasp, had, knowing by experience his brother's mean and base disposition, tried to dissuade the people from electing him. His reign was miserable, the lower orders of the State being by his corruption and inability reduced to a degree of hopeless subjection, while he entrusted the rich noblemen with uncontrollable power, which he had no strength to withdraw from them when danger was coming. Before his accession to the throne, he had to subscribe to a very severe charter, containing, in substance, that the clergy should be preserved in the full possession of all their earlier privileges and immunities; that a clergyman should, on no account, be tried in a civil court, but be subject only to the laws of the ecclesiastical court; that the king should not be permitted to declare war or conclude peace except by consent of the nobility and the clergy; that the noblemen should not be obliged to serve in the wars beyond the frontiers of the kingdom, and that an annual diet should be held at Nyborg. On the whole, the power of the nobility and the clergy attained to such a height as never before or after him. The king and the archbishop, *Esger Juel*, came, through the papal mediation, to an agreement, and from that very time matters assumed a better aspect between the kings and the church, because the clergy, in fear of the increasing power of the nobility, began to attach themselves closer to the kings. Although Christopher II. had promised the nobility, under the sanctity of an oath, that he would inviolably keep the charter to which he had subscribed, he did not do so, but gave a finishing stroke to his wickedness and absurdity by saying, that he did not consider the breaking of an oath of any consequence. Several powerful noblemen, therefore, the bailiff *Lauritz Jonsen*, the field-marshal *Louis Albertson*, and *Canute Porse*, Duke of Halland, flew immediately to arms, and when the king soon after entered into a dispute with Count *Geert* (Gerhard) the Great, of Holstein, concerning the guardianship over the young Duke of Schleswig, Waldemar V., the displeased noblemen joined Count Geert, who raised a body of forces in Holstein, gave battle to the king at Gottorp, defeated him, and raised the siege. Christopher now levied, in spite of his charter, a tax upon his subjects, by renewing the ploughpenning. To this was added another piece of misconduct, which enraged the clergy. He made some alterations in a monastery, without consulting the bishops, who began to fulminate threats, and the king was accused of intending to trample on the neck of liberty. The nobles exclaimed that he aimed at the ruin of the nobility, and the people murmured at the weight of taxes, and especially at the ploughpenning, the most grievous of all taxes, because it fell wholly on the poor laborers. Discontent appeared in every quarter, and a confederacy was formed to depose Christopher, who, finding himself unequal in strength to his subjects, fled to Mechlenburg, after which he was unanimously divested of his royalty, and the young Duke *Waldemar* elected king under the guardianship A.D., 1326. of Count Geert. But a charter was now issued in which it was decreed that as long as the king was alive, his successor could not be elected, nor any certain promise be given of the succession to the throne. The friends of the new king were richly rewarded. He made over to Count Geert the whole Duchy of Schleswig, to be held as a fief of the crown; to Canute, Porse, Halland, Samsö, and the earldom of Kallundborg; to John, a half-brother of the deposed Christopher, Laaland and Falster; and Louis Albertson and Lauritz Jonson were likewise rewarded. Thus a general peace was concluded, to the great satisfaction of the people, who now expected an end to all their calamities. Nevertheless, a dispute soon arising among them about this division, Christopher II. came, by the aid of his half-brother, back again to his kingdom, and an agreement was concluded at *Ripen*, according to which Waldemar again should have Schleswig, and Count Geert, as an equivalent, have Fjunen as a hereditary fief, together with a great part of Jutland; and if Waldemar should die without leaving inheritors behind him, then Schleswig should devolve to Count Geert, and Fjunen to Denmark. John, who had assisted the king in regaining his kingdom, was rewarded with Sjelland (Zealand) and Skane. A new contest, in which Christopher imprudently involved himself with Count Geert, was ended by a decisive defeat of the royal troops on *Loheath*, in Schleswig. The battle continued for a whole day. Geert was near being worsted, but finding means to bribe the king's troops, he soon retrieved his affairs, and gained a complete victory, the king escaping from the field with great difficulty. Next year proved fatal to the liberty and life of Christopher, for, going to the island of Laaland with a small retinue, he was seized by John Ellemose, a friend of Count Geert, and carried prisoner to the strong castle of *Aalholm*, close by the city of Nysted. The king was, however, again set at liberty, but did not live A. D. long to enjoy his freedom. He fell ill, and died 1334. in a few days, and was buried in Soró, in Sjelland, at his death owning only the city of Skanderborg, in Jutland, a piece of Laaland, and a few possessions in Esthonia; the kingdom having thus sunk into nothing. A greater complication of folly and inability than there was about Christopher II., no Danish king has been possessed of, wherefore the account of his death produced the greatest jubilation. *Pontanus* says, that he was so much hated, that his memory was stigmatized with bitter lampoons.

Upon the death of Christopher II., an *interregnum* of seven years ensued. *Erik*, the eldest son of Christopher, had been mortally wounded on Loheath; *Otho*, the next but one, attempting to regain his ancestral kingdom, was defeated and captured on *Tapheath*, by Wiborg; and *Waldemar*, the youngest son, sojourned at the court of Louis of Bavaria. The cruel Geert, pressing and impoverishing the inhabitants, now disposed of the country at pleasure. Skane, Halland and Bleking shook off his cruel yoke, and submitted themselves to *Magnus Smek*, at that time king of Sweden and Norway. A complete annihilation of the Danish kingdom seemed to be unavoidable, the more as Geert enrolled an army of ten thousand German soldiers, and ravaged the whole of Jutland with the utmost cruelty, sparing neither women nor tender children. But the Jutlanders were not inclined to submit to a tyrant upon whom they already had long looked with the greatest aversion, and at the head of them a knight, *Niels Ebbeson* of Nòrrerüs, rose and became the deliverer of his fatherland. Instead of yielding to despondency he employed his hours of retirement to revolve in his mind what was to be done. After debating some time with himself, he rose and called together several of his most esteemed countrymen. He told them that all now depended on their own exertions. If they yielded to the cruel Geert, they had nothing to expect but to be treated tyrannically. But if, on the contrary, they acted with vigor and union, their numbers and courage were still sufficient to rescue them from this scourge of oppression. They willingly adopted the suggestions of the noble knight, who wrote a letter to Geert, in which Niels Ebbeson's plan was communicated to him. Thus says the letter: "To Count Geert: Sir, I hereby swear, by God, in whom I believe, but you do not, thou blood-thirsty tyrant, that wheresoever and whensoever I can get hold of you, be it either at midnight or at cock-crowing, either at your table or in your princely bedchamber, or even at the foot of the holy altar, you shall fall by my hand. Your sworn and mortal enemy, Niels Ebbeson."

Collecting a body of sixty trusty retainers, he left his manor for *Randers*, in Jutland, where Geert had fixed his head-quarters, seized the sentinels, and pushed on to Geert's lodging, which he forced open. Geert was awakened with the noise, and seeing Niels Ebbeson enter with armed men, began to supplicate him, in the most humble terms, to save his life. But considering the life of the tyrant a just atonement for the cruelties the people had suffered, he plunged his sword into his breast, and then made his retreat with all possible expedition, after having given the alarm to the whole army, by sounding horns and beating drums. A. D., 1340.

The notice of the death of the tyrant was followed by a general acclamation. But the brave and fearless deliverer of his fatherland soon after lost his life by Skanderborg in Jutland, in a battle against Geert's sons, who would avenge the death of their father. But Niels Ebbeson has never lost the grateful memory of the Danes, who, in a charming forest, close by his manor-seat, have erected a marble column, on which an inscription, with Spartan brevity, tells his patriotic exploit; and yearly, in the summer-season, the citizens of Aarhus, and the scholars of the Latin school, take a walk to Nòrrerüs, where, by spirited songs, they call back to their minds, his magnanimous and heroic deed.

Geert having been killed, the way to the throne was paved for Christopher's third son, *Waldemar IV. Atterdag*, who was recalled from Bavaria. A.D. 1341. To Waldemar's elevation the emperor Louis, at whose court Waldemar was bred, greatly contributed. His elder brother Otho, having renounced his claims to the throne, Waldemar received the homage in Wiborg. Uniting great vigor with the most refined policy, humanity and affability, he conciliated good will on all sides, and came into possession of a popularity, which gave him means more powerful than arms for the future improvement and extension of his kingdom. His vigilance was equal to his valor, and he quickly made himself master of Jutland, Sjelland, Fjunen, Laaland and Falster; and the Danish dominions, so lately divided among a number of petty tyrants, were now again united into one sovereignty. For a number of years, as we have seen, Denmark had been the theatre of continual domestic and foreign wars, which filled every place with confusion. One of the most powerful kingdoms, after having given laws to such a number of other nations, had at length fallen under the scourge of some petty vassals, who laid desolate her fairest provinces. But now she again began to taste the sweets of liberty and resume her old influence. Waldemar IV. sold immediately the remote Esthonia to the Teutonic Order (a confraternity of German knights, instituted by Pope Celestin III., A. D. 1192,) for nineteen thousand ounces of silver, to be enabled to redeem more important provinces; and by marrying Hedevig, a sister to the duke Waldemar V., of Schleswig, who brought him a considerable dowry, he acquired great wealth. The most considerable enemies he conquered were the invaders of his frontier, or the internal disturbers of his kingdom, and, on the whole, he only made war to secure peace. The Jutlandish nobility, accustomed to disobedience to the laws, headed by *Claus Limbek*, raised a rebellion, and entered into an alliance with the counts of Holstein, and other enemies of the kingdom, but the powerful Waldemar compelled them to comply with his dictates. Among all the exertions of his active life, he was also very attentive to the improvement of the internal welfare of his kingdom. He frequently traveled round to have an eye upon the execution of the laws, he settled the civil concerns, which were in a boundless chaos, he erected castles and fortresses, he laid out highways, and caused canals to be dug, and to his people, who, under such circumstances, were obliged to pay high taxes, he gave a detailed account of the spending of the taxes he had levied.

At this time Magnus Smek was king of Sweden; of whose improvidence and stupidity Waldemar availed himself to regain the Swedish provinces, Skane, A. D., Halland, and Bleking, thus encompassing his 1360.

great aim—the re-union of the Danish kingdom. A marriage was also agreed upon between *Hakon VI.*, king of Norway, and a son of Magnus Smek, and *Margarethe*, a daughter of Waldemar; a basis thereby being laid for a continual union of Norway with Denmark. Next year Waldemar seized upon the Swedish island, *Gulland* (Gothland), the capital of which, Wisby, then one of the richest and most flourishing Hanse towns, he demolished, assuming now the title, "*King of the Goths.*" But, upon the taking of the great island of Gulland, a mighty alliance arose against Waldemar Atterdag, between Magnus Smek, the counts of Holstein, and the Hanseatic towns, (which are said to have sent him at once seventy-seven declarations of war,) and Albrecht the elder, of Mecklenburg. Matters being thus disposed, the allies put to sea, attacked Copenhagen, took the citadel, and plundered the city. But Waldemar rushed fearlessly on his many enemies, attacked the squadron of Lübeck, took six ships, burned several others, and forced the Hanseatic towns and his other enemies to raise the siege. The regency of Lübeck were so incensed at their defeat, that, accusing the admiral of neglect of duty, they ordered his head to be struck off. A peace was concluded between the king and the Hanse towns, Waldemar thus reaping the harvest of glory, and gaining the great honor of having put a prompt end to this dangerous war.

A.D., 1362.

We have seen that the king of Norway, *Hakon VI.*,

was contracted to the princess **Margarethe**. Yet, to oblige the Swedish nation, who insisted on his renouncing the alliance with Denmark, he consented to marry *Elizabeth*, a princess of Holstein, instead of Waldemar's daughter. Every circumstance seemed favorable to the conclusion of this alliance, as both the Swedes and Holsteiners were equally desirous of it. She was now embarked on the Trave, to pass over to Sweden; but Heaven disposed events otherwise. Boisterous weather drove the ship on the coast of Denmark. Waldemar Atterdag received the princess with all the honors due to her rank, but still he kept her under a gentle constraint, in the meantime hurrying Magnus Smek and Hakon VI. to come to Denmark, where then, by consent of the foolish Swedish king, the nuptials between Margarethe and the Norwegian king were celebrated. But this affair deprived Magnus Smek of his throne, the people electing in his stead his nephew, *Albrecht*, duke of Mecklenburg. Nevertheless Magnus resolved to make vigorous efforts for the recovery of his throne. Having received aid from Waldemar and his son, Hakon VI. of Norway, he took the field, gave battle, but was defeated at *Tillinge*, near Jónköping, and conducted prisoner to Stockholm, where he was confined for seven years, till he at length was delivered by his son, Hakon. Upon the whole, the cunning Waldemar bore up well against his many enemies, until the Jutlandish nobility,

A.D.. 1363.

A.D., 1365.

A.D, 1368

headed by Claus Limbek, excited a fresh rebellion, joining *Henry*, duke of Schleswig, the counts of Holstein, the Hanse towns, Sweden and Mecklenburg, who all had concluded a formidable alliance against him. At the sight of such a league Waldemar's courage forsook him. Finding himself unable to resist this cloud of enemies, he determined to abandon all. He left his kingdom for four years, after having previously appointed the sagacious *Henning Podebusk* viceroy—

A. D., 1370. who was happy enough to prevail with the Hanse towns to conclude the peace of Stralsund, after which the other enemies broke off all hostilities. By this peace it was decided that the Hanseatic towns should, for fifteen years, possess the maritime towns of Skane, and enjoy special commercial privileges over the whole of Denmark.

A. D., 1372 Upon his returning home Waldemar found his kingdom in the greatest confusion, but this untiring king signalized himself by a successful and active endeavor to re-establish order, strengthen the enervated country, and infuse into the souls of his subjects a portion of that spirit of independence and patriotism of which he was possessed himself. Henry, duke of Schleswig, being childless, there was a good prospect of again getting this duchy re-united with the kingdom; upon which important point Waldemar, in his last days, directed all his attention; but, unfortunately, he only survived Henry so short a time, that the question whether Schleswig should belong to Denmark or be yielded to the counts of Holstein (who, pursuant to the treaty of Ripen, 1330, laid claim to it,) could not be decided, but was deferred to the following reign. During the thirty-four years he wore his crown, he devoted himself to reform all abuses, and to revive the wholesome laws of the country. He increased the public revenues, and applied them to the adorning of the cities with public buildings, while at the same time he condemned the expenditure of the public money for mere show. He also paid particular attention to the comforts of the poorer citizens, and took care that they should be maintained at the public cost. Altogether, he seems to have been a man superior to the time in which he lived. He had built a beautiful country seat in the neighborhood of Elsinore, called *Gurre*, and there he breathed his last. From the time of his return from abroad, he was constantly afflicted with the gout; recourse was had to a variety of medicines, but without effect. A. D., 1375.

Before leaving Waldemar IV., (surnamed Atterdag, because he used to say, when a misfortune happened, "To-morrow it is again day,") it may be observed, that under his reign an enemy more destructive than war visited both Denmark and Norway. This was a frightful disease, called the *Black Death*, (*den Sorte Död,*) because people, before they died, broke out with black freckles over the whole body. The plague is supposed to have originated in Asia Minor, and to have been transmitted from Constantinople to the European countries. It raged in Denmark with the most destructive effect, taking off a great deal of the population, and the mortality was increased by the crowded and comfortless manner in which the people at that time lived. The plague spread so violently and so rapidly, that physicians were of no use. In Lübeck, for instance, there died in one day to the number of 1,500. There might be seen in one place wretches lying in the streets in the agonies of death, deserted by their nearest friends through fear of infection, or crawling to the brink of some stream or fountain, in the vain hope of quenching the intolerable thirst with which they were parched. By a ship going adrift this horrible disease came, A. D. 1349, to Bergen, Norway, whence it spread round in the country, nearly dispeopled Norway, annihilated all industry, and enervated everything irreparably. But it should be mentioned here, that Waldemar, during the whole time of the plague, regardless of his own safety, was only anxious to lessen its increase and spreading abroad, by unremitting and judicious exertions.

Waldemar Atterdag left no male issue, but his two grandsons, *Albrecht the Younger*, of Mecklenburg, a son of *Ingeborg*, Waldemar's eldest daughter, and of Henry of Mecklenburg, and *Olaf*, a son of *Margarethe*, his younger daughter, and of Hakon VI., of Norway, were now claiming the hereditary succession to the throne.

One party declared for Olaf, but as he was the son of the younger daughter, his right was consequently very doubtful. But because the house of Mecklenburg had acted hostilely towards Denmark, and Olaf had expectation of Norway and claims to the crown of Sweden, as a grandson of Magnus Smek, Denmark was, by his election, in hopes of one day seeing the three crowns united on the same head. It was, therefore, not long before this important affair was determined. The preference was given Olaf, who, although only six years of age, was, under the name of *Olaf V.*, elected king of Denmark, under the guardianship of Margarethe, his mother; and after the death of his father, Hakon VI., he became also king of Norway, the two kingdoms thus being united: a union which, till the expiration of four hundred and thirty-four years, was not dissolved. When Olaf V. seven years after died in Falsterbo, both kingdoms elected *Margarethe* their queen, though custom had not yet authorized the election of a female. A. D., 1376. A. D., 1380. A. D., 1387.

During the reign of this great princess, who deservedly has been called the *Semiramis of the North*, Denmark and Norway exercised an influence in Europe, the effects of which long vibrated throughout the Scandinavian countries, their vast extent and rival races. Uniting wisdom and policy with courage and determination, having strength of mind to preserve her rectitude of character without deviation, and her efforts being crowned by Divine Providence with success, she is duly considered one of the most illustrious female rulers in history, her renown reaching even the Byzantine emperor Emanuel Palæologus, who called her "*Regina sine exemplo maxima.*" But under her successors, destitute of her high sense of duty, great ability and consistent virtue, her triumphs proved a snare instead of a blessing; the great Union she created dissolved in a short time, and its downfall was as sudden as its elevation had been extraordinary. She was born in the year of our Lord 1353. Her father was, as we have seen, Waldemar Atterdag, her mother queen Hedevig, and she became queen of Denmark and Norway in the year 1387. No sooner elected queen of Denmark, and homaged on the hill of Sliparehog, near Lund, in Ringsted, Odensee and Wiborg, than she sailed to Norway to receive its homage. But a remarkable occurrence is mentioned by historians to have occurred about this time. A report prevailed that king Olaf, the queen's son, was not dead; it was propagated by the nobility, and very likely set on foot by them, in order to punish Margarethe for her liberality to the clergy. The impostor claimed the crown of Denmark and Norway, and gained credit every day by making discoveries which could only be known to Olaf and his mother. Margarethe, however, proved him to be a son of the nurse of Olaf, who had a large wart between his shoulders, which mark did not appear on the impostor. In fine, the false Olaf was seized, broken on the wheel, and publicly burnt at a place between Falsterbo and Skanór, in Sweden, and Margarethe continued uninterruptedly her regency.

But the queen not wishing to contract a new marriage, and comprehending the importance of getting a successor elected to the throne, proposed her nephew. *Erik, Duke of Pomerania*, of which proposal A.D., the clergy and nobility approved by electing him 1388. king of Denmark and Norway after Margarethe's death. Meanwhile *Albrecht*, king of Sweden, having, on account of his preference given to his German favorites, incurred the hatred of his people, the Swedes requested Margarethe to assist them against him, which she promised, if they in return would promise to make her queen of Sweden. Moreover, Albrecht had highly offended the Danish queen; had, though hardly able to govern his own kingdom, assumed the title, "King of Denmark," and laid claim to Norway too; and when she blamed him for it he had answered her disdainfully In a letter he had used foul and abusive language, calling her "a king without breeches," and the "abbot's concubine" (abbedfrillen), on account of her particular attachment to a certain abbot of Soró, who was her spiritual director. It is, however, true, that her intimacy with this monk gave room for some suspicion that her privacies with him were not all employed about the care of her soul. Afterwards, to ridicule her yet more, king Albrecht sent her a hone to sharpen her needles, and swore not to put on his night-cap until she had yielded to him. But under perilous circumstances Margarethe was never at a loss how to act. Nevertheless, she acted here with the utmost prudence, trying first to gain the favor of the peers of the state, and solemnly promising to rule according to the Swedish laws. The war now broke out between Albrecht and Margarethe, whose army was commanded by *Jvar Lykke*. The encounter of the two armies, about 12,000 men on each side, took place at Falköping, 21st of September, 1388. A furious battle was fought, in which the victory for a long while hung in suspense. But Margarethe's good fortune prevailed, Albert was routed and his army cut in pieces, and Margarethe was now also mistress of Sweden.

A. D., 1388.

While this was passing, the queen tarried in Wordingborg, Sjelland, longing with ardent desire to learn the result. But no sooner hearing that the victory was gained, and the Swedish king and his son, Erik, taken prisoners, than she hastened to *Bahus*, in Sweden, where the king and his son were brought before her. Lost in joy and amazement at having her enemy in her power, the queen now retorted upon king Albrecht by uttering some reviling and sarcastic expressions, and in causing a large night-cap of paper, nineteen yards long, to be put on him; a retaliation proportioned to his offensive words. He and his son were, thereupon, brought to *Lindholm*, a castle in Skane, where they were kept prisoners for seven years. On entering the castle, a dark, square-shaped room was assigned them, and when the king said, "I hope that this torture against a crowned head will only last a few days," the jailor replied: "I grieve to say that the queen's orders are to the contrary; anger not the queen by any bravado, else you will be placed in the irons, and if these fail, we can have recourse to sharper means." To the excessive self-love, intemperance, conceitedness, and want of foresight, which had characterized all his actions, the unhappy Albrecht had to ascribe his being here.

The year following, the queen stormed the important city of Calmar, yet siding with the imprisoned king, and made several wise alliances with Richard II., of England, and other potentates, and concluded a truce for two years with the princes of Mecklenburg, and the cities of Rostock and Wismar, which had begun to raise fresh levies in favor of the unfortunate Albrecht. This period expired, she laid siege to Stockholm and other fortified places, of which John, Duke of Mecklenburg, and other friends of the imprisoned king had become masters. But the cause of Albrecht was but little forwarded, and his opponent, Margarethe, gained ground every day. She compelled the capital to surrender to her and do homage to her as its sovereign, whereafter a peremptory peace was concluded on Good Friday, which restored tran-

A. D., 1392.

A. D., 1395.

quillity to the three kingdoms. The imprisoned king and his son were delivered up to the Hanseatic towns, and they obtained their liberty for sixty thousand ounces of silver, upon condition that they should resign all claims to Sweden, if said amount were not paid within three years. As soon as the king and his son were delivered to the deputies, they solemnly swore to a strict observance of this article, the Hanse-towns engaging themselves to guarantee the treaty. The money, however, not being paid by the stipulated time, Margarethe became an undisputed sovereign of Sweden, the third Scandinavian kingdom.

About this time the *Victuals-brethren*, called so because they, from the Hanse-towns, brought victuals to Stockholm while besieged, began to imperil Denmark, plundering the Danish and Norwegian coasts, and destroying all commercial business along the Baltic. But Margarethe, always able to act properly in unexpected difficulties, ordered the harbors of the maritime towns to be blocked up, thus putting a quick stop to their cruelties and piracies. The queen's principal care was now to visit the different provinces, to administer justice and redress grievances of every kind. Among other salutary regulations, the affairs of commerce were not forgotten. It was, for instance, decreed that all manner of assistance should be given to foreign merchants and sailors, particularly in case of misfortune and shipwreck, without expectation of reward; and that pirates should be treated with the greatest rigor, in order to deter them from that dishonorable profession.

Erik of Pomerania, was, as we have shown, elected king of Denmark and Norway, after Margarethe's death; but also wishing to have him elected her successor to the Swedish throne, she brought this, her nephew and foster-son, to Sweden, and introduced him to the deputies, one by one, whom she requested to confirm his election to the succession. The majesty of the queen's person, the strength of her arguments, and the sweetness of her eloquence, gained over the deputies, who, on the 22d of July, 1396, elected him at *Morastone*, by Upsala, to succeed her also in Sweden. But Margarethe, soon discovering his inability and impetuousness, took pains to remedy, as much as possible, this evil, by procuring him as a wife, the intelligent and virtuous princess *Philippa*, a daughter of Henry V. of England; and shortly after she got *Catharine*, her niece and Erik's sister, married to Prince *John*, a son of the German emperor, Ruprecht, John being promised to assume the Scandinavian crowns if Erik of Pomerania should die childless. Thus having strengthened and consolidated her power by the way of influential connections and relationships, the queen, upon whose head the three northern crowns were actually united, now proceeded to realize the great plan she already had long cherished: to get a fundamental law established for a perpetual union of the three large

Scandinavian kingdoms—the realization of which has immortalized her, and secured for her admiration in the eyes of the world and of the most thorough historians, who do not hesitate to surname her "the Great," and to compare her with the great Greek and Roman heroes and statesmen. On the 17th of June, 1397, Margarethe summoned to an assembly in *Calmar*, in the province Smaland of Sweden, the clergy and the nobility of Denmark, Norway, and Sweden, and established, by their aid and consent, a fundamental law. This was the law so celebrated in the North under the name of the *Union of Calmar*, which afterwards gave birth to wars between Sweden and Denmark that lasted a whole century. It consisted of three articles. The first provided, that the three kingdoms should, thenceforward, have but one and the same king, who was to be chosen successively by each of the kingdoms. The second article consisted of the obligation upon the sovereign to divide his time equally in the three kingdoms. The third, and most important, was, that each kingdom should retain its own laws, customs, senate, and privileges of every kind; that the highest officers should be taken of the natives; that an alliance being concluded with foreign potentates should be obligatory upon all three kingdoms, when approved of by the council of one kingdom; and that, after the death of the king, his eldest son, or if he died childless, then another wise, intelligent, and able prince, should be chosen common monarch; and if any one, because of high-treason, was banished from one kingdom, then he should be banished from them all. A month after, on the queen's birth-day (13th of July), a legitimate charter was drawn up, to which the queen subscribed and put her seal; on which occasion Erik of Pomerania was anointed and crowned by the archbishops of Upsala and Lund as king of Denmark, Norway, and Sweden. Te Deum was sung in the churches of Calmar, the assembly crying out: "*Hæcce unio esto perpetua! Longe, longe, longe, vivat Margarethe, regina Daniæ, Norvegiæ et Sveciæ!*"

This strict union of the three large states became a potent bulwark for their security, and made them, in more than one century, the arbiter of the European system; the three nations of the northern peninsula presenting a compact and united front, that could bid defiance to any foreign aggression.

III.

1397—1448.

Queen Margarethe—Attempts to regain Schleswig—*Erik of Pomerania*—Dispute about Schleswig—War with the Hanseatic Towns—Rebellion in Sweden—Engelbrechtson—Charles Canutson—Dethronement of the King in Denmark and Sweden—*Christopher of Bavaria* acknowledged King of all three Kingdoms—Rebellion of the Peasantry—The House of Oldenburg.

ALTHOUGH Erik of Pomerania was elected king, and in the year 1407 past minority, Margarethe continued governing until the day of her death. "You have done all well," wrote the people to her, "and we value your services so highly, that we would gladly grant you every thing." The union of the three Scandinavian kingdoms having been established in Calmar, all her efforts now aimed at regaining the duchy of Schleswig, A. D., which circumstances had compelled her to resign 1404. to Gerhard IV., Count of Holstein. For such a reunion with Schleswig a favorable opportunity appeared, when Gerhard was killed in an expedition against the Ditmarshers, leaving behind three sons in minority. Elizabeth, Gerhard's widow, fled to Margarethe, for succor against her violent brother-in-law, Bishop Henry of Osnabrück. Margarethe, fond of fishing in foul water, was very willing to help her, but availed herself of the opportunity to annex, successively, different parts of Schleswig.

The dethroned Swedish king, Albrecht, never able to

forget his anger with Margarethe, or her severity against him, and continually cherishing a hope of re-ascending the Swedish throne, and considering the Union of Calmar a breach of peace, contrived to make the Swedish people displeased with her, and thought it a suitable time to revolt from her dominion. He established a strong camp before Visby, the capital of the island of Gulland, having six thousand foot and, at some distance, nine thousand horse. Determined to engage before this junction could take place, the queen's commander-in-chief, *Abraham Broder*, immediately advanced until in sight of the enemy, and then endeavored to gain possession of Visby and the ground near by. In this he was so far successful, that Albrecht and his army had to leave the camp, and conclude a truce. But, nevertheless, he did not, till after a lapse of seven years, give up his hope of remounting the throne of Sweden, making a final peace with Margarethe, and henceforward living in Gadebush, Mecklenburg, where he, in the year 1412, closed his inglorious life. Soon after (27th of October) queen Margarethe died on board a ship in the harbor of Flensburg, fifty-nine years of age, and after an active and notable reign of thirty-seven years. Her funeral was performed with the greatest solemnity, and her corpse was brought to the cathedral of Roeskilde, where Erik of Pomerania, her successor, in the year 1423, caused her likeness to be carved in alabaster. Her acts show her character:

judiciousness, united with circumspection, wisdom in devising plans, and perseverance in executing them; skill in gaining the confidence of the clergy and peasantry, to have a weight sufficient to counterbalance the imperious nobility. On the whole, she applied herself to the civilization of her three kingdoms, and their improvement by the enactment of excellent laws, the great aim of which was to undermine the nobility. She pursued the plan of her great father, to recall all rights to the crown-lands, which, during the reign of her weak and inefficient predecessors, had been granted the nobility. The prosecution of this plan for the perfect subversion of the feudal aristocracy was unfortunately interrupted by her death; her imprudent and weak successor having no power to restrain the turbulent spirit of a factious nobility. Previous, however, to giving an account of his rule of the internal affairs of the states, it is necessary to take a connected view of the reign at large of this mean and base monarch.

Erik of Pomerania's inability in ruling the three Northern kingdoms, now appeared more and more distinctly; for during the reign of Margarethe, all his undertakings were mostly under her guidance. He possessed no vigor of mind, no bold and enterprising spirit, and was never guided by prudence. The three sons of the duke Gerhard IV. took advantage of his inability, endeavoring to withdraw themselves from his yoke, and to be enfeoffed with the duchy of Schleswig. At a Diet of

Nyborg the king cited the young dukes, and opened the assembly himself with a full explanation of the circumstances of the dispute. A. D., 1413. When he had finished his speech, the archbishop, in a fulminating harangue, declared, that the duchess-dowager, *Elizabeth*, and her brother-in-law, *Henry of Osnabrück*, as tutors and counselors to Gerhard's children, had forfeited all right to the duchy of Schleswig, in consequence of having, before Margarethe's death, taken arms against their lawful sovereign, and that Schleswig should, therefore, be annexed to the crown of Denmark. Scarce had the archbishop pronounced this sentence, when the eldest son of the deceased duke, Gerhard, threw himself at the king's feet, and besought him to grant the investiture of the duchy as a fief; but the king replied in the negative The three young dukes now began to concert measures for shaking off his yoke; and, although Erik of Pomerania had the military power of three large kingdoms at command, and marched an army of a hundred thousand men against them, he was defeated near *Immervad*, in Schleswig, with great loss, insomuch that A. D., 1421. his flight became a proverb: "At Immervad the Danes were driven to the devil." Although this defeat did not terminate the war, it produced a truce, in order to settle preliminaries for a peace. Arbitrators were chosen, and the whole affair of the duchy of Schleswig was again canvassed. Nevertheless, the young dukes embraced every occasion of frustrating the intention of the truce, and chose to decide the difference by the sword. Erik perceived their aim, and equipped a fleet with the design to invade the island of Alsen. Here he met with no success; the admiral, Ivar Brusk, died on board, and a hurricane dispersed and shattered the whole fleet. Erik now took the course of appealing to the German empe-

A. D., 1424. ror, *Sigismund*, and repaired to *Ofen* (Buda), where the emperor then resided. Construing the appeal in favor of the king, Sigismund declared, that all Schleswig should henceforward be annexed in full right to the crown of Denmark, and that the dukes Henry, Adolphus, and Gerhard, had, by their conduct, divested themselves of their right to Schleswig. The king, now

A. D., 1425. believing the whole to be settled, resolved upon a pilgrimage to Palestine. But, after returning, he found the ancient leaven of contest revived and violently fermenting in the breasts of the dukes, who, making alliance with the Hanse-towns, continued the war; and though king Erik collected all his strength to oppose them, and even gained a complete victory over the Hanse fleet, yet at last they overmatched him, and weakened the kingdoms by horrible ravages. However, their attempts to seize upon *Copenhagen* failed; the city being saved by the bravery and intelligent preparations of his queen, *Philippa*, of England. At length the unlucky war with the dukes was ended by the treaty

A. D., 1435. of *Wordingborg*, by which *Adolphus*, the only one yet alive, should enjoy, during his life, the duchy of Schleswig, except the city of Haderslev and the island of Aró, and his heirs, for two years after his decease; Denmark thus again being dispossessed of Schleswig. Some disturbances in Sweden had accelerated the peace of Wordingborg. Sweden, from the very beginning displeased with the Union of Calmar, was embroiled in commotions, which chiefly proceeded from the mean policy of the king in bestowing his offices of trust on foreigners, in usurping the rights and prerogatives of the Swedish people, and from disproportional taxes. Encouraged by the weakness of their sovereign, they resolved to attempt a change in the government, and to wrest the sceptre from the hand of Erik, whom they generally nicknamed "the Pomeranian knave." The circumstance which caused the first operations of the Swedes towards the recovery of their lawful privileges, was the tyrannical oppression exercised by *Jens Erikson*, the royal bailiff, in the province of Dalecarlia. A mountaineer and miner, *Engelbrecht Engelbrechtson*, accused the bailiff before the king. The officer was deposed, but Engelbrechtson had spoken with such ardor and bluntness, that the king forbade him his presence, and ordered him to leave Denmark. "That I will," replied Engelbrechtson, "but to return in a different manner." The Dalecarlians, ever watchful of their liberties, resolved to throw off the Danish yoke, and to die like free men, rather than live like slaves under the lash of Erik's tyranny; and the disturbances were carried on, headed by Engelbrechtson, whom *Erik Puke*, an influential nobleman, had joined. It went so far that Engelbrechtson forced the Senate to send the king a formal sentence of deposition. In a meeting, however, of the Council of all three kingdoms, Erik of Pomerania was again acknowledged King of Sweden. To appease the growing displeasure, the king summoned a Diet at *Vadstena*, where he agreed that *Charles Canutson Bonde* and *Christiern Nielson Vasa* should be appointed to digest a new plan of government. But the rebellion soon broke out with renewed power. A rivalship commenced between Canutson and Engelbrechtson. Both were fired with the glorious emulation of being the deliverer of their country. Engelbrechtson, in particular, was extremely successful, when he was suddenly murdered by the artifice of his rival; between whom and Erik Puke a new dispute arose, that once more restored the king's affairs. Canutson and Christiern Vasa, however, soon seemed resolved to overturn the whole arrangement of the offices of government, and to substitute creatures of their own in place of those who formerly had filled them; wherefore the nobility and the clergy, perceiving their aim, remonstrated against the continuance of this junta in office, and summoned a general Diet at *Calmar*, where the senators of all three kingdoms met together to draw up more precise terms for the Union. Here it was stipulated, that after the death of the king, forty men

A. D., 1436.

A. D., 1437.

of each kingdom should meet together in *Halmstad*, to elect the new ruler; that the king should always have two intelligent men with him, and war could not be declared, or peace concluded, without the consent of all three kingdoms; and that the king should never prefer to the offices of trust any foreigners within the limits of the Swedish monarchy. This delineation, in some respects more accurate and complete than that of Calmar, 1397, never gained, however, any validity; and the rupture between the kingdoms was incurable, until at length the Union of Calmar, which had promised the North so great blessings and stability, after a series of wars and immense bloodshed, and only after a course of one hundred and twenty-three years, was broken and nullified. Even in Denmark a great dissatisfaction with the reign of Erik of Pomerania began to appear, occasioned by the long and unlucky wars, by the debasement of the coin, and by the heavy taxes lavished on unworthy favorites of the king, or wasted in idle exhibitions of magnificence. The people were also highly displeased with his bestowing the highest offices on German noblemen, and with his endeavors to get his cousin-german, Bugislaw of Pomerania, appointed his joint governor and successor. Vexed at the senators' non compliance with his request about that, Erik of Pomerania left Denmark, repairing to the island of Gulland with a large body of troops, with all the jewels of the crown, and with his concubine, *Cecilia*, o

A. D., 1439.

whom he was passionately enamored. He was now dethroned in all three kingdoms, and his name rendered both odious and despicable. It was the time for a competitor to start forth, and to avail himself of this general disaffection to the dethroned king, who had no more expectation of re-ascending the throne.

29th June, A. D., 1439.

This competitor was *Christopher of Bavaria*, a son of Erik's sister, Catharina, and Pfalzgrave John. Erik being childless, Christopher, who now returned from Bavaria, stood thus plainly in the hope of succession, and the regency of the three Scandinavian kingdoms was, at the Diet of *Halmstad*, conferred upon him. The despicable Erik of Pomerania lived for ten years on Gulland, where he, with ignominy, dragged on a life of piracy, from whence he went to Pomerania, where he, having no resource but in the society of his concubine, at the expiration of ten years, died unlamented. His noble and magnanimous queen, Philippa, whom he often had treated unkindly, betook herself to the monastery of *Vadstena*, which she herself had founded, and here she expired, on the fifth of July, 1430. The king perceiving his loss, and repenting of his conduct, caused many requiems to be sung for a speedy entrance of her soul into the dwellings of the blessed.

A. D., 1439.

A. D., 1459.

The taste for classical learning, at this time, was far from being universally diffused in the Scandinavian countries, and it is, therefore, highly to be appreciated that some monkish writers preserved alive the embers of the literary spirit, and contributed to the preservation of such of the Greek and Roman authors as we now possess entire; and however miserable an individual Erik of Pomerania rightly may appear, he seems, nevertheless, to have had some taste for literature, or disposition to patronize science and the arts, since he prevailed with the Pope, Martin V., to permit him to found a University in Copenhagen, which, however, on account of his tumultuous reign, was not carried into effect.

Christopher of Bavaria succeeded now to the throne of his uncle, and received homage in Wiborg. Immediately on his arrival in Denmark, the senate published a decree, whereby all those were declared enemies to their country who should visit Erik's court on Gulland, and a manifesto was issued containing the articles of accusation against Erik of Pomerania, which were affixed on the gates of all the northern Hanse-towns. Although Christopher of Bavaria was elected by the senators, the peasantry being yet regarded as too inconsiderable to have any voice, he followed, nevertheless, the old custom, to travel round to receive homage in the different kingdoms. In Sweden there were some hindrances to his election; but the clergy, taking as much pains in preserving the union of the three kingdoms as the nobility did in nullifying it, prevailed upon the senate to acknowledge Christopher king of Sweden, and to swear allegiance to him as their sovereign, whereafter he was crowned in Stockholm. In the year following Christopher went from Sweden to Norway, and received, at *Opslo*, the crown of that kingdom. Thence he passed to Denmark, and was crowned at Ripen, by the archbishop of Lund. *Charles Canutson Bonde* resigned his office, but the Diet declared, that, in consideration of his services, he should enjoy Finland and the island of Oland, but on condition, that the crown should, at any time, have power to redeem them for the sum of forty thousand marks in silver. Christopher confirmed this donation of the Diet, and granted, thereafter, the investiture of Schleswig, as a hereditary fief, to duke Adolphus, in order to have a support in him, if need be. In the beginning of his reign a violent rebellion broke out amongst the peasantry of Jutland, who refused paying taxes, unless they were permitted to pay them to their late king Erik, of whom they yet were in favor. The peasants, whose army is said to have amounted to the number of twenty-five thousand men, routed the royal troops, slew the commanders, and put to death all the noblemen they could catch, with every circumstance of cruelty. Incensed at their obstinacy, Christopher marched against them in person, gave them battle, and obtained a complete, but bloody victory. Henry Togon, a senator, who had always espoused the cause of the dethroned king, together with several others of his adherents, was taken prisoner, and broken alive upon the wheel. But the main body of the rebellious peasants, called the *Vendelboërs*, who lived north of the Lymfjord, gained a neighboring hill, which they so intrenched with wagons and trains, as to withstand all the attacks of the king's cavalry. At last, Christopher was advised to offer them pardon, if they would submit, which expedient induced them to throw down their arms. To pay tithes to the clergy, of which there so long time had been a dispute, and with which the peasants were yet highly displeased, was decided upon under Christopher, by a sentence from the senate. He also tried to limit the commercial privileges of the Hanse-towns, confirming their privileges only upon condition that they should interpose no obstacles to the trade of other nations, and that Scandinavian merchants should enjoy the same privileges in the Hanseatic harbors. In Sweden they were not satisfied with Christopher's reign, though it came not to any rebellion. He was there surnamed *the bark king* (Barkekongen), because an unfruitful year happened, in which the people, to get sufficient bread, had to grind flour of bark. But, in all reason, his subjects were very much displeased with his connivance at Erik of Pomerania's piracies, which he passed over, saying: "My uncle must also do something for the support of his life." Christopher of Bavaria received an embassy from the Sultan of Turkey,

A. D., 1444. who offered him his daughter; but the king declined accepting the offer, *Dorothea*, a daughter of the markgrave, John of Brandenburg, surnamed the Alchymist, being more agreeable to his inclinations. Before leaving Christopher, it may be added, that he removed the royal residence from Roeskilde to Copenhagen, where, since that time, the kings of Denmark have resided, and that he entered upon a treaty of Roeskilde, whereby Copenhagen, until then a dependency on that diocese, was ceded to the crown. After A. D., 1448. a reign of eight years he died. On assuming the reins of government he gave some indications of a vigorous administration; but this was only of short duration. He was abandoned to his pleasures, and, like most kings, a slave to unworthy favorites.

The prosperity and esteem of the peasantry, who tilled the ground and constituted the majority of the nation, seem to have been very lightly considered in this period. Frequent rebellions of the peasants, quelled by much bloodshed, under Erik Ploughpenning, Christopher I., Erik Glipping, Erik Menved, Waldemar Atterdag, and Christopher of Bavaria, prove that the peasants were sensible of the yoke resting upon them, but in vain tried to shake it off. The almost uninterrupted internal disturbances and external wars, of which the nobility and the clergy availed themselves to enlarge their power and riches, weakened and impoverished the peasantry, and they were considered only a part of the property belonging to the noblemen, transferable along with horses, cows and other movables, at the will of the owner; while, on the other hand, the clergy and the nobility were floating in riches and extensive privileges. The clergy were allowed a free election to all vacant church preferments, the king renouncing his power of presentation. No tax could be imposed upon the clergy, except in one particular case —the king's captivity. No freeman (nobleman) could be taken or imprisoned, or dispossessed of his free tenements or liberties, or outlawed, or banished, or any way hurt or injured, unless by the legal judgment of his equals; the clergy and the nobility thus being set far above the common level.

In this period, about the end of the twelfth century, the commercial spirit had begun to make some progress toward the North. The Baltic was then infested by pirates, who ravaged the coasts. The city of Lübeck, on the Baltic, and Hamburg, at the mouth of the Elbe, were obliged to enter into a league of mutual defence for the protection of their merchantmen against these piracies. This association, which was, as before mentioned, termed the *League of the Hanse-towns*, became soon so formidable in the eyes of the kings and states of Europe, that they even courted its alliance. The burgher class of Scandinavia and the cities were very much pressed by the Hanseatic towns, which had made themselves masters of all trade with foreign countries.

and imported German commodities to the Scandinavian cities; and the condition of the burgher class was about on a level with that of the peasantry. During the greater part of this period, the general state of literature was at a very low ebb; but a brighter period was now at hand, and classical learning began to be universally diffused, and a more genuine taste was revived for polite literature, when the admirable invention of the art of printing was made, in the year 1436, by *John von Sorgenlock*, called Gänsefleisch, from Guttenberg, generally, therefore, called *John Guttenberg*. This invention was, as is well known, considerably improved by *John Faust*, a rich jeweler, and *Peter Schöffer*, an ecclesiastic from Gernsheim. In the year 1457 the first book was printed, in Latin, namely, the Psalms of David, of which five copies yet remain—in Göttingen, Vienna, Mainz, Paris, and in the royal library in Copenhagen

THE HOUSE OF OLDENBURG.

IV.

1448—1536.

Christian I.—Charles Canutson—Archbishop Jens Bengtson—Steno Sture the Elder—Battle on Brunkehill—Pilgrimage to Rome—University of Copenhagen—*Hans*-Charter—Division of the Duchies—Expedition to Ditmarsh—Rebellion in Sweden and Norway—War with the Hanse Towns—*Christian II.*—Expedition against Sweden—Archbishop Gustav Trolle—The Slaughter at Stockholm—Sighrit-Dyveke—Torben Oxe—The Beginning of the Reformation—Rebellion—The King flees—*Frederick I.*—Civil War—Rebellion in Skane—Soren Norby—The Reformation spreads—John Tausen—Diet of Odensee—Diet of Copenhagen—The War of the Count (Grevens Feide)—*Christian III.*—Shipper Clemens—Battle by Oxenhill—Literature and Language.

CHRISTOPHER of Bavaria, dying without issue, the advantages which would have accrued from annexing the duchy of Schleswig to the crown, made the senate first cast their eyes on Adolphus. But because of old age, declining accepting the crown offered him, Adolphus proposed to them his nephew, Christian, a son of Count Diderick the Happy, of Oldenburg, whose answer to the ambassadors is remarkable: "I have three sons," said he, "of very opposite qualities; one is passionately fond of women, another breathes nothing but war, but the third is moderate in his disposition, prefers peace to the din of arms, and is generous and magnanimous." With one voice, of course, the senate declared for that prince whose panegyric the father had drawn; and the house of Oldenburg, at this day seated on the throne of Denmark, assumed the government in the person of *Christian I.*, Count of Oldenburg, and a nephew to Adolphus, duke of Schleswig and count of Holstein Willingly accepting the offer, Christian I. sought to enter into favor with the people by marrying the queen-dowager *Dorothea.* Next he gave a communication in writing to the Diet, declaring Denmark an *elective* kingdom, and binding himself not to impose taxes, not to declare war, and not to grant any deed of feoffment, unless consented to by the Diet; after which he was anointed and crowned in Copenhagen, and received from the archbishop, Yvon, the standard of the kingdom. Christian I. now sought the affection and friendship of the Swedish nation, in order to pave the way for an unshaken union of the three crowns. But the Swedes endeavoring to break the Union of Calmar, which they considered a thorn in their flesh, rose in rebellion, and chose, diametrically opposite to the statutes of said Union, and against the express wish of archbishop Jens Bengtson Oxenstjerna, and the whole Swedish clergy, their grand mareshal, *Charles Canutson*, for their king. Even in Norway, assisted by his kinsman, the archbishop *Aslach Bolt*, Charles Canutson was crowned in Drontheim as king of Norway. But in the following year, at a meeting in Halmstad, the Swedish and Danish senators agreed that Charles Canutson had to renounce all claim to Norway, to which it was certain he had no manner of right, and that Denmark and Sweden, after the death or deposition of Charles Canutson, were to be re-united. Although Charles Canutson did not approve of that agreement, yet Christian I. was declared king of Norway, and crowned in Drontheim. At the same time an agreement was made in Bergen, that Norway and Denmark should always be ruled by one king, happen what might to Sweden. But the Swedes, disgusted with the despotic government of Charles Canutson, determined at length to throw off his yoke. The archbishop Jens Bengtson Oxenstjerna, on account of some personal grievances, headed the insurrection, entered the metropolitan church, put on his high-priest ornaments, and prostrated himself before the high altar; then laying aside his habit, he swore he would never again resume it, until Charles Canutson was driven out of the throne of Sweden. A. D., 1450.

Charles Canutson, finding the greater part of the Swedish nation disaffected, concealed the public treasure in the house of some Dominican friars, and embarked with all his private riches in a ship, with which he set sail to *Dantzic*, in Western Prussia, where he sojourned for seven years. Christian I. was now unanimously elected king of Sweden, conducted into the church by the archbishop, and crowned, amidst A. D., 1457 the acclamations of the people. The crown of all three kingdoms was thus now placed upon his head, and the Union of Calmar re-established. His little son, *Hans*, only three years of age, was elected his successor to all three kingdoms.

Shortly after, at the death of Adolphus, who died without issue, there seemed to be a sure prospect of re-uniting South Jutland (Schleswig) with the kingdom, but instead of incorporating it with the Danish crown as an escheated fief, Christian I. unwisely engaged himself in negotiations with the nobility and the clergy, to be elected duke of Schleswig and count of Holstein, to which latter, however, *Otho of Schaumburg* was more entitled; wherefore he had to purchase Holstein for the sum of forty-three thousand florins, and to buy off the pretensions of Gerhard and Maurice, nephews to the late Adolphus, for an equivalent of forty thousand florins. Christian I. thus became king of Denmark, Norway, and Sweden, duke of Schleswig and count of Holstein; whereupon he forced the Dominicans to refund the treasure lodged in their hands by Charles Canutson, after they had for a long time denied the fact. But in a short time new disturbances broke out in Sweden, where the nobility still sought to prevent a firm union of the three kingdoms, and the people complained of the king's absence from Sweden, and of burdensome taxes. The king, imagining that the archbishop was concerned in it, ordered him to be brought a prisoner to Denmark; whereupon a violent rebellion arose, headed by the archbishop's nephew, *Ketil Carlson Vasa*, bishop of Linköping, who invited Charles Canutson to return to the throne, and he was a second time acknowledged king of Sweden; but his good fortune was of short duration, for when Christian I. released the archbishop, and reconciled himself with him, Charles Canutson had to renounce the crown, and swear that he would never again aspire to re-ascend the throne. Finally, he was sent a prisoner to *Finland*, with a certain appanage for his subsistence. Nevertheless, assisted by the lord high treasurer, *Erik Axelson*, Charles Canutson, whose affairs were ruined in appearance, was a third time called back to the Swedish throne, and died as king of Sweden. His death, however, did not procure Christian I. the Swedish throne, which got a sagacious ruler in *Steno Sture the Elder*, a nephew to Charles Canutson, who for twenty-six years governed the kingdom with wisdom, curbed the insolence of the nobility, elevated the peasantry and the burgher class, and founded the celebrated University of Upsala. Christian I. determined to support his claim to Sweden by force of arms, set a powerful armament on foot, with which he sailed to Stockholm, but was in the bloody battle on *Brunkehill* totally defeated and dangerously wounded, thenceforward desisting from any claim to Sweden.

A.D., 1470

A.D., 1476.

A.D., 1471.

Christian I. had promised to undertake a pilgrimage to the Holy Land, but to be released from it he took a journey to Rome. On his way thither he visited the German emperor Frederick III., who, upon his request, elevated Holstein, Storman, and Ditmarsh to a dukedom, enfeoffing the king with the country last mentioned, which for a long space of time had been a republic. But the Ditmarshians did not submit to Denmark till the next century, after a most bloody contest for their liberty. He then pursued his journey to Rome, where he was received with extraordinary distinction by his Holiness and the College of Cardinals. The Pope, Sixtus IV., permitted him to found a university in Copenhagen. Immediately upon his return from Rome, the king went to Cologne to compose some controversies between the Emperor and *Charles the Bold*, duke of Burgundy. The university was at length established, the bishop of Roeskilde being appointed chancellor, but on account of its narrow means it had in the beginning only three professors, and gained no fame till after the introduction of the Reformation. The young students, therefore, visited so frequently foreign universities, that the king deemed it necessary to lay it upon them as a duty first for some years to be in a course of study at the University of Copenhagen. Christian I. resolved now to strengthen the succession by the marriage of his son, and sent therefore, an embassy to Saxony, to demand *Christina*, daughter to the elector Ernst, for his son. The proposals were accepted, and the marriage ceremony performed, on which occasion the Order of the Elephant was first instituted. Originally this order bore a patriarchal cross, which after the Reformation was changed for a gold chain with an elephant suspended to it. The Danish kings confer this order only upon princes and noblemen of the first distinction, observing, however, one rule, which is, never to confer it upon those who have not first been favored with the order called Dannebrog.

Christian I. was in a continual want of money, occasioned by his two expensive journeys, and by the amount he had to pay for being elected Count of Holstein. The unfavorable consequences of this want of money appeared, when the king's daughter, *Margarethe*, was married to James III. of Scotland; for as the king was not able to pay down more than 2,000 florins of the dowry, which amounted to 60,000 florins, the Orkney and Shetland islands were mortgaged for the 58,000 florins; and as Denmark for a long series of years was not able to redeem them, and Scotland, because this debt had waxen so old, raised difficulties in giving them back, these possessions, which originally belonged to Norway, were lost forever. The power and arbitrariness of the Hanse-towns yet continuing under Christian I. appeared strikingly by the violent acts which their officers and stewards exercised unpunished in

Bergen. Falling upon the royal constable, *Olaf Nielson*, they murdered him, the bishop, and sixty other persons. Their power and tyranny, however, did not long continue, their trade began to be limited, and their declension to draw near, other lands, particularly Holland and England, beginning to trade in the North, and exchange commodities from India and the Orient for the produce and manufactures of the North; and every variety of useful merchandise was now, by means of the Baltic and the great continental rivers, easily conveyed through most of the kingdoms of Europe, all of which successively annihilated the superiority of the Hanse-towns; and in order to destroy entirely their detrimental influence in Denmark, Christian I. entered into alliance with England, Scotland, France, and Burgundy. He also enacted a commercial law containing many regulations favorable to the mercantile affairs of Denmark; for instance, that German merchants should not be permitted to travel round in the country and engross commodities for the purpose of making their profit by enhancing the price, but should buy them in the towns. The Hanseatic confederacy had, from the year 1438, begun to decline, and it is not to be denied, that it is to this decline Scandinavia and many other European states owe their domestic manufactures and the increase of their real wealth. After having pursued the true interests of his people, and sought to establish order, tranquillity, and an equal administration of justice,

Christian I. died, after a reign of thirty-three years, and lies buried in the Cathedral of Roeskilde. <small>May 2, A. D., 1481.</small>

He was succeeded on the throne by his son *Hans* (John), as we have seen, already in his father's lifetime elected successor in all three kingdoms. He was immediately acknowledged king of Denmark, but in the two other kingdoms, especially in Sweden, he met with considerable difficulties, Steno Sturo the Elder not being disposed to resign. Even in Norway the interest of Sténo Sturo was promoted by the aid of the Archbishop of Drontheim. Nevertheless, at a meeting in Halmstad, king Hans was declared king of Norway, <small>A. D., 1483.</small> but had to sign and seal a charter which bears witness to the increasing power of the nobility and the clergy. All the old privileges of the clergy were confirmed; the king could no more meddle with the election of a bishop; the peasants and attendants belonging to the nobility and the clergy were to be exempted from paying taxes. The king could not confer a feoffment upon any one, or deprive any of the fief he had, unless the members of the Diet had consented to it. No serf could obtain a demesne, nor the king himself mortgage it; and the right to fortify manors, abrogated by queen Margarethe, was in this charter restored to the nobility. But about any privileges for the commons, who yet were considered in a very abject and despicable light, was not one word spoken; and if the king, so run the words, should dare to violate this charter, the inhabitants were entitled to apply violent means, without being impeached of having broken their oath of allegiance. In the same year, at a meeting in *Calmar*, the Swedish Diet declared Hans king of Sweden, but Steno Sturo set all engines at work to frustrate the resolution of the Diet, his arts succeeding so happily, that for fourteen years the king hoped in vain to ascend the Swedish throne.

In the duchies, king Hans met with great difficulties in getting elected, his brother *Frederick*, whom the influential queen-dowager ardently assisted, withstanding his election. At length both of them were elected dukes, the duchies being divided into Gottorp and Segeberg. Frederick chose the Gottorp part, but was, however, not satisfied, and continued long to show himself very grasping and presumptuous. He assumed the title, "Inheritor of Norway," and laid claim to the islands of Laaland, Falster, and Mona; but at the Diet of Callundborg these insolent claims were rejected, as being entirely unauthorized. Nevertheless, the two valuable duchies were unfortunately again dismembered from the crown, notwithstanding the inconveniencies lately felt from the grant made to the children of Gerhard. King Hans, having now, through fourteen years, in vain hoped that by the way of negotiations he might ascend the throne of Sweden, resolved to enforce his right by arms. His mother *Dorothea*, who had continually dissuaded him from war,

A. D., 1490.

A. D., 1494.

and entreated him to rest satisfied with his present dominions, was now dead and gone, and Steno Sture the Elder was just now very critically situated, being at variance with several influential members of the senate, and with *Svante Nielson Sture*, who engaged in his interest the archbishop of Upsala, *Jacob Ulfson*, and all the clergy, who upbraided Steno Sture the Elder with having occasioned numberless losses and disgraces to the kingdom. Hans thought it, therefore, a favorable opportunity to try the chances of war. The Danish army advanced upon Stockholm, opened the gates of the capital, and cut to pieces an army from Dalecarlia consisting of thirty thousand men, in the memo- A. D., rable battle of *Ródebro*, where many of the 1496. brave Swedish Dalecarlians sacrificed their lives with the most desperate courage; whereafter Steno Sture, encouraged by the Dalecarlians, attacked the royal Danish army at *Nordermalm*, but was again defeated. Despairing now of being able to make head against the king's army, the administrator, Steno Sture, A. D., signed a treaty, by which he acknowledged king 1497. Hans king of Sweden, agreeable to the Union of Calmar, which thus, a hundred years after its founding, was re-established, Steno Sture getting Finland, the city of Nykòping, and some other lands and cities assigned for his maintenance. King *Hans* was now immediately crowned king of Sweden, and his son *Christian* elected his successor. The king now probed the wounds of the state, applying the most moderate and the wisest remedies to compose the controversies in Sweden, and effect a more friendly spirit.

The Swedish affairs settled, the king engaged in a war, which terminated little to his honor or advantage. It was occasioned by the grant made by the emperor to the late king of that country inhabited by the people called *Ditmarshians*. For many ages this brave people had thrown off the Danish yoke, and aspired to perfect independence. A considerable royal army was now equipped, the greatest part of which consisted of levied troops, under the command of *George Slentz*, a German nobleman. To co-operate with this enormous force, duke Frederick, the king's brother, arrived, together with the flower of the nobility of Schleswig and Holstein. So sure did the Danes make themselves of victory, that they had shared the booty before the engagement, and every one brought carriages for moving off his proportion of the spoil. But their expectation was dissipated like a summer's cloud. In fact, few enterprises were preceded by more immense preparations, and as few, perhaps, attended with a more unfortunate issue, the great object falling altogether short of its aim. It has been mentioned, that Ditmarsh had been a republic (a district not seven Danish miles in extent), which now the Danish king was desirous of subjugating. The Ditmarshians, penetrated with love of liberty, threw down the dykes, which restrained the encroachments of the North Sea, and the whole country was laid under water. A small body of one thousand men, headed by *Wolf Isebrant*, opposed boldly the royal army, and a murderous battle was fought, the Danes attempting all the time to drain off the inundation. But the sluices being opened, and the water gushing in from all parts, the confusion among the Danes reached the highest pitch, and the great royal army was totally routed near *Hemmingsted*, in Holstein. Whole ranks of the Danes were swept down by the grape-shot of the Ditmarshians; king Hans himself made a narrow escape; the old banner, *Dannebrog*, was lost, and an immense number of German and Danish noblemen covered the battle-field. The Ditmarshians committed all sorts of cruelties on the bodies of the wounded; their eyes were plucked out, their noses slit, and their ears cut off.

A.D., 1500.

This great and decisive victory secured the independence of the little republic; and for many years no superiority of numbers could overcome the irresistible bravery of the intrepid Ditmarshians. No sooner the Swedes, dissatisfied with king Hans and with the outrages of the royal bailiffs, had been informed of the defeat of the Danish army at Hemmingsted, than they revolted again, judging this a favorable opportunity to shake off the Danish yoke. Steno Sture was re-elected administrator, and the rebellion increased to such a degree, that soon the king was master of only the castles of Calmar and Stockholm, which, with great courage and perseverance, were defended by Hans's queen, *Christina* of Saxony, until, after a siege of eight months, the whole garrison wasted away by sickness and hunger.

The revolt in Sweden was the signal for another in Norway, which, however, soon ceased, when the plot was discovered, and the ring-leader, *Canute Alfson*, put to death; and a later rebellion, headed by *Herluf Hydefad* and *Bishop Charles of Hammer*, was quelled with great severity and frequent executions, by the king's son, *Christian*, who, since the year 1501 had been appointed administrator of Norway. Prince Christian took Herluf Hydefad and the bishop prisoners, condemned them to death, and ordered them to be broken on the wheel. In a word, the rigor with which his Highness treated the rebels, and especially the nobility, a great number of whom he put to death, gave so rapid a progress to his arms, that he soon saw himself master of all Norway. Meanwhile Steno Sture the elder had died, and was succeeded in the administratorship by *Svante Nielson Sture*.

A. D., 1502.

A. D., 1503.

A new ringleader now appeared in Sweden, *Hemming Gad*, bishop of Linköping. Possessed of engaging manners, of great ingenuity, of military talents, and being a decided adversary of the Union of Calmar, and bearing an inveterate hatred to Denmark, the bishop was very fit for infusing a rebellious spirit into the Swedish nation; upon which, by his uncommon eloquence, he exercised a great influence. The negotiations were carried on through several meetings, but without settling the disputes. At length, at a meeting in Calmar, the council of all three kingdoms agreed to compose and accommodate the differences between king Hans and the disobedient Swedes. The Swedish senators not appearing, the Danish and Norwegian senate pronounced the sentence, that Svante Nielson Sture and his partisans were guilty of high treason and rebellion; and after the scandalous conduct of Sweden had been represented in its strongest colors to the German emperor, *Maximilian*, he confirmed this sentence, and forbade all German countries and cities to have anything to do with the factious Sweden. A war now also broke out between Denmark and the Hanse-towns, which would not break off their commercial connections with Sweden. Moreover, the Hanse-towns were exasperated at the increase of other nations' trade in the North, and especially at a treaty concluded by Hans with England, by which this country was granted the same privileges as the Hanse-towns had hitherto exclusively enjoyed. In this naval war the Danish sea-heroes, *Otto Rud*, *Sören Norby*, *Andrew Bilde*, and *Holger Ulfstand*, signalized themselves by the bravest exploits; and by the peace of *Malmö* a war with the Hanse-towns for the first time ended successfully for Denmark; the merchantmen of which now rode triumphant in the Baltic.

A. D., 1505.

A. D., 1512.

The Hanse-towns had to promise to break off all mercantile connections with Sweden while rebellious, and to defray the charge of war by paying thirty thousand florins. It also came in Malmó to an agreement with Sweden, which, however, put no end to the contests; the Swedes, in spite of this agreement, electing, after the death of Svante Nielson Sture, his son, *Steno Sture the Younger*, administrator. The next year king Hans died, after a reign of thirty-two years. Without any brilliancy of talents, his character is generally said to have been tempered with piety, moderation, and simplicity of manners. He was so great an admirer of the simplicity of the ancient Danes, that he even imitated their dress, and always wore an antique sword hung over his robe. Nevertheless, for having caused his treasurer, *Anders*, to be beheaded, only on account of a loose suspicion of embezzlement, king Hans is blamed very much, the majority considering the treasurer innocent. On his death-bed the king was also so touched with remorse at having been instrumental in the treasurer's death, that he often called upon his name in a kind of frenzy, and ordered, before breathing his last, requiems to be sung for the rest of the soul of the innocent treasurer.

During the reign of king Hans, two Norwegian noblemen stabbed the grand marshal, *Paul Laxmand* (Salmon), as he was passing over a bridge in Copenhagen, and flung his body into the sea, saying that land was not so natural an element for a fish as the sea; alluding to Laxmand, which was the marshal's name. The king commenced a lawsuit against the murdered man, who was declared guilty of treacherous connections with the Swedish rebels, and his large estates were adjudged to the king.

Christian II., his son, in Sweden generally called *Christian the Tyrant*, was now raised to the throne; a man in every respect opposite to his father. He was of high genius, ability and judgment, but not possessed of any mild and humane disposition. His administration was like Cromwell's in England, arbitrary, cruel, and vigorous, and he made no scruple to use religion for reaching his aim. In political matters he was both a leveler and a tyrant. He was born on the 2d of July, 1481, two years before the great reformer, Martin Luther. His father, king Hans, put the young prince out to board with a wealthy citizen in Copenhagen, called *Hans Bookbinder*, where *George Hinze*, an ecclesiastic, daily came to teach him. The prince being of a wild character, and by his dissipations often hazarding his own life, Hans Bookbinder was desirous of being freed from the burden of having supervision over him, and proposed, therefore, to the king, to place him with Hinze. He neither being able to moderate the prince, had to have a watch upon his actions, to take him along with him to church, and make him sing in the choir together with the other singing boys. The king con sidering it below the prince's dignity, took him again to the royal palace, and caused him to be taught by a German master of arts, in general called *Master Conrad*, who instructed him so thoroughly and carefully in Latin, that the young prince spoke it with the greatest volubility and wrote it with classical elegance. On account of his being trained amongst the commons, he had sucked in, as with his mother's milk, a great predilection for the burgher class and the peasantry, while he, on the other hand, cherished a strong antipathy to the nobility and the clergy, who restrained his power and oppressed the lower orders. When twenty years of age, he was, as before mentioned, sent to Norway, to quell a rebellion there, which he performed with great courage, but also with the utmost severity. Thereafter appointed administrator of Norway, he became acquainted with *Dyveke*, a handsome girl, whose mother, *Sigbrit*, had moved from Amsterdam to Bergen, where she kept a tavern. Both of them exercised, from that time, a great but corruptive influence upon Christian II.

A. D., 1513. On the death of king Hans he was, without any opposition, acknowledged king of Denmark and Norway, but Sweden, as usual, raised difficulties concerning his election, and several years passed away before he could ratify his claims there. Meantime

A. D., 1515. Christian resolved to strengthen his power by marrying the noble and gentle princess *Elizabeth*, a sister to the celebrated Charles V., emperor of

Germany and Holland. Studious to please his young queen, the king sent to Holland for gardeners and a colony of Dutch to cultivate all sorts of fruits and other vegetables for her table, and assigned them the little island of Amager, close by Copenhagen, where they highly improved the horticulture, hitherto little known in the North. Notwithstanding his marriage, the king's unlawful connection with his concubine, Dyveka, continued, until a sudden death took her off. Many believed that she had been killed by poison slowly infused into her by the family of a rich nobleman, *Torben Oxen*, who had fallen in love with Dyveka, and would marry her. Torben confessed that he had solicited her favor, but never obtained it. Immediately the king's countenance altered, and he was provoked to such a degree, that he resolved to put Torben Oxen to death without mercy. He was arrested and imprisoned. The affair was tried by the senate, where he was unanimously acquitted, the law having assigned no punishment for simple concupiscence. When the senate's decree was related to the king, he flew into a passion, saying, that if his friends had been as numerous in the senate as Torben's their judgment would have been different; adding: "Even if he had a neck as thick as that of a bull, he shall lose it; and when did I ever say a thing, make a promise, or utter a threat, that I did not fulfill my word?" He proceeded to assemble twelve peasants of the neighborhood before the gate of the citadel, and ordered them to pass sentence on Torben. Dreading his majesty's resentment, and thinking they would be sacrificed, if they did not comply with his humor, they gave their verdict in the following terms: "We do not judge Torben, but his own words condemn him;" whereafter he was immediately beheaded.

This despotic act irritated the nobility yet more with the king, who during his whole reign strove to restrain the extravagant power and influence of the nobility and clergy, and to elevate the peasantry and the burgher class. It is here not out of place to remark, that many of his laws bear witness to a sound judgment, mainly aiming at removing and reforming the degeneracy of manners and morals among the clergy, and at diminishing their exorbitant riches and power, which rendered them odious to the people and prevented them from being examples of the virtues they had to preach. Of the school affairs the king took a peculiar care. He increased the salary of the teachers, and commanded them to prove their qualification by submitting to a public examination. Considering the great influence and power of the nobility and clergy a blight upon the social condition of the mass and an obstacle to the progress of society, he struggled, during his whole reign, against the encroachments of the aristocracy, until, at last, because of his despotism and cruelty, a general insurrection broke out, which retarded him in realizing his many salutary reforms.

But now an epoch commenced, the most important of any in the history of the North. The great Reformation, which Martin Luther had begun in Saxony was early introduced into the Scandinavian countries, and Christian II. received with joy this new religious system of liberty, which he considered conducive to promote his plans. Endeavoring in vain to induce Luther to visit Copenhagen, he prevailed upon his uncle, *Frederick the Wise*, Elector of Saxony, to send him *Martin Reinhardt*, who for a short time preached the new doctrine; but not being able to preach correctly in Danish, and, therefore, often exciting the mirth of his hearers, he left Denmark; whereafter *Carlstadt*, another disciple of Luther's, arrived in Copenhagen; but he also returned soon to Germany without having performed anything worthy of notice. [A. D., 1520.]

Nevertheless, Christian II., though in favor of the Reformation, felt obliged to keep on good terms with the Pope, Leo X., who might perhaps be useful to him in regulating the Swedish concerns, and he permitted, therefore, the abominable *Arcemboldus*, a seller of indulgences, to travel throughout his dominions to make sale of releases from the pains of purgatory, which this pious robber said every one might purchase for a small sum of money. The form of the absolution issued by Arcemboldus was as follows: "I absolve thee from all thy sins, how enormous soever, and remit thee all manner of punishment, which thou oughtest to suffer in purgatory, and at death the gates of paradise shall be opened to receive thee. In the name of the Father, of the Son, and of the Holy Spirit;" even adding, the same as Tetzel, the Dominican friar, in Germany: "As soon as the money clinks in the coffer the soul springs out from purgatory." The king, however, soon fell out with Arcemboldus, and deprived him of a great portion of the money he blasphemously had collected.

The Swedes continued showing themselves unwilling to acknowledge Christian II., who was, however, fortunate enough to find a zealous partisan in *Gustavus Trolle*, Archbishop of Upsala, who carried on a correspondence with the king to extinguish the liberties of his native country. Steno Sture the younger encompassed now the archbishop's castle, *Steka*, and the senate of Sweden deposed him from his dignities. The mighty prelate had immediate recourse to the Pope, Leo X., who granted him a bull, laying the kingdom of Sweden under the sentence of excommunication. The affrighted Swedes returned to their allegiance, Gustavus Trolle was restored to his archiepiscopal functions, and Christian II. succeeded by the aid of the archbishop in establishing the supremacy of Sweden. Seven hostages were given Christian as a security for the loyalty of the Swedes, and amongst these was the young *Gustavus Erikson Vasa*, who was destined by Providence to be the deliverer of his country. Christian ordered the fleet to get under sail, and steered strait to Denmark, where he arrived safe with the hostages. The king perceiving young Gustavus Vasa's patriotic feelings and skill, and, therefore apprehending him, confined him immediately in prison in the castle of *Kaló*, in Jutland, from which this noble youth at a later time found opportunity to escape, and to gain a considerable number of adherents, and take the field against the generals of Christian. A.D. 1519.

The king, whose intention it was now, at one blow, to bring the rebellious Steno Sture to subjection, equipped a powerful armament, and commanded his general, the brave *Otho Krumpen*, to march a numerous army to Sweden, while the fleet was harassing the coasts. Steno Sture gave battle at *Bogesund*, in Visi-Gothland, but fell into an ambush laid for him, and received a wound of which he soon after died. A.D., 1520. Sweden was now left without a head, and the Senate fell into a violent dispute about a successor, while Christian was marching unopposed to Stockholm, which he blockaded on the sea side. After being long and bravely defended by the heroic *Christine Gyldenstar*, Steno Sture's widow, Stockholm had at last to yield to the king, who, by the archbishop, Gustavus Trolle, was proclaimed, in the name of the states, king of Sweden, Denmark and Norway, and crowned with the usual ceremonies, the archbishop of Lund and the bishops of

Roeskilde and Odensee glorifying the solemn act by their presence. Although he, on the day of his coronation, had proclaimed a general pardon of the offences of the Swedish people, he continued to thirst for vengeance, and resolved, if possible, to suffocate in blood the rebellious spirit in Sweden, and extirpate, at one stroke, all the Swedish nobility, in revenge for the troubles they had excited. In his meditated schemes the king got an adviser in *Didrik Slaghak*, doctor of the canon law, whom Arcemboldus had brought along with him to Denmark, and who had attained a very great degree of the king's favor and esteem. He was a man of a deep and subtle reach, and being skilled in kindling discontents, he insinuated himself into the king's mind by soothing flatteries, and persuaded him to use the papal bull as an instrument of vengeance. The third day after the crowning, Christian II. invited the principal senators and nobles to a brilliant entertainment, in the royal palace of Stockholm, and bestowed the Order of the Elephant on a great number of the German and Danish nobility, but not on a single Swede. The gates of the capital were locked, the streets beset with guards, and every citizen, under pain of death, forbidden to leave his house. Amidst the most unbounded festivity, the archbishop, Gustavus Trolle, made his entrance into the great saloon of the palace, the Pope's bull in his hand, and in the name of the Holy Church, demanded satisfaction for the usage he had sustained. The sen-

8th Nov., A. D., 1520.

tence of excommunication was read aloud; the archbishop concluded his crafty oration with a pathetic request that justice might be granted and the criminals punished. The king now ordered his guards to seize the whole senate and nobility and imprison them, and a tribunal was erected to pass sentence. *Jens Anderson Beldenak*, bishop of Odensee, being the only Dane present, now interrogated, by virtue of his office, the rest of the assembly, whether they, who had opposed the Pope in deposing the archbishop, were heretics or not? The answer being in the affirmative, the king considered it a sentence of death, and under the pretence of extirpating heresy and impiety, he ordered ninety-four senators and a great number of the nobility and the clergy to be beheaded on the market-place of Stockholm. Christian made no distinction between friends and enemies, the better to convince the people that he acted less from motives of vengeance than obedience to the Holy See. Only to signify displeasure, or show compassion, cost the life. A citizen of Stockholm was drawn along and beheaded, because he shed tears over these dreadful scenes. Among those who were the victims to this infernal revenge, was *Erik Vasa*, father to young Gustavus Vasa, and nephew to the former Swedish king, Charles Canutson. On the whole, the fortunes and the lives of individuals were entirely at the mercy of the cruel king, who himself witnessed these horrors from a window in the palace. The whole city of Stockholm was a scene of blood and heart-rending calamities. To hold out yet more distinctly the appearance of having exercised, not his own vengeance but that of the Church, Christian II. ordered the noble-minded bishop, *Matthew of Strengnæs*, and bishop *Hemming Gad*, of Finland, to be beheaded; while the subtle Didrik Slaghak, who had aided him in carrying out the *Slaughter of Stockholm* (generally called so), was rewarded with the archbishopric of Lund. Thus having, as he thought, consolidated his supremacy in Sweden, the king left Stockholm for Denmark. In his passage from Sweden, instances of his cruelty are to be met with. Gibbets were erected wheresoever he passed along, and the inhuman tyrant ordered even the mother and sister of Gustavus Vasa, both of whom he had long confined in prison, together with five monks of the monastery of *Nydal*, to be sewed up in a great sack and thrown into the sea. The abbot found means to escape out of the hands of the ruffians employed to bind him. He ran towards the river, but was pursued and murdered by the king's order, before he could save himself by swimming. At Jónköping he caused two noblemen to be scourged to death, and the Swedish historian, *Lagerbring*, says, "Massacres and calamity marked the way wheresoever the Danish monarch passed along." Some Swedish writers even affirm that, not content with the barbarous revenge taken on the living, the king ordered the dead body of Steno Sture to be dug up, and divesting himself of humanity, flew like a wild beast upon the corpse, which he tore and mangled with his teeth and nails. To complete the measure of his barbarity, he ordered the widow of Steno Sture, Christine Gyldenstar, to be brought before him, and asked her whether she chose to be burned, flayed, or buried alive? His savage intention was, however, altered by the strong interest made in behalf of that unfortunate lady.

But the despotism and cruelty of a king is no uncommon prelude to a revolution, which now took place under Christian II., whose cruelty forever dissolved the bonds between Denmark and Sweden, and the Union of Calmar was irreparably broken by the Swedes, who recovered their ancient independence. Young Gustavus Erickson Vasa escaped from his prison in Denmark and from Christian's emissaries, who were continually at his heels, fled disguised to Flensburgh in Schleswig, where he hired himself to some merchants, under whose protection he escaped out from the Danish territories, and arrived in Lübeck, where the regency gave him a ship to convey him to Sweden. He now went to the mountains of Dalecarlia, where he, for some time, concealed himself, in the disguise of a workman, in the mines. He found aid and protection from the valiant inhabitants of Dalecarlia, to whom he opened his project and discovered his name and rank, and with a band of these hardy peasants he repulsed the Danes and took A. D., Upsala. After being elected, at the Diet of 1521.

Vadstena, administrator of Sweden, and two years after, at the Diet of Strengnæs, king, by the unanimous suffrages of his fellow-citizens, *Gustavus Vasa* made his entry into Stockholm, and the words "Saviour and Deliverer," echoed to him from every quarter.

A.D. 1523.

Thus Sweden was now emancipated from Denmark, and the Union of Calmar annihilated. Norway remained connected with Denmark till 1814, when the allied powers, by the treaty of Kiel, gave it to Sweden, as an indemnity for Finland, which Russia had taken. Gustavus Vasa reigned in peace for a long space of years, and is the founder of the celebrated *House of Vasa*, which has given Sweden so many excellent kings, amongst whom was the great and famous Gustavus Adolphus, who made foreign nations sensible of the weight which Sweden might have in the affairs of Europe.

The slaughter of Stockholm had produced a general astonishment throughout all Europe, and had, as even two bishops had been beheaded, exasperated the Pope to such a degree, that he sent a nuncio to Copenhagen, to examine into the death of the bishops who had been massacred at Stockholm. Christian II. treacherously threw the whole blame on his friend Didrik Slaghak, who was sentenced to be beheaded and then to be burnt; which sentence, in the king's justification, was executed in the market-place of

A.D. 1522

Copenhagen; after which the imperious and arbitrary king appointed his personal attendant, *John Veza*, archbishop of Lund.

Christian's outrageous and cruel proceedings had produced, even in the minds of the Danes, the greatest disgust toward him, and rendered his name hateful. He trampled upon all law and government; he endeavored, by menaces, to extort from his uncle, Frederick, his dukedom of Schleswig, and of the archbishopric of Lund he disposed at pleasure. The number of the disaffected increased, therefore, daily; and the Danish nobility, exasperated at his oppressions, and not expecting any good from him, determined to risk all, rather than tolerate so intolerable a yoke. The nobility and clergy of all Jutland rose in one general revolt, and wrote a formal sentence of deposition, which they transmitted to the king in *Veile*, in Jutland. *Mogens Munk*, chief-justice of Jutland, was entrusted with the dangerous commission of making him acquainted with the resolution. A. D., 1523. He dined with the king, and, after dinner, left the decree in a glove on the window. It had not lain long in that place, before the king, observing a large scroll of parchment, ordered it to be read, and no sooner perceived the contents than he ordered search to be made for *Mogens Munk*, but that nobleman had meanwhile removed himself out of the reach of danger. The king now repaired to Copenhagen. Although, as yet, Copenhagen, Malmö, all

Norway, and the whole peasantry and burgher class were loyal to him, he felt discouraged, and behaved like a coward, as he had reigned like a tyrant. Attended by his queen, children, and Sigbrit, the mother of his concubine, he betook himself to Holland, where he, in vain, solicited assistance from his brother-in-law, the emperor Charles V. His uncle, *Frederick*, duke of Schleswig and Holstein, was now offered the throne of Denmark and Norway, which he accepted without any hesitation. Upon his return from Holland, Christian II., however, collected an army to invade Holstein and oppose his uncle, but his troops forsook him, and his general, *Henry Gjóe*, after an obstinate defence of eight months, had to surrender Copenhagen to Frederick I. Nevertheless, a great part of Denmark sided yet with Christian II., and one of his most faithful adherents was the noble and brave *Sòren Norby*, a general of consummate ability and of indefatigable activity. In Skane he collected an army of twelve thousand men, who, however, were entirely cut to pieces by Frederick's general, *John Ranzau*, first at *Lund*, and then at *Brunktoftlund*, near Landscrona, and Sòren Norby was, at length, obliged to leave the country and flee to Russia, where he was imprisoned by the Czar Vasilius Iwanowitch. Being at length set at liberty, he entered into military service under Charles V., and fell at the siege of Florence.

Notwithstanding all these disadvantages, Christian II. hoped and projected to regain his dominions, and went now to Norway, where he was elected in *Opslo*. A.D., 1531. But here his success was of short duration. Bishop Canute Gyldenstar arrived in Norway with troops, and Christian had to submit. Christian II. went now, with a safe-conduct, to Copenhagen, to negotiate in person with his uncle, Frederick I., but anchoring in the harbor of Copenhagen, he was, in spite of the warrant of security given him by the bishop, taken prisoner and carried to Sònderburg, on the island of Alsen, in the Baltic, where he was compelled to pine for seventeen years in a gloomy tower, with no other companion than a Norwegian dwarf. A.D., 1532. Frederick I. and the nobility engaged themselves, reciprocally, never to release him. First when Christian III. had ascended the throne, more freedom was given him; the castle of Callundborg, in Sjelland, was granted to him, where he, under continual inspection, lived ten years, till the beginning of the reign of Frederick II. (1559). A.D., 1549. His body was brought to the church of St. Canute, in Odensee. He left behind him two daughters: Dorothea, married to the elector of Saxony, and Christina, to the duke of Lothringen. The bad use Christian II. made of his many great qualities, of which a single one might have immortalized another prince, became his ruin, and he left a most piteous monument of the effects of cruelty and despotism, exerted over a free-spirited and warlike people.

Immediately after the downfall of Christian's royalty *Frederick I.* ascended the throne of Denmark and Norway. On mounting the throne he had to sign a charter containing several new articles, and he was to be declared an enemy of the kingdoms, and deprived of the throne, in case he manifestly violated his engagements. In this charter it was determined, that bishops and archbishops should be of *noble* descent, and that the king should patrocinate the Romish Church, punish all Lutheran heretics, solemnly promise to show a deadly enmity to the dethroned and imprisoned king, Christian II., and declare Denmark and Norway *elective* kingdoms. The legislative authority was to be in the Diet, which should consist of a certain number of deputies, chosen amongst the nobility and the clergy; but the burgessescould not be invested with any public office, or in any way be on a footing of equality with the nobility. Finally, the king could not declare war or conclude peace without the consent of the nobility; and if the king delayed his signature to laws or ordinances, sixteen noblemen should be empowered to supply the want of it, and sign for him.

Except Copenhagen and Malmö, which still adhered to the dethroned king, and for eight months gallantly bore up against the royal troops, until all hope of assistance was gone, both Denmark and Norway proclaimed

Frederick I. king, with the usual formalities. Besides having an able and courageous general in John Ranzau, Frederick I. was energetically assisted by Lübeck, because he had restored to that city the commercial privileges of which Christian II. had deprived it. Frederick I. of course could not see Gustavus Vasa raised to the throne of Sweden but with an eye of jealousy; he eagerly wished, from motives of ambition and interest, to see the three kingdoms reunited, and with that view he wrote to some of the chief nobility of Sweden. But the answer he received was not agreeable to his wishes, the Swedes being no longer in a disposition to give ear to such hopes. "The Union of Calmar," wrote they, "had more than once proved fatal to their liberties, which they now enjoyed in the greatest felicity, under a king possessed of every quality which could engage their affection." Frederick I., comprehending that there was no hope for him in this respect, made, at Malmö, A. D., a strict alliance with Gustavus Vasa against their 1524. common enemy, Christian II.

Notwithstanding the efforts of the dethroned king to promote the Reformation had almost proved fruitless, yet there were not wanting those who deeply felt the necessity of embracing the new religious principles, which day by day were advancing in strength in Germany, and thence easily propagated to the Scandinavian countries by the young students who pursued their studies at Wittemberg, and other German Universities.

The people's mind had grown weary of the bondage of spiritual despotism which the Popes had established, and a doctrine adulterated and tricked out with false additions, was not more satisfactory to the religious want. The fear of God consisted in external ecclesiastical actions, and remission of sins might be had for money from the seller of indulgences. The public worship was conducted in Latin, and the people were not permitted to read the Bible in the vernacular tongue. The ministerial order did not enjoy any esteem or love, and the lower ranks of the clergy made themselves despicable by their ignorance, drunkenness, and excesses in indulging in concubinage. The higher ranks of the clergy, enjoying at ease their rich revenues, were neglectful of their duties, which very often were discharged not by themselves but by their vicars. Many curateships were often conferred on one curate to enlarge the revenues, the bishops even causing the curateships to be vacant through a whole series of years, in order thereby to arrogate the incomes to themselves. The avarice and extortions of the bishops were excessive almost to a proverb; their wealth was, therefore, often exorbitant, and their power and privileges enormous. All church property was exempt from taxation, while on the other hand the laity were loaded with excessive impositions. All clergymen were exempted from criminal process in the courts of law, and delivered over to the ecclesiastical tribunal, so that the Church alone took cognizance of the crime. Different orders of lazy monks, *Augustinian, Franciscan* and *Dominican* friars, who already during the reign of Waldemar the Conqueror had crept into the country, rambled about and made considerable profit from the sale of indulgences, performing their mean-spirited acts with little regard to discretion or decency, and describing the value of the indulgences in such a disgusting and blasphemous style of exaggeration, that even the ignorant began to suspect the worth of the remission of sins dispensed by them; all of which gathered into a heap, prepared the minds of the people willingly to listen to the bold attacks of Luther and the other great Reformers against all these outrageous and unchristian acts. Even the nobility were in favor of the Reformation, hoping thereby to re-obtain the great property that their ancestors had bestowed upon the Church; and the kings could not but wish the liberal principles of the Reformation introduced into their countries, which would not fail to lessen the exorbitant power and influence of the bishops.

All these causes were adequate to the effects attributed to them, and the Lutheran doctrine and form of worship gained, therefore, very soon a complete triumph in the three Scandinavian kingdoms, and already in the year 1527 the magnanimous Gustavus Vasa obtained from an assembly of the state the declaration, that the Lutheran doctrines should be the established religion of Sweden *Frederick I.*, who previous to his ascending the throne had secretly embraced the Protestant faith, concurred with Gustavus Vasa in the design, and although wanting his spirit and genius, he conducted the religious affairs of Denmark and Norway with more prudence and sagacity than was to be expected. The clergy now lost the greater part of their possessions to the crown and the nobility, and the bishops (whose titles, however, were retained in all three Scandinavian kingdoms, Sweden even keeping the title of archbishop,) fell almost into a complete dependence upon the government, their large revenues and ecclesiastical jurisdictions being considerably retrenched and curtailed.

Next to Switzerland, the Scandinavian kingdoms were the first of the European countries that embraced Lutheranism; and in Denmark, *Hans Tausen*, whose parents were only poor peasants, became the most important instrument in spreading the Protestant faith. While a monk in the cloister of *Antvorskov*, in Sjelland, he won the prior's favor to such a degree, that he allowed Tausen to go abroad at the expense of the cloister. Luther's renown brought him to Wittemberg, where, on hearing his preaching, he became convinced of the truth of the doctrines Luther proclaimed. No sooner had the prior heard it, than he suddenly recalled him from Wittemberg, and committed him to the custody of the abbot of the cloister. The following year he was sent to Wiborg, in Jutland, where the prior of the cloister of the Hospitalers (the Knights of St.

John) promised to keep a strict eye upon him. He was, however, permitted to preach, and interested the citizens of Wiborg so much, that they not only gave him asylum in the city, but even protected him against several attempts of the bishop, *George Früs*, A.D., to lay hold on his person. *Frederick I.*, being 1526. secretly a convert to the doctrines of Luther, and by whose protection *Herman Tast* already had spread the Reformation throughout the Duchies, (1522 – 1525,) interested himself for Hans Tausen, issuing a warrant of security for him, and licensing him to preach the Gospel in Wiborg. At the same time *George Sadolin*, also a hearer of Luther in Wittemberg, appeared, a mighty champion of the Reformation; and the new doctrine soon found advocates and adherents in other cities, particularly in Malmó, where two unlearned but highly gifted and eloquent men, *Claus Mortenson Tóndebinder* (cooper), and *Hans Spandmayer* (pail-maker), assisted by the learned *Franz Wormordson*, rose as undaunted proclaimers of the Reformation, and inveterate enemies of the Pope's jurisdiction and of his sellers of indulgences. But the circumstance which, of all others, most conduced to the advancement and universal dissemination of the Lutheran Reformation, was the excellent translation of the New Testament, which the ex-mayor of Malmó, *John Michaelson*, who had accompanied Christian II. in his exile, published in Leipzic, and which by foreign merchants was brought to Denmark. This translation opened the eyes of the people to the papal deviations from the evangelical truth, and gave security for the perpetuation of the Reformation in the North; and now it profited nothing that the bishops forbade the use of this dangerous book, as they termed it. A mean fellow, *Paul Eliason*, a Carmelite from the cloister of Elsenore, who had embraced Lutheranism, but soon again changed color, and was, therefore, called *Paul Vendekaabe* (turncoat), rambled about in the country and preached violently against the new doctrine; but he performed as little by his denunciatory sermons as the bishops by their fulminating pastoral letters, which they dispatched to their dioceses. The difficult position of the Catholic clergy increased also very much by the dispute about tithe, which the people decidedly declined paying; and the controversies were increasing day by day, and internal disturbances would undoubtedly have broken out, had not both the king and the nobility feared the exiled Christian II., and, therefore, moderated themselves. It came, therefore, to a sort of agreement, when Frederick I., after great opposition, effected the publication of a famous edict, sanctioned at the general *Diet of Odensee*, by which every subject of Denmark and Norway was declared free to adhere either to the tenets of the Church of Rome or to the doctrines of Luther; that no person should be molested on account of his religion, and that the clergy should be permitted to

A. D., 1527.

marry; all of which contributed considerably to promote the Reformation, the adherents to which were daily increasing, both in the country and in the towns. In consequence of this decree of the Diet, all abbeys and cloisters were deserted, and celibacy in particular disregarded. Lutheranism was publicly preached and embraced. At last the city of Malmö erected the standard of Luther, prohibited mass, idols, and the other superstitions of the Romish Church. Also a new and more literal translation of the New Testament and the Psalms of David into the vernacular tongue, published by a canonist, *Christen Pedersen*, likewise one of the guides of the exiled king, conduced to the advancement of this important matter. Hans Tausen, who now had established the Reformation in Wiborg, was by the king called to Copenhagen to preach the new doctrine. A. D., 1529. Finding a better spirit than Reinhardt and Carlstadt eight years before had found, he soon gained the majority of the citizens of the capital over to the new doctrine, the Reformation thus having gained a firm footing in the three most important cities: Copenhagen, Wiborg, and Malmö. The bishops excited an alarm, but could obtain nothing more than that the affairs of religion should receive farther regulation at the next general Diet.

But the Diet of Augsburg, at this time assembled in Germany to try the great cause of the Reformation, and expected to result in condemning the doctrines of the

Protestants, as they were termed since the yea. 1529, was, by the Catholics in Denmark, considered a favorable opportunity to oppress their opponents. No reconciliation, however, of the opposing opinions being effected in Augsburg, the prelates prevailed, therefore, upon the king to convoke a Diet in *Copenhagen*, that the new doctrines might be debated, and, as the Catholics hoped, thoroughly condemned. But the Protestants displayed great power and firmness at the Diet. They gave in their Confession of Faith, consisting of forty-three articles, stirred up the people by ardent sermons, and above all, inveighed bitterly against the traffic in indulgences and the worship of images. The Catholics tried in vain to refute the Protestant Confession of Faith; but their attempt occasioned a defence in writing from the Protestants, accompanied by a vehement complaint of the bad administration and gross immorality of the clergy. The bishops now reminded the king repeatedly of his promise to defend the Catholic doctrine, but without avail. The discussions were carried on in the Danish language; but the Catholics, missing thereby the help they had expected from their pleader, *Dr. Stagefyhr*, whom they had called in from Germany, required the use of the Latin language. But this the Protestants would not grant, as they thereby would lose the important assistance which they hitherto had had from the commonalty. At length the Diet dissolved without having accommodated the

A. D., 1530.

differing points; the king declaring, that he would protect both parties in the free exercise of religion, but that neither party should be allowed to seek proselytes at the expense of the other.

However trifling the result of this Diet of Copenhagen may seem to be, yet it was a clear gain for the Protestants, whose doctrines soon began to prevail in all the cities of the kingdom, and to show the Catholic bishops that the end of the mighty power, which they long had wielded, was fast approaching. But this was not passing without great tumults and violence. The monks particularly, exposed to great persecution, were often so teased and vexed that they left their cloisters. In Copenhagen, the citizens, headed by the mayor of the city, *Ambrosius Bookbinder*, broke, on the 27th of December, into Our Lady's church, causing great devastation, and cutting to pieces all the images of the saints; and the Catholic clergy, were, just now, less able to make sufficient resistance. Their chief, the archbishop *Aage Sparre*, was not acknowledged by the Pope; *Jens Andersen Beldenak*, bishop of Odensee, who, as we have seen, had been present at the slaughter of Stockholm, was, at the Diet of Copenhagen, disgraced with a mark of infamy, for having used injurious language against the king; *George Früs*, bishop of Wiborg, was, for a violation of his duty, excommunicated by the Pope; *Laga Urne*, bishop of Roeskilde, the most undaunted champion of Catholicism, had expired a year

A. D., 1530.

before the Diet of Copenhagen, and his successor, *Joachim Rónnow*, was consecrated, upon condition that he would not impede the spreading of the Reformation in his diocese. The Catholic affairs were thus considerably on the decline, and the Protestant faith commenced to get a permanent footing in Denmark and Norway. It was three years after these important events, that Frederick I., who had openly avowed himself a Protestant, died at Gottorp, close by the city of Schleswig, where he frequently resided and lies buried. He is not mentioned by historians in language of eulogy, but in general considered deficient in moral force and clear judgment. Nevertheless, it is not to be denied that he conducted the religious affairs of his kingdom with much greater prudence than his more talented predecessor, Christian II.; but whether he was a sincere favorer of the Reformation, or not, is very questionable, the more as he seems to have temporized with both parties. At all events, his religious opinions were dim and benighted. He knew the words of Christ, *Matthew* ix. 15: "The devil departs not out of a man but by prayer and fasting." Being prompt in compliance with them, but not finding it convenient or comfortable to fast himself, the king hired seven boys to fast in his place, believing thereby to have done justice to the words of the Saviour. The Roman Catholics detest, of course, his memory, to this day, for having contributed to effect a reformation

[margin: April 13, A. D., 1533.]

in religion, to the utter extinction of their tyrannical superstition and spiritual power. Frederick I. left behind him two sons, Christian and Hans, and one daughter, married to the duke Ulrick, of Schwerin.

Upon the death of Frederick I. an interregnum followed of three years, accompanied by a sanguinary war. At a general Diet assembled in Copenhagen in order to deliberate on the election of a king, the nobility would select Christian, Frederick's eldest son, but the clergy, entertaining fear of him who had been a hearer of Luther in Wittemberg and was in favor of the Reformation, voted for his younger brother, Hans, whom they hoped to bring up in the Catholic faith. A third party were for recalling the imprisoned king, but this faction was yet small, and partly absorbed in the two others. Not being able to agree, the election of the king was postponed to the following year, in order that the senators of Norway might be assembled, and the same king seated on the throne of both kingdoms. The Catholic party now beginning to recover their courage, passed several resolutions tending to stop the spreading of the Reformation. It was determined that no priest could be appointed in any diocese without the consent of the bishop, that the mass should be re-established, and the existing monasteries and ecclesiastical institutions continue uninjured. Hans Tausen, the most dangerous opposer of the Catholic church, was charged with offensive language against the bishops, and sentenced to leave the diocese of Sjelland, and nowhere in the kingdoms, either verbally or in writing, to interfere with religious affairs. The condemnation of the universally esteemed Hans Tausen occasioned a great riot in Copenhagen, the bishop Joachim Rònnow even running the hazard of being mobbed by the exasperated citizens. Tausen, however, left Copenhagen, but Rònnow had, for fear of his own life, to permit him to return.

The burgher class and the peasantry, not having yet forgotten the imprisoned king, Christian II., who so valiantly had taken their part, began, while the nobility and the clergy were at variance concerning the election of the king, to think of restoring him to the crown; the regency of Lübeck, which hitherto had opposed him, but was now displeased with some commercial liberties granted to the Dutch, also projected the restoration of the imprisoned king, and Denmark was in the most perilous and distracted condition. Lübeck was governed by two talented men, the mayor, *George Wullenveber*, and the admiral, *Marc Meyer*, who from an obscure birth had risen to the highest dignities in Lübeck Both of them made an alliance with *Ambrosius Bookbinder*, Mayor of Copenhagen, and with *George Münter*, mayor of Malmó, declaring their object to be to replace Christian II. upon the throne, and to introduce the Reformation. They complained that Christian II. was confined, contrary to the faith of a treaty and to the safe-conduct granted him by Frederick's general, Canute Gyldenstar. Upon receiving intelligence of this design, the senate renewed the alliance with Gustavus Vasa, and concluded a union between Denmark and the Duchies, in order to deter their enemies from attempting the restoration of the imprisoned king, but without effect. The regency of Lübeck and the popular party appointed *Count Christopher of Oldenburg*, a relative to Christian II., commander-in-chief, after whom the whole war is called *Grevens Feide* (the War of the Count). He was a nobleman of great courage, fond of glory, of a most enterprising disposition, and deeply interested in releasing the imprisoned king. He landed troops in Sjelland, and by assistance of the citizens made himself master of Copenhagen and Malmó; all Skane, Sjelland, Fjunen, and the adjacent islands yielded within a short time, and paid their homage to Christian II., who, on hearing what was passing in his favor, exulted for joy, crying: "May be the crown can be replaced upon my head; then once more I shall teach the nobility how to obey." The most horrible outrages were committed on the noblemen, who were filled with astonishment at the arbitrary manner in which they were treated, and with fear of the imprisoned king's reassuming the reins of government. To put a stop, if possible, to these terrible scenes, the nobility and bishops of Jutland resolved to meet for the election of a sovereign. Holstein took the same resolution, and they assembled in a small town, called *Rye*,

June 4th, by the city of Skanderborg, where they elected
A. D., the eldest son of Frederick I., Prince Christian,
1534. king, and committed to him the charge of the war, and transferred to him the whole military and executive power of the crown. He immediately laid hold of the offer, ascended the throne of Denmark and Norway, and was crowned in Horsens, Jutland, by the name of *Christian III.* Troops were now levied with the utmost industry and alacrity, arms provided, and all military stores furnished from the royal magazines of Jutland. Then Christian III. complained to Gustavus Vasa, his brother-in-law, of the irregular conduct of the Lübeckers, in order to exhort him to enter Skane with a force sufficient to wrest that province out of the hands of the enemy, and re-annex it to Denmark. But these measures to affright the rebels had not the effect for which they were intended, but cemented yet more the alliance between the regency of Lübeck and the popular party, which, alarmed by the preparations of the king, transferred their arms to Jutland, which now for a while became the theatre of a bloody war. *Shipper Clement*, an adherent of the imprisoned king and of Count Christopher of Oldenburg, went to Jutland, where he brought the peasantry together, took the city of Aalborg, and defeated the nobility and the royal troops. Christian III., informed of it, marched immediately an army into North Jutland, under the command of the celebrated general *John Ranzaw* The royal

cause was supported by all the nobility, and by a great portion of men of landed property in Jutland, and by all the members of the clergy. The first military operations were favorable to the king. Rantzau took possession of Aalborg, where a great carnage took place; the peasants were forced to submit, and Clement, who escaped out of the battle, was afterwards taken prisoner and beheaded. His head was fixed on a stake in the market-place, and crowned in derision with a leaden crown, on account of his insolence in defending the imprisoned king. In Skane and Halland Christian III. was aided by the noble Gustavus Vasa, who of course did not wish the cause of the imprisoned king to succeed at all. Gustavus Vasa gained a complete victory at Helsingborg, in Skane, over the Count of Oldenburg and the forces of Lübeck, and Mark Meyer was taken prisoner. A.D., 1535. About the same time the brave and undaunted John Rantzau brought the whole island of Fjunen under subjection, in the celebrated battle of *Oxebjerg* (Oxen Hill), A.D., 1535. where an old clergyman, *Hans Madson*, a beautiful model of the most exalted and virtuous patriotism, arrived half naked and barefooted from the hostile camp, disclosing to Rantzau the plans of the enemy, which contributed considerably to the happy issue of the battle. A great number of soldiers and officers were killed or taken prisoners, and among the latter the old archbishop of Upsala, *Gustavus Trolle*, who again had proceeded on the stage to operate in favor of the imprisoned king.

Meanwhile the royal cause had also met with great success from the military abilities of the brave old admiral, *Peter Skram*, surnamed *Danmarks Vovehals*, (the Desperado of Denmark), who won a glorious victory at the island of Bornholm over the Lübeck fleet, and cleared the Baltic, so that John Rantzau could pass over to Sjelland and lay siege to Copenhagen, where Ambrosius Bookbinder was yet defending the cause of the imprisoned king. Also the Southern part of Norway submitted to Christian III.; and the archbishop of Drontheim, *Olaf Engelbrechtson Lunge*, who in the Northern part maintained the cause of Christian II., had to flee from the kingdom to Holland, where he died.

Thus all the schemes of the popular party beginning to prove abortive, *Albrecht of Mecklenburg*, who was married to a niece of the imprisoned king, was appointed lieutenant-colonel to assist the chief-commander, Count Christopher. But this, however, did not alter the circumstances, which day by day turned so much to their disadvantage, that they soon found it necessary to solicit terms of peace. Deputies now met at Hamburg, and ordained, that hostilities should cease between Denmark and Lübeck, and that their ancient friendship should be renewed, upon condition that the island of Bornholm should be ceded to the regency of Lübeck for the space of fifty years. Christian III. acceded readily to this peace. Only Copenhagen and Malmö were yet faithful to the cause of the imprisoned king. At length George Münter surrendered Malmö after a long siege, but Copenhagen held out constantly a whole year, until the famine, which reached such a degree that the inhabitants were reduced to such straits that dogs, cats, rats and the most loathsome animals were used as food, compelled Ambrosius Bookbinder to surrender the capital to Christian III. Albrecht of Mecklenburg and Count Christopher of Oldenburg were forced to throw themselves at the king's feet to obtain pardon. A few of the most stubborn ringleaders were beheaded, but the great body of the revolters were conciliated by an act of amnesty. July 29, A. D., 1536.

The intellectual excitement occasioned by the introduction of the Reformation, exercised a useful influence upon the improvement of the Scandinavian literature, which, as well as all progress of literature, was highly favored by the spirit of free inquiry fostered by the Reformation. In the last centuries of the Middle Ages there was less scientific activity than before; historians, as Saxo Grammaticus, Snorro Sturleson, and Andrew Suneson, appeared no more, and the fatherland's history was only told in brief chronicles and dry annals, mostly written by monks in corrupt Latin. At the foreign universities—Paris, Bologna, Cologne, and Lóven—where young men pursued their studies even after the erection of the universities of Copenhagen and Upsala, only the canon law and scholastic philosophy were taught. But the Reformation, rightly called the great genius of all genuine liberty, emancipated the human mind from the thraldom which ages of spiritual despotism had imposed upon it, discarded the subtleties of the schools, and sent science and the arts forth into the wide world of humanity. Only a few ecclesiastics cultivated medicine. *Henry Harpestreng* canon in Roeskilde, composed in the thirteenth century a remarkable medical work in Danish, yet extant. Danish writings were also very rare, everything being recorded in Latin. King *Olaf*, Margarethe's son, highly disliking this putting aside the mother tongue, enjoined that public documents should be issued in the Danish language; but, however, Latin continued to prevail. German merchants and mechanics settled in almost all cities of the country; German noblemen immigrated in multitudes from Holstein and other German countries, and except king *Hans* and *Christian II.*, all the kings of the fifteenth and sixteenth centuries were Germans, not so much as able to speak Danish with their subjects. Under these circumstances, the Danish language was more and more depraved; German words and phrases crept into it, and the original phrases and forms of expression disappeared.

But the Reformation, that great principle of Christian liberty, which restored to every mother tongue its rights, and the progress of the art of printing, which now also had become known in Scandinavia, arrested the approaching dissolution of the Danish language. The Bible was now translated into Danish, and Danish books were published. *John Snell*, a traveling printer, was the very first who in Denmark printed a Latin book, published in *Odensee*, in the year 1482. The very first printing office was established by *Gotfred of Ghemen* in Copenhagen, where, in the year 1495, the first Danish book was printed and published, by the name of *The Danish Rhyme Chronicle*, i. e., The Danish History put into Rhyme; which, during the reign of Christian I., was composed by the Abbot of *Soró*, Nicolaus. But none has rendered himself more eminent in regenerating the language than *Christen Petersen*, above mentioned, who not only during his exile published a translation of the New Testament and of the Psalms of David, but even upon his return to Denmark continued to enrich the literature with several literary works, all excelling in a pure and elegant style. *Peter Lolle*, also, who collected the heroic songs of the Middle Ages and the old Danish sayings, has distinguished himself by the purity and splendor of his style.

The morality of the Middle Ages could not but suffer by the degeneracy of religion and by the increasing corruption. The scandal of the crimes committed by many of the ecclesiastics, was increased by the facility with which such as committed them obtained pardon.

A bishop, for instance, might assassinate for a small sum of money. Any clergyman might violate his vows of chastity likewise for a little money; and it is, on the whole, easier to conceive than to describe the gross immorality which such a system introduced into society at large. The kings often had the mortification to see all their laws overthrown by insurrections of the peasants, goaded to madness by the oppressions of their lords. Murders, and other dreadful crimes, therefore, occurred frequently, private vengeance often supplying the impotency of the laws.

Scarcely any institutions existing for the instruction of the commonalty, the greatest number of the people were growing up in the deepest ignorance. Through all classes of society gross superstition was prevailing, especially appearing in belief in witchcraft and enchantment. Sorceresses were tried by an ecclesiastical tribunal, condemned and burnt. Christian II. forbade, indeed, that superstitious cruelty; but, however, long after his time, it continued, and even as late as 1675, two sorceresses were burnt alive in *Kjóge*, a few miles from Copenhagen. Intemperance and gluttony, and, among the higher classes of society, an excessive luxury in dress and equipage, were characteristics of the fourteenth and fifteenth centuries. Drunkenness was here, as in other northern countries, a prevailing vice, both among the higher and lower classes, among clergy and laity. Mead and strong beer were the usual drinks to be taken, either for quenching thirst or for medicinal purposes; mead being prepared in the country itself, beer imported from Germany. Beer was taken so excessively, that a man daily consumed twelve pints, and to a nun in a nunnery five hundred and four gallons were annually allotted. Brandy, in the north of Europe, a spirit obtained from grain, was only known as a medicine; and coffee, tea and chocolate were unknown in Scandinavia before the seventeenth century. Vegetables were, comparatively speaking, used very little, whereas fish and meat formed the principal food, strongly seasoned with spices. Luxury in entertainments was very much in use; Christian II., therefore, enacted a law that a wedding-party must not last more than two days. The extravagance of the rich nobility in dress and ornaments exceeded all bounds. Immense amounts of money were squandered away on ornaments of gold and silver, gems, dresses embroidered with pearls, silk, velvet, damask, brocade variegated with gold, and furs of ermine and sable; even the servants of the nobility being sometimes dressed gorgeously, and their horses, on festival occasions, covered with costly cloth and ornaments of gold and silver. The general dwellings in the towns were plain, usually built of timber-work, and thatched, wherefore destructive conflagrations frequently happened. Panes of glass were yet, in the fifteenth century, rare and expensive; skin and horn being, therefore, used instead of glass. The opulent noblemen erected castles, fortified with towers, ramparts and moats, where they lived in princely magnificence. But the Reformation, rightly called the principle of equality, compelled the nobility to renounce a great many prerogatives which they had hitherto exercised over the poor and ignorant population, and to use a more temporizing policy.

THIRD PERIOD.

FROM THE ACKNOWLEDGMENT OF LUTHERANISM AS THE ESTABLISHED RELIGION OF DENMARK UNTIL THE INTRODUCTION OF THE ABSOLUTE SOVEREIGNTY. 1536—1660.

I.

1536—1596.

Christian III.—Diet of Copenhagen—Charter—Bugenhagen—The Reformation introduced into Iceland—Intolerance—University and School Affairs—Alliance with Sweden—New Division of the Duchies—*Frederick II.*—Conquest of Ditmarsh—Three Crowns—The Northern Seven Years' War—Daniel Ranzau—Peace concluded in Stettin—Peter Oxen—Foundation of Kronborg—The Sound Dues—Lübeck—Hamburg—Science and Arts—Henrik Ranzau—Tycho Brahe—*Christian IV.*—Queen-Dowager Sophia of Mecklenburg—Guardianship—Peasantry—Nobility.

THE war now being at an end and Copenhagen surrendered, the king, *Christian III.*, came to an agreement with the senators about abrogating the power and authority the bishops hitherto possessed, thereby facilitating the introduction of the Reformation, and completing the religious revolution. The bishops of the whole kingdom, therefore, were imprisoned, but soon again set at liberty, after, by oath, having promised neither to act nor to speak against the new doctrine. Only *Joachim Rönnov*, bishop of Roeskilde, proving very refractory, was confined in prison till his death. Thereafter, in a general assembly of the states in Copenhagen, at which all the nobility and deputies of the burgher class and peasantry met together, the noble king procured the suppression of the Romish worship, and the abrogation of episcopacy and the episcopal hierarchy; the titles, however, of the bishops being retained, which more easily reconciled the clergy to it. The castles, fortresses, and vast domains of the bishops were now reunited to the crown, and the rest of their revenues applied to the maintenance of Lutheran ministers, the purposes of general education, and charitable institutions.

A. D., 1536.

From Denmark the revolution extended to Norway, where the Reformation was introduced without any opposition; but about the same time this kingdom, for having, as we have seen, supported the deposed Christian II., was deprived of its independence, and reduced to a Danish province; the king of Denmark, however, continuing to call himself king of Norway, but being no more crowned in Trondhjem, only in Copenhagen, the crowning there giving validity to both kingdoms. At that important general assembly, or Diet of Copenhagen, the aristocracy lost the vicious supremacy over the prerogatives of the crown and the rights of the people which they had established; the senate was no more to be composed entirely of nobles; national assemblies should be convoked, and the elections of the kings should not alone be confined to the aristocratic order. Nevertheless the nobility continued to keep a good deal of that ascendency which they had too long maintained; and the royal power, a long time after, was restricted by charters and capitulations, which the nobility prescribed to the kings on their accession to the throne, the burgher class and the peasantry being very little noticed. Before closing the Diet, where the papal hierarchy in Denmark and Norway was entirely overthrown, Christian III. sealed and signed a charter, containing nearly the same clauses and articles as the earlier; yet with the exception that the subjects were not permitted to rebel, even if the king might not rule in conformity with the charter. For the rest, the power of the crown was very much limited by this charter, containing very little to support the dignity of the king, but too much to gratify the nobility and secure to it the chief powers of the state; the whole reign of Christian III., therefore, being a continued struggle against the encroachments of the aristocracy, which had taken too deep root to be eradicated at one blow.

The Lutheran or Evangelical doctrine which, according to the decree of the Diet of Copenhagen, had become the established religion in Denmark and Norway, was, as we have seen, introduced without considerable opposition in both kingdoms; only in *Iceland*, an island in the northern part of the Atlantic ocean, noted for its volcanic mountain, *Hekla*, the Catholic party fell with the sword in their hands; *John Areson*, bishop of Holum, and *Ogmund*, bishop of Skalholt, who withstood the introduction of the Reformation into Iceland, falling by the stroke of an executioner; whereafter the new doctrine got a firm footing, and Iceland fell into complete dependence upon the Danish government, promising never to carry resistance so far as to employ the sword against the king of Denmark. Popery had now been overthrown in Scandinavia, but the Protestantism erected in its stead was for a long time just as bigoted and intolerant as the Catholic creed had been in the worst of times, several severe laws being passed against other Protestant sects, which only in a few points dissented from the established church. There was a division between the Calvinists and Lutherans, and an unhappy animosity of one party against the other, which the Form of Concord, a confession of faith that was subscribed on the 28th of May, 1577, had not been able to compose; and it was in vain that some exiled Calvinists, headed by a Polish nobleman, *John a Lasco*, who had been cruelly persecuted in England, took refuge in Denmark, hoping to induce the else kind-hearted king, Christian III., to show them protection and toleration. But all in vain; and although only disagreeing about a few points concerning the Lord's Supper, and the doctrine of predestination, they were mercilessly banished from Denmark, and, in the midst of the sternest winter, forced, with infants and sick women, to emigrate to

Germany. Flatterers extolled the king as the exterminator of heresy, but sincere and true Christians held Christ's words before him: "Be ye merciful, as your father also is merciful."

In order to regulate the ecclesiastical affairs and compose a liturgy according to the doctrines of the Reformation, Christian III. induced Luther's friend, *John Bugenhagen*, theological professor at Wittemberg, to come to Copenhagen. He crowned and anointed the king, inaugurated the new Protestant bishops, and made himself highly famous by composing a liturgy and ritual conformed to the Lutheran system of reformation. Regarding a strict observance of the Sabbath as a safeguard of public order and virtue, and deeply convinced that God, who is the Giver of all time, never has surrendered to ordinary use this His own reserved season, but appointed it for collective prayers, intercessions, and thanksgivings, and considering the Sabbath Day a season when labor may wipe off its grime, Bugenhagen prevailed upon the king to enact a Sabbath law adapted to the wants of the people, the king himself promising to enforce by his own example the observance of the Lord's Day. For the rest, the meek and pious Bugenhagen advised against persecution of those who proved themselves good and quiet subjects, whatever were their opinions on controverted points of theology; a warning, however, very little listened to in Scandinavia. [A. D., 1537.]

The ecclesiastical affairs having now been regulated,

and the laws having given their countenance to the established mode of worship, the king abolished the cloisters of the mendicant monks, the Dominicans and Franciscans, applying the revenues of their large estates to the maintenance of literary men, Protestant ministers, and school affairs, and teaching those idle, rebellious, and licentious friars how to submit themselves to his decision with unconditional compliance. Also, the prebends granted to the cathedral churches of Lund, Roeskilde, Ribe, Aarhuus and Wiborg, were confiscated, and applied to literary purposes, especially to the advancement of the University of Copenhagen, which, during the civil disturbances, had sunk into nothing; Christian III., therefore, in all reason, being considered the proper founder of the University, which now from this period slowly advanced for about two centuries, till it was brought to great perfection in the age of Christian VI. He appointed a greater number of professors than before, and applied the estates of the cathedral churches to pay the salaries of the professors, and to exempt meritorious and suitably qualified young students, whose circumstances required it, from charge for tuition.

A.D., 1539.

The efforts of Christian II. for improving the school affairs being broken off by his banishment, it was reserved to Christian III. to give the *Latin schools* a better regulation by proposing more proper school-books and a better method of instruction. But it was a pity that in these schools, of which one was erected in each commercial town, the Latin language continued, almost exclusively, to be cultivated, the other branches being neglected altogether. In this manner the Latin language was strained to the highest pitch, and a classical Latin style became the distinguishing mark of profound scholarship: an opinion which, although somewhat modified, has been maintained in the Scandinavian countries. Of erecting country schools, no mention was made in this period.

But civilization and religious enlightenment received a mighty impulse in Denmark during the sixteenth century by that translation of the Bible, which Christian III. ordered, and which *Palladius*, theological professor at the University of Copenhagen, performed in a masterly manner; it being thus the first Danish translation of the Bible, which, hitherto, had been a book unknown to the commonalty and the burgher class. A.D., 1550.

Although Christian III. had not been involved in any war since the civil war had terminated, yet the peace of the kingdom had a long time been threatened by Duke *Franz of Lothringen*, and *Frederick*, Elector of Saxony, sons-in-law of the imprisoned king, both laying claim to the throne, and both having a powerful support in the emperor, Charles V., brother-in-law of Christian II. To strengthen himself against these pretenders, Christian III. entered into an alliance with Francis I.

of France, an enemy of the emperor, and with Gustavus Vasa of Sweden, with whom he, of late, had had some discord concerning the possession of Gulland. These contests, however, were soon composed, a strict alliance was made between Denmark and Sweden, in A.D. 1541. *Brómsebro*, and the plans of the two pretenders did not conduce to the desired result. This alliance, so promising for the strength and harmony of the North, and affording so just expectations of a permanent peace, soon lost its effect, the Danish king assuming three crowns in his coat of arms, thereby indicating his pretensions to all three kingdoms. The inveterate jealousy anew broke out, and although the peace of Brómsebro had put an end to the open contest between the two monarchs, the hereditary animosity between the royal houses of Denmark and Sweden was not extinguished, but, after a few decennaries, broke out in a destructive seven years' war, exhausting the resources of both kingdoms, and at last forcing Denmark to recognize the independence of Sweden by the treaty of Stettin.

The emperor, Charles V., at length withdrawing from all fellowship with his brother-in-law, Christian II., made peace with Denmark, in Spire, where A.D. 1544. Christian III. had to promise to mitigate the rigid imprisonment of Christian II., in the gloomy A.D. 1549. tower in Sònderburg, where he already had pined away for seventeen years. He was now brought to

Kallundborg, in Sjelland, where he ended his days after he had attained his seventy-eighth year. A. D. 1559.

Christian III. was a member of the *League of Smalcald*, which the Protestant princes had formed for their mutual defence, in case any of them should be attacked for the Word of God's sake; but as the war of Smalcald broke out between Charles V. and the Protestant princes, the situation of the Danish king, who had lately made peace with the emperor, became very critical. He sent, therefore, no troops to Germany, but instead, a sum of money, which yet the royal embassador wisely withheld, the war being ended in the battle of *Mühlberg*, where the elector of Saxony, John Frederick, an intimate friend of the Danish king, was taken prisoner after a brave defence. A. D., 1547. Christian III. purchased for the crown the two dioceses, Oesel and Curland; but to avoid offending the Russian Czar, *Ivan Vasilievitch*, declined accepting the large city of Reval, which voluntarily offered to submit to Denmark.

That division of the duchies, Schleswig and Holstein, which had taken place during the reign of king Hans, was again annulled, at the accession of Frederick I., to the Danish crown; but Christian III. undertook a new division between his brethren, although the old and expert general and statesman, *John Ranzau*, strongly advised against this imprudent step. *Adolph*, obtaining the *Gottorp* part, became founder of the house of

Holstein-Gottorp, the dukes of which so often waged war with Denmark; *Hans the Elder* got the *Haderslev* part, and the king himself the Sónderburg part. To the fourth brother, *Frederick*, was only given the diocese of Schleswig, and later, that of Hildesheim. Owing to these divisions and parties, the affairs in Schleswig-Holstein have often taken a disastrous turn for Denmark, and occasioned sanguinary national wars, the kings often not knowing how to keep the rebellious dukes within due bounds; and I grieve to say, that Christian III., in many other respects so invaluable a king, by that division of the duchies between his brethren, has sown the seeds of that spirit of resistance and discord, which, though it did not break out in his time into acts of violence, afterwards proved fatal to his successors, and became the principal cause of the violent revolutionary storms and convulsions in the years 1848, '49 and '50.

The commercial industry in Denmark was roused considerably in every quarter of the country during the reign of Christian III., and not only foreign trade, but domestic manufactures made a rapid progress. Copenhagen, Aalborg, and Kjóge, hitherto having manifested very little of the spirit of commerce, began to be remarkably distinguished for their trade and manufactures; and the international trade between Denmark and Norway was considerably increasing, the favorable location of Denmark and Norway at the Baltic and the

North sea, giving them every advantage in mercantile respects. The herring-fishery in the Lymfjord, and the salmon in Guden river, at Randers, were sources of riches for Denmark, as iron, copper, lead and potashes were for Norway. The Hanseatic League, which had begun to decline from the year 1428, and was now fast sinking into decay, transferred to Denmark and Norway a great part of their trade, and the declension of the Hanseatic Confederacy, the unwise attempt of which to enforce monopoly proved fatal to their privileges and their power, was the commencement of the splendor of Copenhagen, that for a long series of years rivaled the most eminent commercial cities of Europe, and speedily attained to a very high degree of wealth and elegance. A general commercial intercourse began between the North and other countries, and Denmark and Norway found London, Antwerp and Amsterdam the most convenient entrepôts in transmitting their productions. Christian III. encouraged, also, domestic manufactures by many excellent laws, and it became of great consequence for the increase and growth of commercial affairs, that he caused good money to be coined, and made weights and measures uniform for both kingdoms.

It may not be improper to conclude this sketch of the reign of Christian III. with a few observations on his character and private life. During his whole reign he proved intent on projects of real utility, and distinguished himself by rectitude of mind and conduct, by unfeigned piety to God and love to men, and by carefulness for the prosperity and well-being of his kingdom; he loved the arts and sciences, and promoted them; his habits were economical, and his manners plain and familiar; he was a decided hater of falsehood and low flatteries, which he on taking the Lord's Supper strikingly exemplified. The court chaplain addressed the king while kneeling before the altar: "Most high and mighty Prince, most gracious King;" but Christian, rising, reprimanded him directly, saying, "I have knelt down here as a poor sinner; here I am neither high nor mighty. Don't address me in such a manner; call me here plainly Christian." He exhibited himself often to his people, conversed with them, and shared in their innocent tastes and amusements. His queen, *Dorothea*, exercised perhaps a greater influence over him than was desirable, the king's severity against the exiled Calvinists, who had taken refuge in Denmark, being mainly ascribed to her. Being jealous of the great consideration and honor conferred upon the eminent financier and statesman, *Peter Oxen*, she prevailed also with the king to banish him.

A. D., 1559.

On new-year's day Christian III. died in Copenhagen, after having borne the agonies of protracted sickness with Christian patience and resignation. He is buried in the Cathedral of Roeskilde, where a splendid vaulted marble repository is erected to receive the earthly remains of the kings and queens of the house of Oldenburg.

The crown of Denmark and Norway was now conferred upon his son, who was elected and crowned by the name of *Frederick II.*, after having subscribed to a charter not very different from that of his father. Having as crown-prince always been on the best terms with the Danish and Norwegian people, his accession gave great satisfaction. He was soon crowned, and commenced his reign by liberal promises, and showed a wise policy in weakening the powers of the nobility and reuniting the great fiefs to the crown; the nobility, however, understanding how to turn something to their advantage.

Anxious to relieve Denmark from the ignominy it had undergone in Ditmarsh at *Hemmingsted* under king Hans, and at the same time desirous to subdue that rebellious little republic, the king, in conjunction with his uncles, Hans and Adolph, made the most vigorous military preparations for washing out the ignominy and subjugating the unmanageable inhabitants. The warlike duke, Adolph, had already often tried to influence Christian III. to make an expedition against Ditmarsh, but this peaceable king could not be induced to take any part in the contest; after his death, Adolph proposed to make himself master of the republic; but Frederick II. being seasonably informed of it, resolved to lead the undertaking himself, and go in front of his army. War was declared, of which the object and prize was the sovereignty of Ditmarsh.

Though alarmed at the prospect of their destruction, the valiant Ditmarshians would listen to neither reasons nor suggestions, but with desperate bravery defended their liberty against the superior royal army, headed by the old *John Ranzau*. After a most heroic resistance at *Heide*, where women fought as well as men, they were forced to succumb to overwhelming numbers, and with white staffs in their hands to implore the king's mercy; after which peace was soon concluded on terms advantageous to the king and the dukes, who now divided the country between themselves. The talented historian, Professor Molbech, of Copenhagen, has eloquently described and particularized that heroic defence of the little people, who had determined either to conquer or to die; and he has properly compared their heroism with that of the immortal three hundred, who at Thermopylæ, under Leonidas, gloriously fell, opposing the countless hosts of Xerxes. A marble column, as we know, was erected in honor of Leonidas and his brave Lacedæmonians, but no monument has pointed out to the traveler the spot where the heroic band of the Ditmarshians fell.

A. D., 1560.

About the same time as the war against Ditmarsh was ended, A. D., 1560, the noble-minded Gustavus Erikson Vasa, of Sweden, died, sixty-four years of age, having established Sweden's prosperity by wise laws, and founded the hereditary succession of the crown, which afterwards was extended to females. His son, the passionate, cruel, and at last almost insane *Erik XIV.*, ascended the throne, during whose reign the horrible *Danish Seven Year's War* broke out. A. D., 1563-70. A dispute about the use of the three crowns in the Danish coat of arms was the main motive of the war; to which may be added, that the Swedish king would usurp feudal rights over the dioceses of Oesel and Curland, which the Danish king, Frederick II., had resigned to his brother, *Magnus*, who in return renounced all claim to the duchies. Besides that, Erik XIV. had personally offended Magnus. The Seven Year's War now breaking out between Denmark and Sweden, was waged both on land and sea. A. D., 1563. At sea the Danes were led by the great sea heroes, *Peter Skram, Herluf Trolle*, and *Otto Rud;* but the first one being ninety years of age, soon resigned the staff of command. In a naval engagement at Oeland the Danes, indeed, captured the Swedish admiral's ship, called the *Matchless*, having three benches of oars, an equipment of 1,800 marines and 120 pieces of ordnance, but Herluf Trolle was soon after mortally wounded on the Pomeranian coast, and Otto Rud was made prisoner in a battle by Bornholm, and carried to Sweden, where the enraged and cruel king, Erik XIV., would have killed him with his sword, had not Otto Rud undauntedly addressed him, saying: "Be not wholly guided by your passionate temper, but remember, I pray your royal Majesty, what you owe to a warrior, who has discharged his duty to his king and fatherland." Afterwards the Danish fleet was destroyed by a violent hurricane, not far from Gulland. In consequence of all these misfortunes, the Swedes were, beyond doubt, superior to the Danes at sea.

The land force performed nothing as long as it was conducted by the inefficient general, Count *Günther of Schwarzburg;* the command was therefore given to *Otto Krumpen,* who, forty years before, during the reign of Christian II., had conquered Stockholm, but on account of old age he soon retired to private life, whereupon the chief command was entrusted to the brave and magnanimous *Daniel Ranzau,* who immortalized his name in the battle of *Svarteraa,* in Sweden, where he, with five thousand Danes, totally defeated the Swedish army, consisting of twenty-five thousand well disciplined soldiers. Notwithstanding this prodigious inequality, Daniel Ranzau resolved to indulge the ardor of his few troops, but before commencing the battle he tried to inspire them with still more courage, by addressing them as follows: "Soldiers! The enemy, whose cruel hands are reeking with the blood of your brethren, is impending over your heads. You must either battle as heroes or fight as poltroons. On the one hand is honor and a clear conscience; on the other, infamy and remorse. It concerns your king and your fatherland. Therefore, join together in the bravest defence. keep your eyes undauntedly fixed on the enemy, and have a watch upon all his evolutions. In me you will find both the soldier and the general. I shall conduct myself in such a manner that I may be accountable for my conduct, here to my king, and in heaven to my God. Now, soldiers, forward; let the ememy see the white of your eyes; rush straightway on him. The Lord of Hosts will be with us!" The Danish soldiers, animated by these words, fought like lions, and gained a complete victory; and the celebrated Swedish historian, Dr. Gejer, says, that the Danish infantry wrought miracles. Within three hours four thousand Swedish bodies covered the battle-field.

Having thus triumphed over that great superiority, Daniel Ranzau, together with *Franzis Brockenhuus*, another famous Danish commander, made an inroad into Smaland, a province of Sweden; and, having passed into the interior of the country, he defeated, after sanguinary engagements, two Swedish armies; whereafter both those generals undertook a most difficult retreat, in the heart of the winter, through regions filled with mountains, forests, and hollows; a retreat often compared by historians with that of the Ten Thousand from Cunaxa to Colchis, on the Euxine, and thence along the Euxine to the Hellespont, about the year 400 B. C. Unfortunately for Denmark, both Daniel Ranzau and Francis Brockenhuus fell at the close of the war in the siege of *Varberg*, in the province of Halland, in Sweden; but the successful issue of the

A. D., 1569.

war was chiefly owing to their skillful tactics. Erik XIV., of Sweden, having reigned very imprudently and cruelly, and even having with his own hand murdered the young Niels Sture, a grandson of Steno Sture the Younger, before mentioned, and having caused all the nobles to tremble in anticipation of a similar fate, was placed in confinement by his brothers, *John* and *Charles*, and sentenced to suffer death. The only favor shown him was to choose the manner of it, and he chose to empty the cup of poison. On his confinement *John III.* had ascended the Swedish throne in the year 1569. He wished to make peace with Denmark, and after one year of negotiations the seven years' war ended in the peace of *Stettin*. Sweden had to pay down to Denmark one hundred and fifty thousand rixdollars; each kingdom should be entitled to use three crowns in its coat-of-arms, and the pretensions which both kingdoms, since the Union of Calmar had been irreparably broken, had still mutually made to each other, should cease: Denmark recognizing the independence of Sweden, and Sweden, in return, disclaiming every pretension to Norway, Skane, Halland, Bleking, and the island of Gulland.

A.D, 1577.

A D., 1570

The happy issue of the war was owing, in a great measure, to the wisdom, firmness, and prudence of the skillful statesman, *Peter Oxen*, who had been recalled from his exile, and now, by his judicious management of finances and taxes, procured means of defraying the great charges of the war. He also made himself well known by introducing several fruit trees, as also the carp, the pike, and the craw-fish.

The little sconce or fortification called *Krogen*, at Earsound, (the small Sound between Denmark and Sweden), having proved insufficient to command the navigation through the Sound, Frederic II. built the strong fortress called *Kronborg*, close by the city of Elsenore. The origin of the tax known as the *Sound Dues of Earsound*, goes back upwards of six hundred years, and is founded in that ascendency which the kings of Denmark, from time out of mind, have exercised over the narrow and small sounds and belts streaming through their lands; an ascendency which the principal maritime powers, through a series of treaties, have acknowledged, and the tolls levied by the Danish Government on all ships passing through the Sound, were considered an equitable compensation for the expenses which Denmark incurred in the erection and maintenance of light-houses, buoys, and landmarks, to protect the navigation of the different sounds; and this compensation has been paid to Denmark by the several nations interested, according to a graduated scale, but always, however, considered a thorn in the side of the commercial nations of Europe. During the reign of king *Hans* it was decided, by a commercial treaty made with England, that the ships only in cases of utmost necessity could pass through the Danish sounds and belts, and should then pay tolls in

Nyborg, situated on the large belt. From the time of *Christian II.* the sound dues were paid down in pure silver, while in earlier times goods were taken. The enhancing of the Sound Dues in the following age occasioned many complaints, and as Frederick II. raised it considerably, the Lübeckers made a complaint to the German emperor, which, however, resulted in its enhancement particularly for the Lübeckers, who had to submit, their political influence being now almost undone. But *Hamburg* commencing again to occupy an influential rank amongst the commercial towns, had already, during the reign of Christian III., arrogated a right, called the *compulsive* right, in pursuance of which Hamburg would compel the Holsteinish towns situated on the Elbe to carry their grain and other merchandises to this city. But Frederic II. forced Hamburg to give up that usurped right, and pay ten thousand rixdollars, and afterwards one hundred thousand rixdollars.

Yet older than the sound dues at Elsenore is the *Stade* toll levied by the Hanoverian Government on all ships passing up the river Elbe. Stade is a small town situated on the Elbe. It originally belonged to the king of Sweden, but was subsequently seized by Denmark and sold to the elector of Hanover (George I. of England) in 1715. In the time of *Conrad II.*, emperor of Germany (1040), permission was given to the archbishop of Hamburg to establish a market in Stade, and to levy a tax on all goods offered for sale there, with the understanding that the revenue of the tax should be devoted to the use of the Roman Catholic Church in Hamburg. But the toll thus established as a market tax for religious purposes, has been enforced by the successive owners of Stade down to the present day, and has been converted into a transit duty on all vessels bound for the large cities of Hamburg and Altona, which yields the kingdom of Hanover an enormous annual income, for which it returns no compensation of any sort. But Hanover's pretended right to exact a tax for the navigation of the Elbe, is not entitled even to the consideration extended to Denmark; because Hanover does not contribute a single dollar towards keeping the river in a navigable condition, or maintaining light-houses and buoys, the free city of Hamburg having for centuries borne all such expenses.

The fatal division of the two southern duchies of Denmark, was continued under Frederick II., he granting to his brother, *Hans the Younger*, who A. D., became the founder of the *Sónderburg* lineage, 1564. the counties of Sónderburg, Nordburg, and Aró, a small island in the Baltic. Upon the death of this Hans the Younger, this house was divided even into four others: *Sónderburg*, *Nordburg*, *Plóen* and *Glücksburg;* the first of which was afterwards divided into five new lines, all, however, now extinct, with the exception of the *Sónderburg* (Augustenburg), and the *Glücksburg* (Beck), the possessions of the extinct lineages successively being reunited to the crown. Nevertheless, Hans the Younger and his successors took no share in ruling the duchies, but were only considered proprietors of the allodial estates. The protracted disputes between the king and his uncles, concerning the enfeoffment of Schleswig, were ended at an agreement in *Odensee*, after which the dukes, Adolph and Hans the Elder, took the oath of allegiance, thirty-six years after they had received their fiefs. Upon the death of Hans the Elder, his possessions were, after some variance, divided between the king himself and Adolph: Hans the Younger obtained nothing but, in compensation, some scattered possessions of the royal part of the duchies. It is easy to see of what vast detriment this division was to the solid interests of the Danish body.

A. D., 1579.

A. D., 1580.

Frederick II. was, like his father, liberally disposed to encourage science and art, and, by his own example, to promote a fashionable relish for literary productions. He founded a *cloister*, also called the *Community*, a massive building, where a hundred students received free house and board; and in *Soró*, a town forty English miles from Copenhagen, he established an academy for thirty children of noble descent and for thirty descended from the burgher class. *The Academy of Herlufsholm*, the environs of which are celebrated for their beauty, was founded by the great sea hero, Herluf Trolle, who liberally spent all his great riches to establish this yet celebrated institution. At this time lived also several men eminent in the various departments of literature, sciences, and the arts; as *Henry Ranzau, Tycho Brahe, Niels Hemmingson* and *Anders Sórenson Vedel,* the latter of whom has deserved well by an excellent translation of the Latin original of Saxo Grammaticus. Henrik Ranzau, surnamed *the Learned,* a son of the celebrated commander, John Ranzau, rendered himself known, both by his extensive learning and immense riches, which he applied to promote and encourage science and the arts, and to bring about undertakings of general usefulness. The great astronomer, *Tycho Brahe,* has gained the most unlimited reputation abroad, his name being known to the whole civilized world. In the thirteenth year of his age he entered the University of Copenhagen, and after there having passed his examination highly satisfactorily to his examiners, whose attention he attracted, particularly by his deep knowledge in the classics and mathematics, he visited several foreign Universities. Upon his return, the king, Frederic II., presented him with *Hwén,* a beautiful little rock-island, in the sound between Denmark and Sweden, where Tycho Brahe erected a castle named *Uraniaburg,* and an observatory called *Stjerneburg* (star-burg). He occupied these for twenty-one years in profound studies concerning the motions of the planets and the form of the heavens. This great man, whose genius far outshone all who had gone before him in the path of astronomy, so as not to leave to posterity the possibility of eclipsing his fame, discovered that the planets moved in a circular orbit round the sun; and he discovered, likewise, the analogy between the distances of the several planets from the sun and their periodical revolutions, thus paving the way for the immortal Newton. He not only influenced his contemporaries by astronomical works, but instructed, also, many young men; and he enjoyed so high a reputation, that even foreign potentates visited him on his astronomical island, amongst others, *James VI.* of Scotland, who had come to Denmark to celebrate his marriage with princess Anna, daughter of Frederick II. The Scottish king requested Tycho Brahe to ask a favor of him, and Tycho begged two English dogs, which became the innocent cause of his ruin. The lord high chancellor, *Christopher Walkendorph*, visiting him, the dogs, lying at the door, barked at the chancellor, who kicked them. Tycho Brahe, in general easily provoked, was so exasperated, that he severely rebuked Walkendorph, who, greatly offended by this harsh language, tried to disgrace him with the young king, Christian IV. At Walkendorph's request, the king sent *Thomas Finche*, professor of mathematics at the University of Copenhagen, to Hwén, to examine Brahe's astronomical instruments. The Professor, jealous of all the honor and esteem conferred upon Brahe, declared that they were too expensive and superfluous; all which mortified the latter so much as to make him weary of his fatherland, which he left in the month of April, 1597. He now repaired to Bohemia, where the emperor, *Rudolph II.*, highly instructed in learning and science, cordially received him, and gave him a large yearly salary, and a palace called *Benach*, close by Prague, where he lived till his death, 1601. His cotemporary, the great astronomer, John Kepler, lodged in Brahe's house in Benach, both applying themselves to the deepest astronomical speculations. The emperor caused him to be buried with great pomp, in the principal church of Prague, called *Church am Thein*, where a marble monument is erected, on which his image is engraven, as also his usual motto: "*Non videri, sed esse.*" *Dr. Jessen* delivered the funeral sermon, explaining in classical Latin, how his great genius had proceeded, step by step, from the simplest principles to the most sublime conclusions. The emperor, Rudolph II., bought his astronomical instruments. Notwithstanding his high genius and deep erudition, he wanted very much of that which is consistent with real greatness of soul. He was, for instance, very superstitious, considering certain days of the year pregnant with misfortune; wherefore it has become a proverb in the Scandinavian countries, when an unhappy accident happens, "This day is a Tycho Brahe's day."

Niels Hemmingson (Hemmingius), one, for his age,

of the most learned and talented divines, renowned, both in his fatherland and foreign lands, met with the same bitter fate, with the same disappointments and neglect of merit, as Tycho Brahe. Suspected of being inclined to adopt the Calvinistic meaning about the Lord's Supper in the sense of "This represents my body," and of not asserting, as Luther, the bodily presence of Christ in the Sacrament, and arraigned by *August*, elector of Saxony, and brother-in-law to the Danish king Frederic II., for this crime, the generous and learned Niels Hemmingson was suddenly, in the sixty-third year of his age, without proof and passing of any sentence, deposed from his professorship at the university, it being the reward with which Denmark, both now and afterwards, has often distinguished literary genius.

Upon the whole, intolerance was a prominent feature of this period. The Form of Concord (*Formula Concordiæ*), a book in which the Lutheran doctrines, together with some new subtle additions, were explained, which *James Andrea*, professor at the University in Tübingen, Wirtemberg, tried to introduce into Denmark, was not only not introduced, but the king himself, with his own royal hand throwing a copy of that book into the fire, even commanded that clergymen, in whose houses it was found, should be deposed from the ministry, and booksellers attempting to sell it should suffer death without mercy. Already Christian III. had passed a law forbidding any foreigner to settle in the country before he was examined in the Creed, and Frederick II. issued twenty-five articles, which every foreigner intending to settle in Denmark should affirm by oath; whosoever might decline doing so, had to leave the country within three days, and for apostacy capital punishment was to be inflicted.

Frederick II. was married to *Sophia of Mecklenburg*, a daughter of Ulrich of Schwerin; a wise, pious, and intelligent queen, by whom he became father of the famous king of Denmark, Christian IV. He died in Copenhagen, fifty-three years of age, his son Christian yet being a minor, only ten years of age. (A.D., 1588.) Upon the whole, Frederick II. ruled his kingdoms with justice, vigor, and vigilance. In his private life he was frugal without avarice, enterprising without temerity, and of an active and pious temper. The king drawing his last breath, and the court physician who came to feel his pulse remarking, "The beating of the pulse is weak," he answered, "Be it as it may, but we know the mercy of God shall not fail;" and when he had said this he fell asleep. But it was his misfortune, that with his many good qualities, and a large share of mental endowments, he wanted that toleration towards other religious denominations, which should have taught him moderation; and it was his misfortune, too, that in his latter days he indulged in the frequent use of strong spirituous liquors, which abridged his life and undermined his naturally healthy constitution.

Christian IV. now mounted the throne, with the entire approbation and even affection of his subjects; but, being a minor, a guardianship was appointed, consisting of *Niels Kaas,* counsellor of state, *Peter Munk,* admiral, *Christopher Walkendorph,* superintendent of finance, and baron *George Rosenkranz,* lord high chancellor; all ruling the kingdoms carefully, and taking the utmost interest in educating the young king, and inspiring him with good and firm principles. He was not only taught Latin, German, French, Italian, and Spanish, but also mathematics, in which he made great proficiency. Early manifesting a great propensity to naval affairs, he exercised himself in them on *Lake Skanderburg,* in Jutland, where a ship was built for that purpose; thus in his youthful years acquiring no little insight into the science of naval affairs. He was often charged, under his minority, to consider and make answer to embassies, and give audience to the foreign officers who came to Denmark; and he often sat in council to profit by what passed. After having attained the legal age prescribed by the Danish law (eighteen),

A. D., 1596. *Christian IV.* assumed the government; the old, dignified counsellor of state, *Niels Kaas,* addressing him in the following soul-moving words: " By virtue of my office, I hereby deliver to your Majesty the key to that vault, where the royal crown, the imperial globe, and the golden sceptre have been preserved since the death of your royal father of glorious memory. Let the crown never fall from your head, grasp the globe with genius and circumspection, wield the sceptre with wisdom and justice, and impair no man's well won privileges. May our God, the King of kings, and the Lord of lords enlighten you, and fill you with wisdom to promote the welfare of your two kingdoms, and may you never forget the great account you have to make in the last day. May your Majesty be crowned abundantly with all the blessings of this life!" Christian IV. now commenced his reign, after having sealed and subscribed a charter corresponding altogether with that of his father, and has distinguished himself among the sovereigns of the North by the superiority of his talents, and the zeal that he showed in reforming the different branches of the administration. He is often compared by historians with his cotemporary, the magnanimous Gustavus Adolphus, who raised Sweden to the summit of its greatness, and whose very name has awakened in generous hearts the liveliest emotions of respect and admiration. Christian IV. was a remarkable linguist, illustrious commander, and an indomitable, fearless soldier; but whether he was, as Gustavus Adolphus, an exemplary Christian, we are permitted to entertain some doubts; and when, therefore, a Danish historian, Frederick Snedorph, says: "I boldly, in every respect, compare him with Gustavus Adolphus," we believe he asserts too much. After having assumed the government himself, he married the Prussian princess, *Anna Catharina*, whereafter his mother, the noble-minded queen-dowager Sophia, repaired to *Nykjóbing* palace, on the island of Falster, with which the king, her son, had presented her, and where she lived in the exercise of secret charity till her death, in 1631.

II.

1596—1660.

Christian IV.—Care and interest for Norway—Variance with Sweden—Calmar War—Peace at *Knœród*—He encourages Science and the Arts—Commercial Affairs—Discoveries—Regulation of the Post Affairs—Manufactures—Buildings—Participation in the Thirty Years' War—Battle by Lutter, near the Barenberg—Peace of Lübeck—Dissatisfaction amongst the Peasantry and Burgher Class with the Aristocracy—Dispute with Hamburg—Sound Dues at Elsenore—War with Sweden—Inroad of the Swedish General, Torstenson—Battle at Colberg—Peace of Brómsebro—*Frederick III.*—Election of King—The Charter—Alliance with Holland—Corfitz Ulfeldt—Rupture with Sweden—Peace of Roeskilde—Renewal of the War—Siege of Copenhagen—Admiral *Opdam*—Battle at Nyborg—Peace of Copenhagen.

AFTER having taken his seat at the helm of government, Christian IV. commenced to act with great diligence and vigor, paying a particular attention to the many complaints that in Norway had been put up against the oppressive treatment of the royal bailiffs, who, when found guilty, were punished and deposed. Upon the whole, there was a prepossession of mind about him in favor of this kingdom, which he during his reign visited fifty times. Under the title of Captain, he sailed straight to *Kola*, in Russia, and

A. D., 1599.

at *Vardó* ran the risk even of his life, his ship running aground and losing the keel; but he succeeded in getting off, without receiving any injury. Sweden for some time having disagreed with Denmark concerning the northern bounds of Norway, Christian IV., for getting an exact knowledge about this important matter, sailed himself by North Cape and along the coast of Finnmark, where the Norwegian, Swedish, and Russian borders are adjoining to each other. The misunderstanding increased, when *Charles IX.*, a son of Gustavus Erikson Vasa, having received the Swedish crown, which he had long been striving for, assumed the title, "King of the Norwegian Laplanders," and even levied taxes in Finnmark, and posted placards on the customhouse of Elsenore, forbidding the Danish vessels to trade in Lifland and Curland. The dignity of the Danish crown being hereby highly offended, Christian IV. declared war against Sweden, and A. D., 1611. marched a powerful army against the strong fortress, *Calmar*, which after a terrible siege of three months had to surrender, although the old and brave Swedish king, Charles IX., spared no labor, and even hazarded his own person, in rescuing this principal Swedish place of arms. The taking of Calmar, which has given this war the name of the *Calmar War*, exasperated the old Charles IX. to such a degree, that he wrote a very unpolite letter to Christian IV., in which he even challenged the Danish king to fight a duel. In reply to this letter, Christian told him, that it would be much better for him, being now so far advanced in years, to sit like an old woman behind a warm stove, than to risk a blow with a vigorous man, even abusing him in calling him a crafty old knave. Shortly after, October 30th, 1611, died Charles IX., his son, the great Gustavus Adolphus now assuming the Swedish government on the 26th of December, 1611. Quitting now the council board for the scene of battle, Gustavus Adolphus stormed *Christianopel*, the principal depôt of arms in Skane, and re-conquered *Oeland*. Nevertheless, the war continued successful for Denmark, Christian IV. taking by storm the Swedish fortresses, *Guldborg* and *Elfsborg*, and demolishing the large city, *Gothenborg*, which Charles IX. had erected; also at sea the Danes had the preponderancy in this war. The king of Sweden had now levied 1,400 Scottish soldiers, as auxiliary troops, who, headed by Colonel *Sinclair*, landed in Norway, devastating wheresoever they went, and rushing forth like madmen. The Norwegian peasants, highly provoked at their plunderings and cruelties, took up whatsoever arms they could lay hold of, boldly encountering the Colonel and his Scotsmen in *Guld-*

A. D., *brandsdalen* (the Guldbrand valley), south of the
1612. mountain *Dovrefield*, where the Scottish chief and his 1,400 soldiers, save two, in the most horrible massacre were formally butchered. The one went home to Scotland to tell his countrymen of the desperate

bravery with which the people of the North had defended their national rights; the other remained in Norway, where he founded a glass furnace. In memory of that heroic exploit, a monument has been erected with the following plain inscription: "Here was Colonel *Sinclair* shot on the 26th of August, 1612." Upon the intelligence of that frightful defeat, Gustavus Adolphus made peace with Denmark in *Knæród*, in the province of Halland, on the following terms, so advantageous for Denmark: both kingdoms were permitted to use three crowns in their coat of arms; the king of Sweden was not to call himself king of the Laplanders, nor to exact tribute in the Norwegian Finnmark; Sweden had to pay to Denmark one million of rix-dollars. [A.D., 1613.]

But Christian IV. was not so successful in the Thirty Year's War, during which he undertook the defence of the Protestant party against the German emperor *Ferdinand* of Steiermark, who was a zealous Catholic; and the Protestants of Bohemia, who had suffered under the government of his predecessor, Matthias, were apprehensive of still greater restraint under Ferdinand. The religious dissensions continued daily to increase in acrimony and animosity, and at length the Catholic and Protestant leagues plunged Germany into a civil war of thirty year's continuance (1618–1648), the horrors of which make the very flesh quiver. The Bohemians deposed Ferdinand II., and chose Frederick V., of Pfalz, the elector Palatine, son-in-law of the English king, James I., for their sovereign; but Frederick soon lost the battle of White Hill, near Prague, 7th November, 1620, where the imperialists determined the fate of Protestantism in Bohemia, the emperor compelling Frederick to seek refuge in Holland, and banishing the Protestant clergy from the country. Thirty thousand families were driven out, and had to flee to the Protestant states of Saxony and Brandenburg. The Protestant party now seeing its future shrouded in the darkest gloom of an impending tempest, and almost overpowered by the imperialists, formed a new Protestant union, of which *Christian IV.* was chosen the head, and the war burst forth with fresh violence. England, Holland and France also encouraged the gallant Danish king to defend the oppressed Protestants, promising him support of money and troops. Relying on these promises, and actuated by compassion toward the un-

A. D., 1625. happy Protestants, the Danish king was made captain-general of Lower Saxony, and crossed the Elbe with an army of 25,000 men, joined by 7,000 Saxons; but, after some successes, the king fell headlong with his horse from the high ramparts of the fortress, *Hameln*, in Hanover, which accident for a time disabled him from leading his army, and shortly after he

A. D., 1626. was defeated by the imperial general, *Tilly*, near Lutter-am-Barenberg, (August 26, 1626,) with the loss of 4,000 men, the imperial general being far

superior to his Protestant adversaries. Nevertheless it deserves to be remarked, that the Danish army fought with the most undaunted bravery, the king himself setting forth a glorious example. By the two imperial commanders, *Tilly* and *Wallenstein*, the Danes were in the following year driven from Germany, and the imperial troops, consisting of 100,000 men, overflowed the whole of Holstein, Schleswig and Jutland, so that Christian IV., threatened with the loss of his own dominions, was forced to purchase peace in Lübeck by renouncing all right to interfere in the affairs of Germany, and on the condition of abandoning his German allies, especially the Duke of Mecklenburg. Furthermore, Christian had to resign his pretensions to the dioceses of *Bremen*, *Verden*, and *Schwerin*, which he had acquired for his sons, Frederick and Ulrik. {A. D. 1629.}

Thus ended the Danish period of the thirty years' war, which undoubtedly would have been more successful for the brave Danish king had he been assisted by his allies according to their promise; but the Duke of *Lüneburg* treacherously fell off, and *Charles I.*, of England, who in 1625 had ascended the British throne, was almost immediately involved in a contest with his parliament, which diverted his attention from foreign affairs. But to *Gustavus Adolphus*, king of Sweden, perhaps the greatest and noblest warrior the world has seen, often called the *Lion of the North* and the *bulwark of the Protestant faith*—to him it was reserved to be the deliverer of the Protestants. He taught the haughty emperor, whose general, Wallenstein, in derision called him the Snow-King, that the snow does not easily thaw in the North, defeating his mighty armies in almost every engagement, until at *Lützen*, a small town of the present Prussian Saxony, on the 16th of November, 1632, he was shot through the left arm, body and head, and wounded in four other places before he died. But even in death he conquered, and for about sixteen years after, his spirit led his country's hosts to victory, until the emperor, tired of an unsuccessful war, concluded the remarkable peace of Westphalia, in the year 1648, the religious dissensions being finally put an end to. The three religions, the Catholic, the Lutheran, and the Reformed, were equally established.

Although the terms of peace were not severe for Denmark, yet this war of four years' continuance, made with great efforts and enormous expenses, had desolated the Danish countries and destroyed some of the most opulent and flourishing towns. Industry was at a stand, agriculture neglected, commerce and manufactures totally annihilated. Hamburg had arrogated to itself a right called *jus restringendi;* that is, that all the inhabitants along the Elbe should carry their merchandises to Hamburg and there sell them for such a price as the Hamburg merchants thought proper to prescribe. To this despotic act the vigilant and active king Christian sought to put a stop by erecting the fortress *Glückstadt,* where he levied toll on all the vessels which trafficked with Hamburg, which now, after its fleet was defeated on the Elbe, had to submit, and even pay down an indemnity of two hundred and eighty thousand rix-dollars. Denmark, at length, gradually recovering from her wounds and misfortunes, became again a powerful and wealthy nation, so much the more as Christian IV., for remedying the evils of the war and the scarcity of money, through several years had raised the sound dues at Elsenore. But Holland and Sweden, highly displeased with this, watched eagerly for a proper opportunity to deprive Denmark of the Eastern Sound provinces, and a most formidable combination seemed now ready to overwhelm Christian IV., under which a monarch of less spirit and ability than himself must certainly have succumbed at once. *Axel Oxenstjern*, chancellor of the kingdom of Sweden, and during the minority of queen Christina, daughter of Gustavus Adolphus, commissioned governor of the Swedish realm, a statesman whom posterity considers a man second to none, resolved to weaken the power of Denmark by a sudden invasion, commanding the famous Swedish general, *Lennert Torstenson*, to leave Germany, and, without any declaration of hostilities, to carry the torch of war, into the very heart of Denmark. Christian IV. had, indeed, long dreaded Sweden's hostile intentions, but the careless senate and nobility, having placed too many restrictions on his power, would not grant him the

A.D., 1643

necessary pecuniary means to put the kingdom into a due posture of defence. Torstenson, therefore, meeting with no obstacles, burst with the rapidity of lightning into Holstein, Schleswig and Jutland, another division of the Swedish army making an inroad into the Danish provinces in Sweden, Skane, Halland and Bleking; and had these two mighty armies jointly come over to the Danish islands, which, however, the insecure state of the ice and the activity of the Danish fleet prevented, it had been all over with Denmark. But all the towns and castles in the two duchies of Holstein and Schleswig, except Glückstadt, had to surrender to the advancing Swedes; and Rendsburg, on the Eider, one of the strongest Danish fortresses, opened its gates to the enemy, and in the month of January, 1644, Torstenson stood on the Middlefartssound, a point of the island of Funen. Under all these perilous circumstances the old king, Christian, did not relax in any of his royal duties, but evinced the most indefatigable activity, making everywhere in the provinces the most needful defensive preparations, and despite his advanced age, now almost seventy years old, going on board his fleet to command in person, and keeping a strict eye upon the movements of the enemy. But everything seemed to look very gloomy for Denmark. On the other side of the Kattegat, in the Swedish peninsula, *Gustavus Horn*, field-marshal of Sweden, and general *Lars Kagge*, with an army of fourteen thousand horse and foot, had made an irruption into Skane, in the beginning of the year 1644. *Horn* occupied *Helsingborg*, situated on the sound, across from Elsenore, and after having defeated the Danish troops who ventured into the field, he took *Landscrona*, a seaport in Skane, whence he advanced to the siege of *Malmó*, a very strong fortress, defended on the landside with walls, ditches and bastions, and on the seaside by a strong castle, whither the brave old Danish king, with numerous forces, had repaired, which enabled the garrison to defy the utmost efforts of the Swedes. But in the meantime a fleet arrived from Holland to assist the Swedes, obliging the Danes to raise the blockade of Gothenburg, which king Christian had commenced; but the Danish fleet encountering it off the coast of Jutland, prevented it from transporting Swedish troops into the island of *Funen*, and compelled the Hollanders to take refuge under the island of *Sylt*, on the west coast of Schleswig, where they were cannonaded by the gallant Danish king. Meanwhile the Swedish fleet, numbering forty men-of-war, put to sea, under the command of Admiral *Claus Flemming*, a tried naval officer, and having arrived on the coast of Holstein, near the island of *Femern*, met the Danish fleet, numbering thirty men-of-war. On the 6th of July a terrible engagement took place, king Christian, despite his old age, commanding in person. The king himself, standing at the foot of the mast of his admiral ship, and

A.D., 1644.

encouraging his mariners to persevere manfully to the end, was dangerously wounded, losing an eye and two teeth, a splinter from the ship having killed twelve men immediately around him. The king, however, continued to command until the enemy was put to flight.

This glorious victory has given rise to the magnificent Danish war-song, composed by the Danish poet, Ewald, of which the following is a translation, made by Prof. Longfellow:

KONG CHRISTIAN STOD VED HOIEN MAST.

(King Christian stood by the High Mast.)

King Christian stood by the high mast,
   'Mid smoke and spray;
His fierce artillery flashed so fast
That Swedish wrecks were round him cast,
And lost each hostile stern and mast
   'Mid smoke and spray.
Fly, Swedes, fly! No hope to win
Where Christian dauntless mingles in
     The fray!

Niels Juul beheld the tempest grow.
   "The day is right!"
Aloft he bade the red flag glow,
And shot for shot he dealt the foe.
They shout, whilst fiercest perils grow,
   "The day is right!"
Fly, Swedes, in safest refuge hide;
What arm shall stand 'gainst Christian's pride
     In fight?

O North Sea! Vessel's thunders light
   Thy murky sky!

His foemen shrunk with strange affright,
For death and terror round him fight;
Sad Gothland hears the bolts that light
    Thy murky sky!
He gleams, proud Denmark's shaft of war.
The foe must own his brightest star:
    They fly!

Thou road for Danes to power and praise,
    Dark heaving wave!
Receive thy friend, by valor's rays
Led through thy wild and boisterous ways!
Guide the bold youth to power and praise,
    Dark heaving wave;
And free, through storm and tempest, through
Dangers and glory, waft him to
    His grave!

It affords me much pleasure to quote this excellent translation, in which the Danish original has not lost more of its power than is the case with every translation. But, as previously stated, everything seemed to look dark for Denmark, and the victory gained by Femern was only a momentary blaze. After being defeated, the Swedish high admiral, Flemming, repaired to *Christiansprüs*, now called *Fredericksort*, to repair damages, where he, in the bay of Kiel, was immediately blockaded by the Danish fleet, whence the Swedes could not escape on account of the adverse wind. King Christian opened a fierce cannonade upon the Swedish fleet in the harbor, in which bloody engagement the valiant Swedish admiral, Flemming, fell, turning over the command, before he expired, into the hands of *Charles Gustavus Wrangel*, who had acquitted himself in the most satisfactory manner in the battle of Lützen.

1632, where his master, the great and noble Gustavus Adolphus, breathed out his illustrious life. It being, of course, of the greatest consequence to keep the Swedish fleet enclosed in the bay of Kiel, to prevent it from uniting with the Hollandish fleet, commanded by *Martin Thysen*, Christian IV. entrusted this important matter to the charge of admiral *Peter Galt*, and had he acted with due vigilance, the Swedish fleet would have been irretrievably lost. But an unpardonable negligence of Galt, for which king Christian immediately ordered the admiral, although seventy-two years of age, to be beheaded, united the Swedish naval forces with the Dutch squadron. The combined fleet, consisting of sixty-four men-of-war in all, met that of Denmark, numbering seventeen ships-of-war, between the islands of Femern and Laaland, on the 13th of October, 1644, and obtained over it so complete a victory that only two men-of-war escaped, and the heroic Danish admiral, *Prosmund*, fell, after having given the most extraordinary proofs of dauntless spirit. The combined fleet then sailed for Kieler harbor to refit, after which the Hollanders returned home. At length the emperor, *Ferdinand III.*, envious and jealous of the progress of the Swedes in Denmark, ordered his general, *Matthias Gallas*, to collect all his available forces in Bohemia, and move towards Holstein. He entered Kiel, and obtained some few other unimportant advantages, but the Swedish general, Torstenson, offered him battle, which he did not dare to accept;

and Gallas, says a German historian, made his way out of Holstein, having actually been of more detriment than benefit to the Danes, whom he had been sent to assist. The misery of Denmark increasing day by day, and the Swedish general, *Wrangel*, in the spring of 1645, as soon as the season would permit, taking the island of Bornholm, and disputing successfully the sovereignty of the Danish seas, while Torstenson, on the land, kept most of the Danish islands blockaded, the gallant Danish monarch, Christian IV., was compelled to make a disadvantageous peace at *Brómsebro*, on the following terms: Sweden should be exempted from paying Sound Dues; Denmark should forever renounce her claims to *Herjedalen* and *Jemteland*, (two provinces in the Swedish district, Northland, *Norlandia*), also to the two islands in the Baltic, *Oeland* and *Gulland*. In the same year the Danish king was also compelled to adjust a pacification with Holland in *Christianopel*, where the Sound Dues for the Dutch merchantmen were considerably abated. _{Aug. 13th A. D., 1645.}

When the sanguinary and expensive wars, mainly arising out of the thirty years' war, terminated, the Danish and Norwegian kingdoms were so enfeebled and harassed, that they, during the last three years of the reign of Christian IV., sunk into inactive repose. Such a complete change in all commercial transactions had taken place, that credit was shaken, trade injured, manufactures checked, the public treasury exhausted, and thousands reduced to beggary. Several energetic measures for remedying the evils of the war, and bringing the countries into a better condition, were taken by the active old king; but meeting with opposition and obstinacy on the part of the senate and the nobility, which had been invested with undue power and influence, they all sunk into nothing. The nobility were displeased with the king for bestowing the highest offices alone on his sons-in-law, who were married to daughters of his concubine, *Christine Munck*, with whom the king, upon the death of his queen, *Anna Catharina*, had contracted a morganatic marriage. Thus, for instance, Count *Pentz* was governor of Holstein, *Hannibal Sehestedt* governor of Norway, and *Corfitz Ulfeldt*, married to the king's dearest daughter, *Eleonora Christina*, was lord high chancellor, exercising an all-powerful influence upon state affairs. Although the nobility might have some reason for complaining of the favor shown to the king's bastards, yet it is not to be denied, that the sad condition of the kingdoms was owing rather to the many restrictions which the nobility had placed on his power, than to any want of talent in the king himself; the nobility continually trying to restrict the royal authority, to secure the chief powers of the state to the aristocracy, and destroy even the best plans of the king. The noblemen had brought their influence even to that point that neither the clergy nor the burgher class and peasantry could write any application to the king unless signed by a nobleman. *George Dybvad*, theological professor at the University of Copenhagen, published a work about this unjust tyranny, but the nobility convinced the king that Dybvad's *modus operandi* was not in accordance with the spirit of the times, and that it was repugnant to their privileges, and the king, had to depose him from his office. *Christopher Dybvad*, not intimidated by his father's fate, spoke of the nobility in the bitterest terms, and composed a work in which he condemned the prerogatives of the nobility as destructive to the kingdom; but he was imprisoned for life. Even the best efforts of the king for the improvement of his country were opposed by the nobility. He tried to improve the circumstances of the peasantry, but met with so much opposition, that he was forced to give it up; and his anger was often wound up to such a pitch as to exercise despotic authority against some noblemen. Thus, for instance, baron *Christopher Rosenkrantz* was beheaded for having committed only a trifling fraud. Besides all these disagreeable terms on which he was with the nobility, and which often darkened his days. he had, in his old age, the heart-rending grief A.D., to lose his eldest son, crown-prince *Christian*, 1647. his long elected successor to the throne.

We have next to examine the king's conspicuous abilities in leading the internal affairs of his kingdom. In peace he was as unceasingly active as in war and military preparations. Having enjoyed, himself, a careful education, and being well versed in languages, both the ancient and modern, he had a high appreciation of learning, and was, therefore, a judicious and munificent patron of science and literature. He appointed more professors at the University of Copenhagen than before, furnished the University with new incomes taken from the ecclesiastical estates, which were vacant from the time of the Reformation, enlarged the University library, and built a spacious building called *Regentsen* (*domus regia*), for indigent students. The Royal Observatory of Copenhagen, called the *round tower*, was built at the king's expense, and a botanic garden and an anatomical theatre were founded. In order to give the young noblemen that education at home which they frequently sought at foreign Universities, Christian IV. erected in the town of *Sorò* an Academy (*Academia Sorana*), exclusively for noblemen, commanding that for the future no nobleman should go abroad before reaching the nineteenth year of his age. Among the learned men who lived during the reign of Christian IV., we ought not to forget to name *Ole Worm*, distinguished both as physician and antiquarian; *Caspar Bartholin*, a famous anatomist, has become progenitor of a whole generation of learned men; *Tycho Brahe*, above mentioned, acquired an immortal renown by his astronomical researches and discoveries. *Longomantanus*, a disciple of Tycho Brahe, gained reputation as a great mathematician. *Hans Paulson Resen* and *Brochman*, bishops in Denmark, have signalized themselves by deep theological learning, of whom the first translated the Bible out of the original tongues; the learned Icelandic clergyman, *Arngrim Jonson*, commenced fundamentally to explain the remarkable *Icelandic Edda*, composed by *Snorro Sturleson*, A. D. 1218, and containing the system of the Scandinavian mythology, and specimens of the poetry of the ancient Northern Skalds. Of consequence for the history of the fatherland was the *Chronicle of Denmark*, composed and published by *Arild Hvitfeld*, a short time lord high chancellor of the kingdom. Also royal historiographers were appointed; but it is remarkable that it was incumbent on them, as a duty, to write in Latin, and several of them, as *Meursius* and *Pontanus*, were foreigners. The mother tongue as yet enjoyed very little esteem, nearly all books being written in Latin. Christian IV. being also a promoter of fine arts, prevailed upon *Charles van Mandern*, the famous Dutch painter, to visit Denmark, to whom the church of *Soró* owes its greatest beauty. He left many scholars of great reputation, who distinguished themselves by a graceful and correct design, and several, that, in one single department, may be found to surpass even Charles van Mandern. The active king also invited foreign enterprising merchants and mechanics to Denmark, and established salt and saltpetre manufactories, paper mills, sugar houses, powder mills, and several copper works in Norway. Under him, also, were the important silver mines near *Kongsberg* in Norway discovered. In his reign, also, the Danes first directed their attention to the *Asiatic* trade, and founded an *East India* Company, and tried to procure possessions in the East Indies, the king dispatching, for that purpose, the Admiral *Ove Gjedde*, to the island of *Ceylon*, situated in the Indian ocean. This attempt, however, proving abortive, the admiral formed a commercial establishment at *Tranquebar*, on the coast of Coromandel, which was ceded to the company by the rajah of Tanjore. The king also attempting all means possible for renewing the navigation to *Greenland*, which already in the tenth century was discovered and peopled by Norwegians from Iceland, the navigation to it, however, being interrupted by the frightful disease called the Black Plague, under Waldemar IV., dispatched the captain, *Jens Munk*. to Greenland, where he established the Company of Greenland, which carried on a profitable whale fishery in those regions.

A. D., 1623.

That Denmark's own inhabitants might profit by the Icelandic trade, which the greedy Hanse towns and the English had almost exclusively appropriated, Christian IV. founded the *Icelandic* Company. Also, many public buildings, cities, and fortresses were founded by this wise monarch: as the *Merchants' Exchange*, the *Church of the Trinity*, the *Church for Seamen*, the

Palace of Rosenborg, and the splendid *palace of Fredericksborg*, sixteen English miles from Copenhagen, which his father, Frederick II., had commenced. He founded, in Norway, *Christiania*, the present capital of Norway, *Christiansand*, and *Kongsberg;* and the following fortresses: *Glückstadt*, on the Elbe, *Christianspriis*, now called Fredericksort, at the bay of Kiel, *Christianopel*, in Bleking, and *Christianstad*, in Skane; for the greater number of which the king himself made the plans. He established a school for the art of navigation, and raised a standing army, consisting of five thousand foot, steadily trained in military exercises. The king himself, very skillful in the art of ship-building, modeled many of his men-of-war, which were considered the most beautiful and the best in Europe; and the Danish navy was in an excellent condition, and the strongest bulwark of both kingdoms. He also distinguished himself by his zeal for the propagation of the Christian religion, and notwithstanding his limited means, he succeeded in diffusing the Christian principles through a considerable portion of the East Indies; and if the Danish East India Company had not been injured by the pertinacious jealousy of the Dutch, who excluded them from the most profitable branches of trade, he would have been able to do much more. It may not be without interest to learn that Christian IV. was a warm advocate of colonial enterprise, and considering America a gold mine, the idea of planting a colony in the new world held a conspicuous place in the mind of the Danish monarch; and the State of New Jersey was first settled by the Danes, about the year 1624, making their abode in the town of *Bergen;* but as *Peter Stuyvesant*, the Dutch Governor of New-York, conquered New Jersey in 1655, most of the Danes left the country. The great Gustavus Adolphus, of Sweden, conceived the same idea, and a Swedish colony was planted in 1627 in the State of Delaware; but the Dutch disputing the possession of it with them, the Swedes, after the Dutch conquest, 1655, returned to Sweden.

He was a great hater of superstition and deceitful dealing, and the years 1572–1648 were signalized in the annals of Denmark by vehement and severe trials for *witchcraft*. This fanatic and shameful delusion went on increasing until, in the city of *Ribe*, in Jutland, not less than twelve women were burned alive. After a memorable reign of sixty years, and after having himself governed his kingdoms through half a century,

A. D., 1648. Christian IV. died on the 28th of February, 1648, aged seventy-one years, an object of the love and affection of his subjects, and of the honor and regard of the whole of Europe, the policy of which he often had powerfully influenced.

Frederick III. After an interregnum of three months Christian IV.'s second son succeeded his father to the throne of both kingdoms, by the name of *Frederick III.;* during which interval the state affairs were controlled by *Corfitz Ulfeldt*, lord high chancellor, *Christian Sehested*, lord high treasurer, *Ove Gjedde*, lord high admiral, and *Anders Bilde*, commander-in-chief; and having first sealed and subscribed a very severe charter, restricting the royal authority much more than before, and increasing the power of the nobility, which charter has mainly been ascribed to Ulfeldt, Frederick III. ascended the throne. The events of the last time having shown how dangerous the enmity of Holland was, the king wisely sought to persuade that realm to join his party; the more since Sweden, because of her triumphs in the thirty year's war, and last successful war with Denmark, almost became the arbiter of the European destiny, and was elevated to a pinnacle of glory and power which proved dangerous to Denmark's peace and security. The learned and intelligent Corfitz Ulfeldt, therefore, was sent to Holland to negotiate an alliance of mutual defence against every enemy. The alliance made, a *Treaty of Redemption* was concluded, according to which Holland, instead of Sound Dues yearly, had to pay one hundred and fifty thousand florins. Corfitz Ulfeldt, towards the close of the reign of Christian IV., having often given the king reason to be displeased with him, and lost very much of his affection, occupied a position yet more dangerous and slippery during Frederick III. The great power his high office gave him, his immense riches and high connections, struck with fear and jealousy both the king and his proud queen, *Sophia*

Amalia, a princess of Brunswick Lüneburg, who all the time was cherishing a personal aversion and dislike to Ulfeldt's lady, *Eleonora Christina*, the virtuous, handsome, and ingenuous daughter of Christian IV.

A. D., 1649. Upon his return from his embassy, with the result of which the king on the whole was displeased, an action at law was entered against him, as he had, during his administration of the finances, been suspected of embezzlement and peculation; both of which, together with other humiliations, induced him to leave the court entirely, and retire to private life. About the same time a lascivious girl, *Dina Winhofer*, being in an unbecoming intimacy with Colonel *Walter*, informed the king, that Ulfeldt and his lady had prepared a subtle draught for his Majesty. This, however, being proved false, *Dina*, on the 11th of July, 1651, was publicly beheaded, and Walter banished; but Corfitz Ulfeldt continued to be suspected and disliked, wherefore he, with his wife and four sons, suddenly left Denmark for Holland. King Frederick, highly exasperated at his leaving without permission, deposed him from his dignities and deprived him of his estates of *Hirchholm*. Corfitz Ulfeldt, however, not thinking himself safe in Holland, fled for shelter to Sweden, where queen *Christina*, fondly attached to learned and talented men, received him and his family with every circumstance of honor. But here he became guilty of treason, not alone provoking the Swedish king, *Charles Gustavus X.*, Christina's successor, to war against Denmark, but even aiding him in making inroads into the Danish dominions.

Charles Gustavus X., a nephew of the great Gustavus Adolphus, who, at the abdication of Christina, A. D., 1655. seized the reins of government of Sweden, possessed all the qualities and talents requisite to follow in the footsteps of his uncle, his reign being one succession of hardy enterprises and remarkable exploits. He indulged the martial spirit of his people by declaring war against *Poland;* where *John Casimir*, descended through Sigismund, his father, from the race of Vasa, revived his pretensions to the throne of Sweden, protesting against the nomination of Charles X. Poland was then invaded by Charles; the progress of the Swedes was rapid; they obtained two brilliant victories in the field, captured *Cracow*, the former capital of Poland, and compelled the terrified John Casimir to fly into Silesia. Thereafter the king entered Prussia, where he compelled *Frederick William*, elector of Brandenburg, to acknowledge himself the vassal of Sweden. Meanwhile, John Casimir having returned to Poland, the people rushed to arms, and the country was on the point of being reconquered from the Swedes, when Charles X. led back an army to the assistance of his troops, and fought a terrible battle near *Warsaw*, 1656, which, after having lasted three days, was ultimately decided in favor of the Swedes, and Poland had again to submit. His great success in Poland had already excited the apprehensions of the emperor of Austria, of Holland, and Brandenburg, and rekindled the jealousy of Denmark, which, desirous of profiting by the complicated embarrassments of Sweden, and hoping now easily to regain the lost provinces, declared war against Sweden, although her defensive affairs were in the most miserable condition. But Charles Gustavus, who had fought in Germany under the illustrious Torstenson, soon convinced the Danish king, *Frederick III.*, that he was able to chastise his temerity. Concluding an armistice with Poland, he repaired to Pomerania, and then into the duchy of Bremen, which the Danish army had conquered. Thence he marched with 12,000 men into Jutland, where the Danish commander-in-chief, *Anders Bilde*, defended the fortress of *Fredericia*, which, however, was taken by the Swedish general, *Herman Wrangel*, who was now made Lord High Admiral of Sweden. Charles Gustavus X., with astonishing rapidity, made himself undisputed master of Holstein, Schleswig, and Jutland, the treacherous Ulfeldt, who was minutely acquainted with the interior parts of the country, assisting him with his advice and actual help. But Charles X. could not yet pass over to the small islands, as his fleet, numbering fifty-nine men-of-war, in a horrible engagement with the Danish navy close by the island of *Falster*, was so cut up and crippled as to be obliged to make port to refit, this disadvantage being about

A. D., 1657.

the only one he had in this war, while the prospects of the Danish king had become dark as midnight.

After being defeated at the island of Falster, A.D., 1658. Charles Gustavus, in the month of January, drew up his victorious forces on the shore of the Little Belt, which was completely bridged with ice. The extremely rigorous cold, twenty-four degrees of Reaumur, which had thus fettered the strait, still continuing, and giving no signs of relaxing in severity, *Charles*, having tested the strength of the ice, and measured its thickness, weighed the matter carefully for a short time in his mind, and determined to pass over it with his army. With the king at their head, the Swedish troops, numbering 20,000 men, advanced, in separate columns, accompanied by all their horses, baggage, trains and artillery, combating, even upon the ice, (where two divisions of his dragoons were submerged and drowned,) the detachments of the Danish troops, which bravely endeavored to arrest their advance, and at last, victorious over the enemy and the elements, Charles Gustavus entered the island of *Fyén* (Funen). At the eastern coast of Fyen, separated from the island of *Sjelland* (Zealand) by the Great Belt, the Swedes discovered this water, sixteen English miles wide, likewise entirely frozen. Charles at once determined to attempt the passage, taking, nevertheless, such precautions as prudence demanded. In place of crossing directly from Fyen to Sjelland, where the currents are too rapid to afford sure passage on the ice, he marched his army by a circuitous route between the islands of *Langeland, Falster* and *Lauland,* where the well fortified city of *Nakskov,* imprudently listening to the crafty and subtle demonstrations of the treacherous Ulfeldt, unresistingly surrendered to the Swedish king, whose cards were almost all trumps in this war. Only the Danish Admiral *Bredahl* distinguished himself by heroically and successfully defending the Danish fleet, which was ice-bound in the gulf of *Nyborg*. At length, arrived in the island of Sjelland, the Swedes, to whom the ice and the deep snow presented no obstacles, advanced upon Copenhagen, a prey to the greatest terror, and unprepared for the event of a siege. In fact, so general was the consternation, that, within ten days after the landing of the Swedish army in Sjelland, Frederick III. sent commissioners to the city of *Wordingbórg* to negotiate with Charles Gustavus, whose conditions, however, were too severe to be agreed to by the Danish commissioners. But Charles Gustavus, *tenax propositi*, advanced further towards Copenhagen, and Frederick III. had to offer humiliating proposals of peace, signed by the commissioners at the small village of *Hóie Tostrup*, eight English miles from Copenhagen, and afterwards affirmed and signed by the king himself in the definite treaty subsequently concluded at *Roeskilde,* on the 26th of February,

A. D., 1658. 1658. So humiliating were the conditions for

Denmark, and so glorious for Sweden, that one of the Danish envoys exclaimed, as he affixed his signature, like the usually cruel Roman emperor, Nero, when a warrant for the execution of a criminal was brought to be signed: "Would to Heaven that I had never learned to write." Said peace of Roeskilde was concluded on the following terms: Denmark should give over to Sweden *Skane, Halland, Bleking, Bahus, Trondhjem*, in Norway, and the island of *Bornholm*, in the Baltic; as also deliver twelve men-of-war and two thousand horsemen, and, finally, replace the treacherous Corfitz Ulfeldt in his dignities. Shortly after both monarchs met together, for the first time, with great pomp and ceremony, at a splendid entertainment in the royal palace of Fredericksborg, amusing themselves by friendly conversation, as though living in the best harmony. The base and contemptible Corfitz Ulfeldt was now replaced in his dignities, his estate, *Hirchholm*, restored to him, and his lady, Eleonora Christina, was granted the title of Countess of Schleswig-Holstein.

But to return to Charles Gustavus. Repenting that he had omitted the convenient opportunity of subduing all Denmark and Norway, and pleading that the two thousand horsemen had not been delivered duly equipped, he broke the peace a few months after, landed with his army in Korsór, and advanced upon Copenhagen. But this insincere peace, which proved to be only a suspension of arms, stirred up a new spirit among the

Danish people, now uniting the most enterprising and heroic spirit with the greatest prudence and moderation, and clearly comprehending, that it had come to sad extremities, and that the existence of Denmark and Norway, as independent states, was at stake. In Copenhagen every one prepared himself for the most determined defence; no one spared himself; even the young students of the University took up arms, the king's own example being the most effectual encouragement to the promotion of a courageous defence. Several citizens advised the king to leave the capital, but he answered: "Even if the worst comes to the worst, I will not leave, but die in my nest."

Charles Gustavus X. commenced to lay siege to Copenhagen, and also sent a body of hardy Swedish soldiers to take possession of the important fortress, *Kronborg;* it being of the more consequence, as a strong Dutch fleet was expected to relieve the besieged city of Copenhagen. *Wrangel* was sent to besiege the fortress of Kronborg, which he took from Colonel *Beenfeldt* in less than three weeks' siege, acquiring thereby enormous booty of cannons and powder, which enabled the Swedes to carry on the siege of the Danish capital with yet more energy; Charles Gustavus being so confident of winning the horrible game, as to write to king Frederick III. that his life and liberty lay at the mercy of the Swedes, and that he (Frederick) might easily comprehend that Denmark was undone, and like a patient past recovery.

But king Frederick did not despair; the citizens and students of Copenhagen made several sudden and successful sallies on the enemy; and three patriots, the engineer *Steenwinkel*, the bailiff *Hans Rostgaard*, and the clergyman *Henry Gerner*, hazarded their lives for reconquering Kronborg, which, however, fell short of success, their patriotic design being too early discovered. Steenwinkel was decapitated by the enraged Charles Gustavus, Hans Rostgaard escaped by flight, but the magnanimous minister of the gospel, Henry Gerner, was put on the rack, and asked questions about the plans and operations of the Danish army, which he, nevertheless, obstinately declined revealing.

Under command of the generals *Schack* and *Gyldenlóve*, the chief captain of the city, *Thureson* and the king himself, the citizens of Copenhagen continued to defend the city in the most heroic manner, but began soon to suffer from want of provisions. Meanwhile the Dutch fleet arrived, under Admiral *Opdam*, to the assistance of the Danes, carrying brave soldiers and plenty of victuals. On the 24th of October the fleet came booming through the narrow sound, under a terrible shower of cannon balls from Kronborg, whence the Swedish general, Wrangel, tried to prevent the passage of Opdam and his fleet, but in vain. After having totally defeated Wrangel, Opdam arrived safe in Copenhagen, where the most boundless rejoicing took place. *Te Deums* were sung in all the churches, and fresh spirit and courage quickened every soul.

A.D. 1658.

The siege having lasted half a year without any issue, Charles Gustavus now resolved to take the capital by a general storm and a violent onset, making the most desperate preparations, and promising his troops, if victorious, the plunder of Copenhagen for three days. He ordered his soldiers to put on white shirts, that the besieged might not distinguish them on the snow-covered ground, and bade them not to spare even the child in the mother's womb. The night between the 10th and 11th of February was appointed for that wholesale slaughter, which he had in view. But the result disappointed his expectations. The undaunted *Frederick III.* being informed of the plans of the Swedes by the patriotic *Lorentz Tuxen*, receiver of taxes in Hirchholm, made the most skillful preparations, and his military talents had here, undeniably, the noblest field for their exertion, as his antagonist, Charles Gustavus, was deservedly ranked among the greatest commanders in Europe. In that frightful night king Frederick III. was present himself wheresoever the danger was greatest, and the talent he displayed in bringing the siege of Copenhagen to a happy issue has immortalized his memory, as well as that of its brave citizens. Even the queen, the proud *Sophia Amalia*, arrayed in a military dress, was all the night on horseback, encouraging both the soldiers and citizens to shed the last drop of their blood for king and fatherland.

A.D., 1659

Maddened by the thirst for victory, the Swedish soldiers fought with a bravery almost unheard of; the massacre was dreadful, and the Swedish historian, Lagerbring, says, that Charles Gustavus kept up so constant a discharge of artillery, that had each hundredth ball hit the mark, not a single Dane would have been left. The Danes, excited to frenzy by the agonies their eyes beheld and the lamentations their ears drank in, fought with the most desperate bravery, and after a heroic resistance forced Charles Gustavus to raise the siege of Copenhagen.

For the important services the citizens of Copenhagen had rendered, Frederick III. conferred upon them great prerogatives and privileges, equal to those of the nobility. Few enterprises were ever more deeply weighed than that of Charles Gustavus, few preceded by more immense preparations, and few, perhaps, ever attended with a more unfortunate issue. And here it may not be out of place to use the words of the Spanish writer, Bentivoglio: "So often the Divine Providence, in the wisdom of his impenetrable decrees, has determined the fate of an enterprise quite contrary to the presumptuous expectations of human foresight." Also, in other places did the Swedes suffer great losses. The inhabitants of the island of *Bornholm* drove out the Swedish garrison, and threw off the Swedish yoke. Likewise, from the diocese of *Trondhjem*, Norway, the Swedes were turned out, and the citizens of *Frederikshald*, Norway, bravely defended their town against three different attacks of the Swedes. *Nakskow,* on the island of Laaland, which in the former war so rashly had surrendered, now compensated for it by a heroic and obstinate defence of thirteen weeks; even the small island *Móen,* South of Sjelland, made a valiant resistance. Finally, the confederated troops arrived to the assistance of Denmark; the elector *Frederick Wilhelm,* of Brandenburg, at the head of thirty thousand men, clearing almost the whole peninsula of Jutland from enemies.

Undaunted by all these misfortunes, Charles Gustavus, although finding himself surrounded with mighty enemies, formed a new plan for the destruction of his hated rival, Frederick III. Marching a considerable body of soldiers to the island of Fyen (Funen), where, close by the city of *Nyborg,* a Danish army of ten thousand men was encamped, Charles ordered his general, Count *Steenbuck,* to attack the Danes in their intrenchments. A battle was now inevitable, and both armies prepared for the contest with equal courage. The battle was brief, but fierce, and after a dreadful combat of about four hours' duration, the Swedish army was irretrievably ruined; four thousand of their best troops were left dead on the field, three thousand were taken prisoners, and about two thousand of the fugitives were soon after forced to surrender on the coast, from want of boats to cross the Great Belt. Only General *Steenbuck* escaped by flight. When intelligence of this defeat was conveyed to Charles Gustavus, who tarried in *Korsór* in Sjelland, he laconically exclaimed: "Since the devil has taken away the sheep, he might as well also have taken the buck." Charles Gustavus now repaired to Gothenburg, from whence he made an irruption into Norway, but without avail, only to learn the downfall of all his expectations. Shortly after, he died, in the year 1660, full of grief that his visionary designs had proved unsuccessful; whereafter negotiations for peace were commenced with Sweden, and a treaty was concluded in Copenhagen on the 27th of May, on terms, which, though severe, were more favorable than *Frederick III.*, under the circumstances, could reasonably have hoped. *Sweden* retained *Bahus*, as also the three fertile provinces, *Skane*, *Halland* and *Bleking*, which Denmark never has got again; only *Trondhjem* in Norway, and the island of *Bornholm* were restored to Denmark, the execution of this treaty being guaranteed by Holland, England and France. Thus the bloody war with Sweden terminated, just as Denmark was upon the very brink of her ruin.

A. D., 1660.

FOURTH PERIOD.

FROM THE INTRODUCTION OF THE ABSOLUTE SOVEREIGNTY UNTIL THE YEAR 1852. 1660—1852.

I.

1660—1766.

Frederick III.—The Diet of Copenhagen—The Charter annihilated and Absolute Sovereignty introduced—Kay Lykke—Corfitz Ulfeldt—Eleonora Christina—Dispute with Christian Albrecht of Gottorp—*Christian V.*—Acquisition of Oldenburg and Delmenhorst—War with Sweden and France—Niels Juel—Peace of Lund and Fontainebleau—Griffenfeldt—Ole Rómer—The Peasantry—Oluf Rosenkranz—Masius and Bagger—*Frederick IV.*—War with the Duke of Gottorp—Peace of Travendal—Eleven Years' War with Sweden—Tordenskjold—Peace of Fredericsborg—Hostile Terms with Russia—Hans Egede—Science and the Arts—*Christian VI.*—The Peasantry—Ecclesiastical Affairs—School Affairs—Science and the Arts—The Navy—Count Danneskjold Samsö—*Frederick V.*—Hostile Terms with Russia—Peter III.—Manufactures—Commercial and Financial Affairs—The Peasantry—Science and the Arts.

THE sanguinary struggle ended, a period followed, scarcely to be called a peace, although there was a cessation from open hostilities. Both kingdoms, Denmark and Norway, were in a sadly depressed condition; the scene, that was everywhere presented, was a wide waste of ruin; the countries were sunk in debt, and the soldiers had not received their wages, the commercial affairs were decaying, and the agriculture, of course, neglected. The nobility, enjoying all privileges and prerogatives, would, as usual, be exempted from taxes, although best capable of paying them, and the popular frenzy was inflamed to the highest pitch. To pacify the minds and to find out means to remedy the miserable condition of his kingdoms, King Frederick III. convoked a Diet at Copenhagen on the 8th of September, being called the Revolution of Denmark. A. D., 1660. During the sitting of the Diet the tyranny and unbecoming haughtiness of the aristocracy arose to such a height, that the clergy, the burgher class, and the peasantry, headed by *Hannibal Sehested*, the only nobleman siding with the king, the senator, *Henrik Bjelke*, the honest mayor of Copenhagen, *Nanson*, the learned bishop *Svane*, and pastor *Willadson* of Slagelse, voted for the surrender of sovereignty to the king, and Frederick III., at the close of the Diet, almost without any effort of his own, was thus invested Jan. 10, A. D., 1661. with absolute power, Denmark being now as absolute a monarchy as any other in the world. But it deserves here to be remarked, that the Danish sovereigns have generally exercised their extensive power with great moderation. Nevertheless, this excessive power of the crown, produced, at length, in the year 1849, the liberty of the people, gave rise to a spirit of union, and opened their eyes to the natural rights of mankind.

The sovereignty thus surrendered to the king, a new and solemn contract between the king and the people, called *Law for the King*, and composed by the talented secretary, *Peter Schumacher*, under the following king Nov. 14, ennobled by the name of *Griffenfeldt*, was subscribed to by Frederick III., and declared an inviolable law for both kingdoms, the principal articles of which law were:

A. D. 1665.

1. The king of Denmark and Norway shall indispensably profess the articles of the Lutheran creed, known by the name of the *Confession of Augsburg* (*Confessio Augustana*).

2. The king must neither divide the kingdoms nor separate any province from them, but shall preserve their integrity.

3. The king shall reside in Copenhagen, Denmark.

4. The king is of age at thirteen years old, to contro' all affairs.

5. The throne is hereditary, both in the male and female line, but it being never vacant in the eye of the law, the queen-dowager shall, if the king before his death should not have regulated the guardianship, from the very moment of his death, in conjunction with seven counselors of state, assume the reins of government as long as the young king is in his minority, and take care of his education.

6. The most unlimited power of the government, both in ecclesiastical and secular matters, shall be

lodged in the person of the king, who is above the reach of all courts of law, and not personally responsible to any judicature but the bar of God for his acts and conduct in the administration of government.

It need not be explained how greatly this investment of the king with absolute sovereignty curbed the nobility, whose shameful ignorance, meanness and rebellious spirit had rendered them useless and contemptible both to the king and the nation.

The praiseworthy men, above mentioned, who had mainly raised the king to an absolute sovereignty, obtained the most palpable evidences of his gratitude: *Svane* being given the title of archbishop and extensive real estates; and *Nanson, Hannibal Sehestedt,* and *Willadson* likewise presented with donations and high offices, in reward of their important services. New measures for improving the administration of the state affairs were now taken. The whole frame of government was altered altogether, many affairs, which before had belonged to the senate, being divided amongst various *colleges* (*collegia*), in which, by authority of the king's writ, the burgher class as well as the nobility could be invested with offices. Said colleges were: *the college of state*, intrusted with the administration of foreign affairs and with the care of maintaining the new constitution and the interests of the royal house; *the sacred college*, invested with power to confer the ecclesiastical offices on qualified persons; *the college of justice*, to which pertained the judicial power and the regulation of the police; *the college of treasury*, to administer the finances and the levying of taxes; *the college of war*, to which the army was subject; and *the admiralty college*, having the naval affairs under its direction. But whatsoever the colleges had decided upon, was, for getting legal strength and force, first to be laid before the king himself, and have his signature affixed to it. The legislative power belonged to the king alone, that is, the power of making laws, of abrogating them, or of changing them.

Besides these colleges, the *supreme court* was instituted, which became the highest tribunal, its president being the king himself. Frederick III. now employed all his efforts for introducing a more economical system, and remedying the prevailing scarcity of money, the proud nobility, hitherto exempt from taxes, being declared tributary as well as the peasantry, which considerably contributed to settle the confused financial affairs. There remains to be mentioned, that the code of positive law needed a transformation according to the material alteration the government had undergone, for the performance of which the king appointed a committee, which reviewed the earlier laws and elaborated a new code or collection of laws; which important work was finished in the space of eight years by *Rasmus Winding*, professor of law, and *Peter Lasson*, justiciary of the supreme court, the code itself, however, first being published during the reign of Christian V.

We must now take a brief retrospect of the affairs of the treacherous *Corfitz Ulfeldt*, one of the most extraordinary men that ever appeared on the stage of human life. After the peace was concluded in the year 1660, Ulfeldt had made himself suspected even in Sweden of being a clandestine adherent of Denmark. His property, therefore, being confiscated in Sweden, he fled with wife and children to Copenhagen, just at the time the sovereignty was to be surrendered to the king. Being here at liberty for a short time, he and his wife, through the instrumentality of his sworn enemy, *Hannibal Sehestedt*, were suddenly imprisoned in the castle of Rosenborg, on the 3d of March, 1660, from whence they soon after were brought to the castle of *Hammershus*, on the island of Bornholm, and locked up in a dark, subterranean prison, where *Henry Fuchs*, the lieutenant of the castle, for a time of fifteen months, treated them with such inhumanity and severity that Ulfeldt had to make a very submissive request to the king himself for a mitigation of their severe treatment. Count *Frederick Ranzau* was now sent to Bornholm to inquire into the matter. Ulfeldt and his wife were set at liberty on condition that he would solemnly promise never to undertake anything detrimental to the sovereign power of the king, and never, without permission, to leave the country. They arrived now again in Copenhagen, whence they, on the 27th of December, 1661, went to the island of Fyen, to their beautiful manor

Ellensborg. Some time after, Ulfeldt, upon request, obtained permission to go to *Spaa*, a celebrated watering-place in Belgium, but instead of it, he went with his wife and four sons to Amsterdam, where his lady, the magnanimous and faithful Christina Eleonora, left him for England, in order to claim a large amount of money with which Ulfeldt had supplied Charles II. On taking leave of her, 7th July, 1662, his parting words were as follows: "You have been united with me in love, you have suffered with me in patience, you have shared my hardships with manly perseverance, you have assisted me with kind advices in difficult cases, you have tried to lead my heart unto Him by whom kings reign and princes decree justice; you have loved me even in the utmost miseries. I am now parting with you, but whatsoever might happen, do not forget to adhere to Him who is the ruler of adversities and the strengthener of love." They never more met each other on this side the grave.

After she left, Ulfeldt, whose heart was full of hatred against the Danish king, engaged himself in treacherous negotiations with Holland, France, and Brandenburg, aiming at overthrowing the new constitution of Denmark. But the elector of Brandenburg, *Frederick Wilhelm*, a personal and intimate friend of Frederick III., informed, without delay, the Danish court of Ulfeldt's high treason, who instantly was sentenced to suffer death; but it being impossible to get hold of him, he was decapitated in effigy, his sentence of condemnation being written on the scaffold, his house in Copenhagen pulled down, and a monument of infamy erected on the void place.

No sooner was Ulfeldt informed of the sentence of death pronounced against him in Denmark, than he left Amsterdam and fled, crossing the Rhine to *Brisac*, where he died, aged sixty years, his conscience A.D., being burdened with the memory of crimes of 1664. the deepest dye. His corpse was brought to a cloister near *Neuburg*, in Bavaria, whence his sons brought it, interring it secretly under a tree. He was a man of the greatest talents, a great linguist, an accomplished nobleman, and a sagacious diplomate; but he was headstrong in his passions, imprudent, treacherous, and capricious, and his romantic spirit often led him into the most extravagant excesses. Ulfeldt's wife, the noble-minded *Eleonora Christina*, a splendid example of conjugal love, was by the English government delivered up to Denmark, and sent on board of a ship to Copenhagen, where the queen, *Sophia Amalia*, ordered her maid of honor to strip Eleonora of her clothes, after which she was imprisoned for twenty-three years in *Bluetower*, and all the time treated with every circumstance of severity. This action is the greatest stain upon the memory of the queen, who ought to have respected the unhappy lady for that which was her only offence—a noble faithfulness in sharing the fate of her husband.

Immediately after the death of the queen, the succeeding king released Eleonora from imprisonment, in 1685, presenting her with the palace of *Maribo*, on the island of Laaland, and with an annual allowance of fifteen hundred rixdollars. Here she lived for thirteen years in literary occupations and pious contemplations, until she died on the 16th of May, 1698, aged seventy-seven years. Her biography, composed by herself, she finishes with the following words: "Persecutions followed my husband of blessed memory; I followed him, and afflictions, therefore, followed me: *mais la tristesse donne occasion a la patience*. Death will be acceptable to me; nevertheless I do not wish for it, but agree with the Latin proverb:

> Rebus in adversis facile est contemnere mortem:
> Fortius ille facit qui miser esse potest."

She is buried in Maribo cemetery, the words she herself had wished being engraved on the tombstone: "Unless Thy law had been my delight, I should have perished in mine affliction. *Ps.* cxix. 93."

Although the absolute power, as above mentioned, was generally exercised by Frederick III. and his successors with great moderation, he seems, nevertheless, especially immediately after having obtained this power, to have held the highest notions of his sovereignty, and to have exerted his authority with rigor. A rich and esteemed nobleman, *Kay Lykke*, had in a private letter mentioned the queen in offensive terms. Though humbly imploring mercy and forgiveness for his temerity and inconsiderateness, he was sentenced to suffer death; but having seasonably escaped by flight the capital punishment, he was executed in effigy, his large estates being confiscated in behalf of the crown. *Gunde Rosenkranz*, an accomplished and honest nobleman and senator, having often deserved well of his country, was without mercy banished, only for being at variance with the king's favorite, *Henry Gabel;* and for the unexampled severity shown against the innocent countess, Eleonora Christina Ulfeldt, the king is highly to be blamed.

For the rest, Frederick III. took energetic care for the welfare of his kingdoms, commencing rapidly, during his reign, to emerge from the weakness and enervation into which they had been plunged by the Swedish invasion and subsequent wars. He reformed the laws, and encouraged commerce by establishing trade with Guinea, on the western coast of Africa, and with the West Indies. The king himself, being a man of letters, patronized science and the arts, and established the royal library, one of the greatest in Europe, now containing four hundred thousand volumes, and the university library was considerably enlarged. The fleet, almost entirely disabled in the last war, was excellently fitted up by a Norwegian, *Cort Adler*, who in Venetian service against the Turks, had immortalized himself by the most undaunted courage in many naval engagements. But a most heavy burden on the country was the standing army, which was now augmented to twenty-four thousand men, kept in constant pay; and the king, who, with all his superiority of genius and extensive knowledge, firmly believed in the possibility of the transmutation of metals into gold, wasted not a little of the national revenue in vain on costly alchemical experiments, conducted by Burrhi, an Italian professor of that imaginary science, with which so many of even the superior minds were in that age infatuated.

Frederick III. inherited Oldenburg and Delmenhorst and bought Sónderborg, Nordborg, and the island of Aró, in the Baltic. In the latter part of his reign hostilities were about to break out with Charles II. of England, as an English admiral had attacked a Dutch commercial fleet, which had fled for refuge to a harbor in Norway; A. D., 1667. the conclusion, however, of a peace at *Breda*, in Holland, dissipating the alarm. But soon a serious misunderstanding arose between Frederick and *Christian Albrecht*, duke of Gottorp. The new relation into which the dukes of Gottorp, because of the sovereignty surrendered to the king, had come to Denmark, occasioned frequent collisions; and Christian Albrecht, having made an alliance with Charles XI. of Sweden, was more prone to strife than to submission. The dispute, however, was settled by the *Recess of* A. D., *Glückstadt*, the friendship being confirmed by a 1667. marriage between the duke and the daughter of the king, *Fredericka Amalia*.

Frederick III. died after a remarkable reign A. D., of twenty-two years. Upon the whole, having 1670. distinguished himself by firm principles, manliness, prudence, and judiciousness, he nevertheless often showed, as above mentioned, a blamable severity, mainly, perhaps, to be ascribed to the undue influence his queen, the haughty *Sophie Amalia*, exercised upon him. He is also to be blamed for having surrounded himself too much with German favorites, and neglected the mother tongue to such a degree, that the crown prince for a long while did not understand Danish. Neither was it slightly to his discredit that he nearly all the time lived in prohibited sexual commerce with different concubines.

Christian V. succeeded to the Danish crown A. D, on the death of his father. He commenced his 1670. reign by adopting a policy entirely contrary to that system of equality, which had begun to take place during the reign of Frederick III., the new king being unfavorable, as it will appear, to the people's liberties, but in favor of the higher orders of the state, which now again would have everything at their disposal. The nobility, having been made tributary from compulsion, during the reign of Frederick III., was now, by Christian V., exempted from paying taxes, and not alone restored to their ancient rights and privileges, but several new prerogatives were conferred upon counts and barons, the lower orders of the state being considered only as a part of the property belonging to the real estates. Amongst these prerogatives were:

Right of patronage (jus vocandi), consisting in freedom to confer a vacant pastorate on their estates upon any candidate for orders the nobleman might please to select—a right very often misapplied in the most shameful and conscienceless manner, the nobleman frequently offering a pastorate to a young candidate upon condition that he should marry a woman debauched by the lewd nobleman himself; *right of jurisdiction*, that is, an exclusive privilege of appointing any judge on their estates they might wish—a right, likewise, often misused; *exemption from paying tithes of their manors to the clergy;* and *power of life and death* over their peasants, that is, it was left to the disposition of the nobleman to order a peasant to be scourged and beheaded.

All these shameful privileges granted to these dregs of society were, in fact, the very cause of the subsequent freedom of the Danish nation, which at length, roused out of sleep, shook off the unjust yoke to which they, for centuries, had been subjected.

Christian V. established also a *distinction of ranks and honor*, which he considered an essential benefit to the state, as furnishing a reward for public services and captivating to the ambition of individuals, who thereby might be prompted to distinguish themselves in service of their country; but although undeniably thereby was given an incitement to many to exert themselves laudably, it nevertheless imposed a great burden on the community, a new order thereby being established, invested with new privileges and immunities, not to mention the impure emulation and vanity it produced. He also instituted two new orders of knighthood: the orders of *Dannebrog* and of the *Elephant*, with the latter of which only kings, princes, dukes and noblemen were decorated. Upon the whole, the gay humor of the French, and that spirit of levity and luxury which was prevailing at the court of Louis XIV., was never more conspicuous in Denmark than during the reign of Christian V., who himself loved the lusts of the flesh and the lust of the eyes and the pride of life, but cared not very much for matters relative to salvation.

. The good terms on which Denmark, by the Recess of Glückstadt, had come to Christian Albrecht, duke of Gottorp, commenced now again to be subverted by disputes concerning Oldenburg and Delmenhorst, which the last count, *Anthon Günther*, by his will before his death, had divided between the king of Denmark and the duke of Gottorp; but *Joachim Ernst*, duke of Plóen, in Holstein, believing himself more entitled, laid claims to the said earldoms, and appealed to the emperor's bench. For averting the danger, which was threatening, the wise diplomate, Griffenfeldt, whom Louis XIV. called the world's greatest statesman, negotiated with the duke of Plöen and prevailed upon him to resign his claims, by which means Christian V. decidedly became the master of both earldoms; which exasperated Christian Albrecht to such a degree as to prepare himself to strike a decisive blow against Denmark. But Christian V., by virtue of his authority as sovereign king, cited him to meet in *Rendsburg*, where he was compelled to make an agreement, according to which he had to give up his troops and fortresses to the king, as also to pass his word for refraining from all hostilities. A.D., 1675.

At the same time the arbitrary designs of Louis XIV. had excited universal dissatisfaction, and alliances were formed to resist his designs and successes, which alarmed all Europe. A triple alliance was formed between England, Holland and Sweden, to compel Louis to make peace with Spain, and the union of these powers being too formidable to be opposed, a treaty was signed. But other projects soon occupied the monarch of France, whose designs against the dominions of Spain had been checked by means of the triple alliance. He meditated now the conquest of Holland, and took every measure necessary for so great an enterprise. England and Sweden entered into his views, while the German emperor, *Leopold I.*, and the Elector of Brandenburg,

Frederick Wilhelm, took up arms to protect Holland and rescue it from destruction. *Griffenfeldt* advised the Danish king, Christian V., to maintain a wise neutrality, and keep up good terms with Sweden, which had joined the mighty France.

But from an ardent desire of reconquering the lost provinces in Sweden, *Christian V.*, disposed to war himself, and instigated by the Elector of Brandenburg, declared war against France and Charles XI. of Sweden, whose troops lately had been defeated at *Fehrbellin* in Brandenburg, Denmark thus again being involved in a horrible war. A. D., 1675. The Danish king, not daunted by the power of his enemies, opened the theatre of the war in Germany, although Griffenfeldt advised the king rather to invade Skane, the inhabitants of which were yet in favor of Denmark. After many toilsome tasks, the strong fortress, *Wismar*, was taken, especially by Griffenfeldt's constancy, and *Bremen* and *Werden* were also conquered by the Danish and Brandenburg troops. Next year the war commenced in Skane, and *Christian V.* launched his fleet, now excellently equipped and fitted out, into the Baltic, and during the continuance of this war, the Danish navy rode triumphant, and gained a decided superiority over the Swedish fleet. The great Danish admiral *Niels Juel*, in whom every endowment of nature necessary to form a consummate warrior seems to have been centered, conquered the important island, *Gulland*, and

A. D., co-operating with the Dutch admiral, *Tromp*, he
1676. totally defeated, in a most desperate engagement,
the whole Swedish fleet at the island of *Oeland*, whereby
the king was enabled to carry his army to *Skane*, where
in the beginning, he went on with brilliant success,
conquering the greatest part of Skane and Bleking, and
several strong fortresses.

But fortune soon turned her back upon him. The
Swedish king, Charles XI., endowed with military talent,
as were almost all the kings of the illustrious house of
Vasa, and with an intrepid and enterprising mind, arose
now like a phenix from its ashes, and defended himself
with great ability and success. A Danish army was
A. D., defeated by Charles, at *Halmstad*, and in the
1676. next year two battles were fought near *Lund*
and *Landscrona*, where both kings commanded in per-
A. D., son. The battles were brief, but, for their dura-
1677. tion, the most sanguinary on record; the victory,
towards the last, remained doubtful, when suddenly,
Charles XI., amusing the Danish left wing by a feigned
attack, poured his infantry, in masses, on the centre;
they encountered the bravest resistance, but the Swedish
king, bringing up the cavalry just as the Danish lines
began to waver, broke through them with a headlong
charge, and in a few moments the Danish army was a
helpless mass of confusion.

The result of this brilliant victory was the immediate
conquest of the lost fortresses, except *Christianstad*,

26 *

which for a long time was defended with great heroism by the Danish general, *Von Osten;* who, nevertheless, as his assistant, General Ahrensdorff, neglected his duty altogether, had to surrender that strong fortress to the Swedish king, and every thing now seemed short of success for Denmark. The wise and intelligent Griffenfeldt stood no more by the king's side; he had been removed partly by his own crimes, partly by secret intrigues of his enemies, the king now trusting only in his inefficient German favorites, *Hahn*, *Ahlefeldt*, and *Ahrensdorff*, who assisted him in his immoral dissipations and irregular course of life.

Notwithstanding all looking very dark for Denmark, Christian V. attempted to retrieve his losses in a new campaign, and sent his half brother, *Ulrik Frederick Güldenlóve*, a natural son of Frederick III., to Norway, which had been attacked by the Swedes. Güldenlóve acquitted himself bravely and with success, soon after conquered Jemteland, made his way through Bahus and Halland, and took by storm the strong rocky fortress, *Carlsteen*, situated by the Cattegat, while at the same time the brave General *Lóvenhjelm* entirely defeated a superior Swedish army at *Uddevalle*, in the province of Bahus. The rays of the sun seemed again to smile on Denmark, her navy continuing to ride triumphant wheresoever she came in engagement. The celebrated Niels Juel gained a new victory over the Swedes at *Kolberg Rhed*, close by the island of Femern, and a

A. D., month after, he immortalized his name by en-
1677. tirely destroying the Swedish fleet in the bay of *Kjóge*, by Sjelland. The latter, numbering forty-six men-of-war, attacked the Danish fleet, moored in a formidable position in the bay, but, after a desperate contest, every Swedish ship that had a share in the engagement was taken or destroyed, the Swedes being humbled considerably by this loss.

A. D., In the meantime, conferences taking place at
1678. *Nimvegen*, and peace with France being made, Denmark also had to consent to peace with Sweden, in
A. D., *Lund*, and the same year with France, at *Fon-*
1679. *tainebleau*. On account of the interference of France, who would not permit her ally, Sweden, to suffer any loss, Denmark got nothing for all her great victories at sea, but had even to promise to replace the rebellious Christian Albrecht of Gottorp in his former rights. The good footing between the two neighboring kingdoms now seemed to be firmly established, Charles V. marrying *Ulrikka Eleonora*, a sister of the Danish king. After the restoration of peace, the king of Sweden tried to make himself as absolute as the kings of Denmark, but he died prematurely, leaving his crown to his son, *Charles XII.*, who has deservedly been styled the Alexander of the North, and who rivaled the fame of the most celebrated conquerors of antiquity.

We shall now dwell a little on the fortunes and fate of the chief minister of Christian V., the great *Peter*

Griffenfeldt, whose Christian name was *Schumacker.* His father was a wine merchant in Copenhagen. His education commenced in the house of bishop Brockman, where king Frederick III. saw him, bestowed his favor upon him, and, perceiving him to be a young man possessed of a very considerable share of learning, and of uncommon acuteness of understanding, permitted him, at royal expense, to visit foreign universities. Upon his return he was ennobled by Christian V., decorated with the order of the Elephant, and made lord high chancellor. Even the German emperor, Leopold I., conferred upon him the title of landgrave.

But there are never wanting those who are envious and jealous. His success procured him powerful enemies, who tried to get rid of him, and cast an aspersion upon his honor in the eyes of the king, who was weak and of a changeable mind. Güldenlóve, half-brother of the king, bore an inveterate hatred against Griffenfeldt, because the latter had tried to counteract the detrimental influence Güldenlóve exercised on the king's morality. Another dangerous enemy was *John Adolph,* duke of Plóen, whose daughter he had refused to marry; *Ahlefeldt, Hahn, Knuth,* and other German favorites, also tried to undermine Griffenfeldt, in hope of profiting by his declension from greatness; and the king himself appears not to have seen through the ungenerous policy of these crafty knaves, who were possessed of neither abilities nor virtue. Griffenfeldt was suddenly impris-

A.D., oned, charged with leze majesty and simony, 1676. and also with using abusive language against the king himself, the following words being found in his diary: "To-day the king has spoken as a child in the council of state;" a circumstance which contributed in no slight degree to heighten the king's animosity against Griffenfeldt. He was sentenced to suffer death, and his property to be confiscated; a sentence, however, which three members of the Supreme Court deemed so iniquitous that they refused to subscribe to it. But only the minority of the court being in his favor, the king said, "Justice will take its course," and signed the warrant for the execution of the great statesman. A high scaffold was erected, but just as the executioner was about to strike the mortal blow, voices were heard on the staircase, crying "Pardon, in the name of his Majesty!" Griffenfeldt, on hearing that the sentence of death was commuted to imprisonment for life, cried, "This mercy is more cruel than the capital punishment." Then he was brought to the citadel of Copenhagen, where he was imprisoned for four years, whence he was sent to a prison on the island of *Munkholm*, in Drontheim Fjord, Norway, where he was kept for eighteen years, (1679–1698), and treated there all the time with the utmost degree of barbarous cruelty. He was set at liberty only a few months before his death, and died in Jutland, on *Steensballe*, a beautiful manor belonging to his son-in-law, baron *Krag*, with whom he passed the last days of his wretched and toilsome life. From his early youth he distinguished himself by remarkable talents; he spoke almost all modern languages, and even in his fourteenth year he wrote Latin with Ciceronian perfection; as a statesman he has never been surpassed. Louis XIV., of France, looked upon him as a genius of the highest order, and he undeniably wielded the diplomatic sceptre with a discrimination which no doubt saved Denmark and Norway from being involved in one common ruin. After his fall, the want of his rare talents was often deeply felt, the king himself saying, "Griffenfeldt alone better understood the welfare of my states than all my other counsellors together." His administration was vigorous and useful, but his haughtiness and imprudence gave great offence to the Danish nobles, and was mainly the cause of the conspiracy being formed against him, of which Güldenlóve, above mentioned, was the principal instigator; and it is not to be denied that he wanted that prudence which should have taught him rather to yield to the necessity of the times, than, by obstinately maintaining his power, to risk an entire deprivation of it.

According to the pacification of Lund, Christian Albrecht was as we have seen to be replaced in his former rights, but new disputes arising, Christian V. marched his army into Schleswig, when, by the interference of other realms, the treaty of *Altona* was brought about; agreeably to which the

A. D., 1679.

A. D., 1689

rudely treated duke was allowed to return to his dukedom from Hamburg, where for several years he had lived a retired life. Upon his death his son *Frederick*, married to *Hedevig Sophia*, a sister to Sweden's warlike king, Charles XII., succeeded to the rule of the duchy, and relying upon his affinity to the king of Sweden, he picked a new quarrel with Denmark, which shortly after the death of Christian V. created a most dangerous war. [A.D. 1694.]

Like many of his predecessors, Christian V. had earnest controversies with Hamburg, which were composed, however, by an agreement of *Pinneberg*, Hamburg obliging herself to pay Denmark two hundred and twenty thousand rixdollars. The mighty Hanse Confederacy now gradually declined, and this league, once so extensive as to preserve a monopoly of the Baltic trade, was now forced to share it with the merchants of England, Holland, Sweden, and Denmark, and included, in the seventeenth century, only the cities of Hamburg, Lübeck, and Bremen.

In many branches of the internal administration of Denmark and Norway, important improvements were made during the reign of Christian V. The new code, published in 1683, by name of *Christian V.'s Danish Law*, has been before mentioned. The celebrated mathematician, *Ole Römer*, acquired great fame throughout Europe, by his ingenious astronomical instruments, and by discovering the swiftness of the emanation of light from the sun, from whence the most important conclusions have been deduced. He also composed a new *terrier*, which became the basis of a more exact taxation of the lands of private persons. The navy and admiralty were excellently administered by *Span* and *Janus Juel*, a brother of the great admiral, and at the close of the Swedish war the Danish fleet numbered forty-eight men-of-war, duly equipped and fitted out.

The able statesman, *Sigfried Pless*, regulated skillfully the financial affairs, which had fallen into great disorder during the war with Sweden. Nevertheless, at the death of Christian V., Denmark had run into a debt of one million of rixdollars, mainly to be ascribed to the king's military enterprises, which had been attended with a prodigious waste of treasure. To improve *trade* and *manufactures*, a *College of Commerce* was established, the East India Company was renewed, and commercial houses erected for Iceland, the Faroe isles, and Greenland. The trade with the West Indies was enlarged by acquiring the two islands of *St. Thomas* and *St. John;* and, on the whole, the Danish commerce was vigorously promoted in the latter part of the reign of Christian V., while most other maritime powers of Europe were entangled in wars. Fairs, or great markets, were held at stated times, to which traders resorted from different quarters, and interchanged their several products or manufactures. This trade, however, being

A. D. 1691. exposed to much trouble from the privateers of the belligerent nations, Denmark made an alliance with Sweden, for the mutual protection of their commerce. For defence the old fortresses were refitted and some new ones founded; amongst others, the fortress of *Christiansö*, near the island of Bornholm. The police and the fire-companies were better regulated, and Copenhagen was beautified by laying out new streets and by the erection of the splendid palaces, *Charlottenborg* and *Amaliénborg*. Uniform measures and weights were fully introduced, the common roads measured, and the means of conveyance bettered.

But the peasantry and agriculture, during the reign of Christian V., were in a most lamentable condition, the country not producing sufficient to satisfy her own necessities. The peasants were compelled to serve without wages, whenever the noblemen thought it proper to send for them, their own work often thereby being neglected. The overweening self-confidence and pride of the nobles disdained any co-operation with the lower orders; the nobles filled the highest offices in the state; they appointed judges in their domains for the cognizance of certain civil causes, and exercised an unlimited criminal jurisdiction over their peasants, on whom they occasionally inflicted even capital punishment. The nobility were also exempt from taxation, except in case of war, nor could they be imprisoned, though their estates might be sequestered for debt. The peasants were in perfect bondage to their masters, who, when displeased with them, could, without any judicial inquiry, fetter them, and send them for one year to the house of correction. The whole was a system of oppression, and exerted a fatal influence on the character of society in general, the great mass of the population, under the thraldom of this system, sinking into the deepest ignorance.

Nevertheless, while inhumanity and oppression held undisputed sway, the sentiment of independence, and the feelings of personal consequence and dignity, were fermenting in the mass of the people, and at length let in those first rays of light, which dispelled barbarism, and introduced that liberty of which the Danish nation, since the year 1849, can rightfully boast.

Science and the arts were not patronized by Christian V., who himself had no relish at all for them, whereas some private men protected literature and took care of its cultivators. *Ole Borch* erected a spacious building, called the *Collegium Mediceum*, appropriated to the use of sixteen indigent students, and *George Ehlers*, a like edifice, called *Collegium Ehlertii*, both of them bequeathing rich legacies to the students. But the liberty of the press was under the severest control, censors being appointed and empowered to examine all manuscripts before they were printed, and to see that they did not contain anything offensive to the king's absolute power, every expression containing the least opposition to the sovereignty being looked suspiciously upon, and at times severely punished. A learned nobleman, *Oluf Rosenkranz*, published a small book entitled, " Defence of the Danish Nobility," which historical work caused a law suit against him, and by the supreme court he was sentenced to be deposed from his office, to recant, and his fief to be confiscated, all of which was executed except the forfeiture of the fief, which was commuted for a penalty of twenty thousand rixdollars. A like instance did appear in a literary controversy between *Masius*, court-chaplain of Copenhagen, and the great philosopher, *Thomasius*, of Halle, Germany: Masius having explained, that the king's absolute power originated immediately from God, while Thomasius insisted that it was originally yielded to the king by the people. This work of Thomasius was publicly burnt by the executioner.

In reference to religious matters a mean intolerance prevailed. The celebrated edict of Nantes, 1598, had, as we know, been issued by Henry IV., of France, giving the Huguenots (Protestants) liberty of conscience, and had been confirmed by Louis XIII., under certain restrictions with regard to public worship. But Louis XIV., by a display of ferocious bigotry, revoked the edict, and nearly four hundred thousand of the Huguenots abandoned their country, some of whom solicited the Danish king, Christian V., for permission to settle in Denmark. The Huguenots being of the Reformed

Church, were, however, by the bigoted interposition of Bishop *Bagger*, and the court chaplain, *Masius*, not granted their request, but had to remove into other lands, Denmark thus losing many subjects of wealth, commercial intelligence, and manufacturing industry. Nevertheless, some time after, the queen, *Charlotte Amalia*, belonging herself to the Reformed Church, interceded for them with the king, and procured them permission to settle in Copenhagen, and a Reformed church was erected, the queen herself paying two clergymen, a Frenchman and a German, a yearly salary, and at her death bequeathing a considerable sum of money to the congregation. But not many availed themselves of this permission, and those who arrived in Copenhagen were oppressed in different ways. Christian V. was married to Charlotte Amalia, a daughter of Landegrave Wilhelm IV., of Hesse Cassel, an intelligent, pious, and virtuous queen, exercising, however, only a little influence upon the king, who lived in open concubinage with a lascivious girl, *Sophia Amalia Moth*, whom he exalted to be Countess of *Samsó*, and by whom he begot several spurious children. After a reign of twenty-nine years, Christian V. died, leaving his kingdom greatly indebted, and a court highly corrupted in morals. The German language got a greater ascendency over the mother tongue than ever before; German was the court language, and Germans filled the highest offices in the state.

A. D., 1698.

A. D., 1699.

After the death of Christian V., the sceptre passed to the hands of his son, *Frederick IV.*, who, notwithstanding the rudeness and imperfection of his education, very soon exhibited proofs of that genius, frugality, and assiduity by which he became one of Denmark's most able and excellent kings. The first object of his attention was how to manage the rebellious duke, Frederick of Gottorp, who, relying on his affinity to Charles XII., of Sweden, defied Denmark in every way, made alliance with Hanover, erected fortifications, and carried Swedish troops into the country. To compel the duke to submit, Frederick IV. entered into a secret alliance against Sweden with *Peter the Great*, of Russia, and *Augustus*, elector of Saxony, who had succeeded John Sobiesky on the throne of Poland, marched an army to the duchy of Schleswig, and commenced to lay siege to the fortress of *Tonningen*, and it was not doubted, that the duke and Sweden both would fall victims to so formidable an alliance. But the progress of the Danes was slower than they expected, the duke being supported by Swedish and Hanoverian troops, and, in the midst of his career, the Danish king was arrested in his operations by intelligence of the dangers which menaced his own capital, which was just now on the point of being taken. The young king of Sweden, Charles XII., only eighteen years of age, soon unveiling his admirable military talents, and undaunted by the power of the league, resolved to carry the war into the dominions of Denmark, and landed immediately upon the island of Sjelland, on which Copenhagen is situated, while his fleet, strengthened by a Dutch and English squadron of ships, which William III., king of England and stadtholder of Holland had sent, bombarded Copenhagen. Frederick IV., cut off from his dominions by the Swedish cruisers, and alarmed by the imminent danger of his navy and beautiful capital, thought himself happy to save his kingdom by indemnifying the Duke of Gottorp, and purchasing a peace at *Travendal*, highly honorable to the Swedes, and left his Russian and Polish allies, who had not duly assisted him, to continue the contest with Charles XII., the young Alexander of the North, who for a long time did not permit them to enjoy a moment of ease or relaxation. The terms of peace were: Denmark should acknowledge the Duke's sovereignty in his dukedom, and his right to erect fortresses, keep troops, and make alliances with foreign powers, and pay him two hundred and sixty thousand rixdollars, to defray the charges of the war. But two years after the peace of Travendal, duke Frederick of Gottorp, who fought for his brother-in-law, Charles XII., fell in the battle of *Clissaw*, in Poland, and the duchess-dowager governed the dukedom in the minority of her son, Charles Frederick, when events soon now came to pass, unexpectedly deciding the long contests between the dukes

A. D., 1700.

A. D., 1702.

of Gottorp and the kings of Denmark. After having humbled Denmark, and already, at the age of eighteen, rendered his name the terror of the North, and the admiration of Europe, Charles XII. resolved to turn his arms against the Russians, whom the heroic king of Sweden totally defeated at *Narva*, after a contest of three hours' duration, all the artillery, baggage, and ammunition of the Russians becoming the prey of the Swedes.

Having wintered at Narva, Charles XII. marched against the Poles and Saxons, and formed the project of dethroning king Augustus, and placing another upon the throne. His designs were seconded by the miserable state of Poland, and by the dissatisfaction of the Poles with their king, Augustus, from the undisguised preference which he showed for his Saxon subjects; and to add to this, the primate of Poland, *Radzrewisky*, secretly meditated a revolution, and entered immediately into the views of the king of Sweden, who, without difficulty, made himself master of Warsaw, in July, 1702. Augustus, convinced that he could only protect his crown by the sword, led his army to meet the Swedes at *Clissaw*, above mentioned, where he, however, was forced to fly, after having made in vain the most heroic efforts to rally his troops.

A second triumph at *Pultusk* gave such encouragement to the enemies of Augustus, that in the year 1704 the throne of Poland was declared vacant, which Charles

XII. now gave to *Stanislaus Leczinski*, a young nobleman of Posnania; and when the Poles hesitated a little on account of his youth, Charles XII. said: "If I am not mistaken, he is as old as I am." Then the king of Sweden turned his arms against Peter the Great of Russia, who was making some ineffectual efforts to revive the party of Augustus, and at the head of forty-five thousand men he entered Lithuania, and carried everything before him, defeating an army of twenty thousand Russians, strongly intrenched.

Intoxicated by success, he rejected the Czar's offers of peace, bluntly declaring that he would negotiate with the Czar in his capital of Moscow. When Peter the Great was informed of this haughty answer, he coolly replied: "My brother Charles affects to play the part of Alexander, but I hope he will not find in me a Darius." Peter prevented the advance of the Swedes, on the direct line, by breaking up the roads and wasting the country, and Charles XII., after crossing the Dnieper, and enduring great privations in the midst of a hostile and almost desolate country, and in the midst of one of the severest winters ever known in Europe, found it impracticable to continue his march to Moscow.

Nevertheless, undaunted by these obstacles, he adopted the extraordinary resolution of passing into the Ukraine, and laying siege to *Pultowa*, a fortified city on the frontier. Leaving some thousand men to guard the works, Charles ordered his soldiers to march and meet

A. D. 1709. the Russians, who were advancing to raise the siege. On the 8th of July, a desperate contest took place, but after a dreadful combat of two hours the Swedish army was irretrievably ruined, and Charles XII., who thus in one day had lost the fruits of nearly nine years of successful warfare, had to escape as a helpless fugitive with three hundred horsemen to *Bender*, a Turkish town in Bessarabia, abandoning all his treasures to his rival, Peter the Great, whom he now had taught how to conquer him.

Under these circumstances, Denmark thought it a proper opportunity to regain the lost provinces of Skane, Halland, and Bleking, and king Frederic IV., after a short interview with Augustus in Dresden, entered into a league with Poland, Saxony, and Russia against Sweden. The Danish monarch invaded Skane, but his troops were in the beginning of the following year defeated by the Swedish army, principally consisting of young boys, commanded by the brave General *Steenbuck*. This victory again quickening the Swedes, was

A. D., 1710. won close by *Helsingborg*, over against Elsenore, and transported Charles XII. to such a degree, that when intelligence of it was conveyed to him in his exile he exclaimed, "My brave Swedes! should God permit me to join you once more, we will beat them all!" Then the war was carried over to Germany, where the Danes conquered the two counties, Bremen and Werden, together with other Swedish possessions, while the fortresses, Stettin and Stralsund, in Swedish Pomerania, were besieged in vain; and next year the Swedes, under General Steenbuck, gained a brilliant victory over the united forces of the Danes and Saxons, at *Gadebusch*, in the duchy of Mecklenburg. A.D., 1712. Not able, however, to master the troops of the allied powers, Steenbuck had to retire to the fortress of *Tónning*, in Schleswig, but on the way thither he sullied his fame by burning the defenceless city of Altona, an outrage which excited the indignation not only of the king of Denmark, but of all Europe.

Although the government of Gottorp had engaged itself to maintain a strong neutrality, Steenbuck, nevertheless, was received into Tónning. In retaliation, Frederick IV. immediately took possession of the Gottorp part of the duchy of Schleswig. The burning of Altona, however, was the last service that the cruel general could perform for his exiled master; unable to prevent the junction of the Russians with the Danes and Saxons, he retreated before superior numbers, and the brave king Frederick IV., of Denmark, pursued his advantages so vigorously, that Steenbuck, at Tónningen, was forced to yield himself a prisoner of war to the Danish king in person, who carried him to Copenhagen, where he died in captivity in the citadel. A.D. 1713.

The Danish fleet, commanded by the illustrious heroes, *Gabel, Sehested, Raben,* and *Tordenskjold,* rode triumphantly throughout nearly the whole of this war. Gabel annihilated a Swedish fleet in Femern Sound, and Sehested and Raben discomfited, off the island of Rügen. another Swedish fleet, which had to retire to the harbor of Carlscrona to refit. The commander, *Hvitfeldt,* has left behind him a never-dying remembrance in the mind of the Danish nation by heroically sacrificing his life in the desperate battle in the bay of Kjóge. Dannebrog, the admiral ship, on which he was, had taken fire. Hvitfeldt could have saved his life, but in fear of thereby setting the whole Danish fleet on fire, he resolved heroically to sustain the whole fury of the assault, till he, with three hundred men, was blown up. The young Norwegian, *Peter Vessel,* so distinguished himself by heroic exploits, that he from a low office rose to the dignity of an admiral, and was ennobled by the name of *Tordenskjold* (thundershield). On receiving this honor, he exclaimed: " Tordenskjold! A beautiful name, your Majesty; and I promise to thunder so in the ears of the Swedes, that your Majesty shall not have to say that you have given me that name in vain."

A. D., 1714.

The Swedish monarch continued to linger in Turkey until the end of 1714; but when he then learned that the Swedish senate intended to make his sister regent in his absence, and to make peace with Russia and Denmark, his indignation induced him to return home.

He traversed Germany *incognito*, and toward the close of the year reached *Stralsund*, the capital of Swedish Pomerania, which was besieged by the united armies of the Prussians, Danes, and Saxons. After an obstinate defence, in which Charles XII. displayed all his accustomed bravery, Stralsund was compelled to capitulate after a siege of two months, while at the same time the Danish and Russian fleets swept the Baltic and threatened Stockholm.

A firmer alliance was now concluded between Denmark, Saxony, and Russia, which also soon after was joined by Prussia and Hanover, the elector of which had ascended the throne of England under the name of *George I*. Stralsund having surrendered, Charles escaped in a small boat to his native shores, and now prepared himself to pass over the ice and make an irruption into Sjelland, from which he, however, was prevented by an unexpected thaw. All Europe believed Charles XII. undone, when, to the inexpressible astonishment of every one, it was announced that he, whose anger with Denmark was now wound up to the highest pitch, had declared war against Denmark, and invaded Norway. But his army was soon driven back, greatly diminished in numbers. *Anna Colbjörnsen*, a clergyman's wife, a patriotic, fearless woman, led astray by cunning pretences the Swedish colonel, *Löwen*, so that he desisted from his plans to destroy the silver mines of Kongsberg.

Charles XII. now laid siege to the city of *Fredericks-*
A.D., *hald*, a maritime town of Norway, near the Skag-
1716. gerack, defended by the strong fortress of *Frede-
ricksteen*, but the two brothers, *John* and *Peter Colbjórnsen*, prevailed on the inhabitants to fire the city, to
prevent the Swedes from having any hold there. A
bloody battle ensued; Charles galled the Danes and
Norwegians with a continual fire; the slaughter was
equal on both sides, till at last, however, the Danes
claimed the victory. Crowds of hungry wolves, issuing
in the midst of the severe winter from the Norwegian
forests, howled over the dying remains of the Swedish
soldiers. Charles XII. was driven to seek a temporary
refuge for his army in the country.

In the meantime, the vigilant Danish admiral, *Tor-
denksjold*, with a daring hardly ever heard of, running
a Danish fleet into the harbor of *Dynekiel*, and, after a
desperate contest of a few hours, destroying the Swedish
men-of-war and store-ships, Charles XII. was compelled,
for this time, to leave Norway. But no way yet intimidated by his misfortunes, and still determined upon
taking Denmark, he commanded his mariners to seize
every Danish vessel, even if the king of Denmark himself might be on board. Frederick IV. now launched
into the Baltic a mighty fleet, commanded by Tordenskjold, who acquired great fame for his courage and
strategic skill in conquering *Marstrand*, and the strong
rocky fortress, *Carlsteen*, although meeting with the

most terrible fire from the Swedish batteries. While Charles XII. had been taken up with his attempts at conquering Norway, Frederick IV. and Peter the Great of Russia prepared themselves to march an army to Sweden, Peter himself arriving in Copenhagen with a fleet, and disembarking a powerful Russian army on the shores of Sjelland, seemingly in assistance of the Danes. But soon learning that the cunning Czar, who, under the mask of friendship, requested the keys to the four gates of Copenhagen, intended to seize upon the Danish capital and the fortress of Kronborg, the necessary preparations were made to oppose this treacherous plan, Peter the Great being suddenly compelled to leave Sjelland. Then secret negotiations commenced between Russia and Sweden, conducted by the Swedish prime minister, Baron de *Görtz*, a native of Franconia, a man of an artful, active, and comprehensive genius, whose plan was to unite the king of Sweden and the Russian Czar in strict amity, who then not only would dictate laws to Europe, but wrest the kingdom of Norway from Denmark, and force the Danish king to renounce the duchies of Schleswig and Holstein to the Duke of Gottorp. The Czar readily joined in the scheme, and a dark storm was gathering for Denmark, when the sudden death of Charles XII. rendered abortive a plan that might have thrown Denmark, and perhaps all Europe, into a state of political combustion.

Charles XII., in the prosecution of his views against

Norway, a second time invested the castle of Frederickshald, in the very depth of winter, but while engaged in viewing the works, and in conversation with his engineer, in the midst of a tremendous fire from the enemy,

A. D., 1718. he was struck dead by a ball from the Danish batteries. His sister, *Ulrikka Eleonora*, succeeded to the throne, and raised to it her husband, *Frederick of Hesse Cassel*, who first had to swear, that he never would attempt the re-establishment of absolute power, which was now fully abolished in Sweden, and a new form of government modeled.

The Swedish senate showed little grief for the loss of this warlike king, who had only involved Sweden in miseries and wars. Upon the intelligence of the death of Gustavus Adolphus at Lützen, 1632, the inhabitants of Stockholm shed tears; upon that of Charles XII. they jubilated. Some have believed, that he was not struck by a cannon ball from the Danish artillery, but was shot by a traitor, a Swedish Colonel *Secker*, which, however, has never been proved. Be it as it may, the kingdom of Sweden gained by his death.

On the first news of the king's death, his favorite minister, Baron *Görtz*, was arrested, brought to trial for having projected a dangerous war when the Swedish nation was exhausted and ruined, and was publicly beheaded in Stockholm. The death of Charles XII. was a great relief to Denmark, and when Tordenskjold, the very first who conveyed the intelligence of it, entered the king's audience chamber, saying, "Charles XII. is dead, and there is not one Swede in the whole of Norway," Frederick IV. embraced him joyfully, and hung a gold chain round his neck.

The new government of Sweden now looked with an ardent desire for peace with Denmark, which was established by the treaty of *Fredericksborg*, the terms of which were, that Sweden should pay Denmark six hundred thousand rixdollars to defray the charges of the war, and acknowledge the sale of Bremen and Verden, which, with their dependencies, George I., king of England and elector of Hanover, had purchased from Denmark for eight hundred thousand rixdollars; Sweden should renounce her exemption from paying Sound Dues, which she had enjoyed since the peace of Brömsebro, 1645; and finally Sweden pledged herself not to assist any more the Duke of Gottorp; France and England securing to Denmark the permanent possession of the duchy of Schleswig. So happy an issue for Denmark had this eleven years' war, though no accession of territory was gained.

A.D., 1720.

The appearance of an English fleet in the Baltic, coming to aid Sweden, finally disposed Czar Peter to measures, and he consented to grant peace in a town of Finland, 1721, on condition of being to retain Esthonia, Livonia, Ingria, part of and dominion over the Gulf of Finland, a high- commerce to the Baltic ocean.

The war thus being ended between Denmark and Sweden, a profound peace ensued. Denmark, however, had soon after to empty a bitter cup. The patriotic, brave, and magnanimous Tordenskjold, who had raised his fatherland by many victories to a great height of naval glory and greatness, and was almost adored by the king and the people, asked permission to go abroad. In Hamburg he met with a Swedish colonel, *Stahl*, a mean-spirited scoundrel, who tried to impose upon a young rich Danish nobleman, by name of *Lehn*, who accompanied Tordenskjold. Exasperated at such conduct, and exchanging high words with Stahl, who called the admiral a vulgar sailor, Tordenskjold gave him a sound beating, and knocked him down in the kennel, after which he left Hamburg for Hanover. A few weeks after, he unfortunately met here again with Stahl, who, bringing the old quarrel again upon the carpet, challenged Tordenskjold to answer for his offence by a duel with rapiers, in using which Stahl was a great master. Tordenskjold of course, answering the challenge in the affirmative, appeared the next morning at the appointed place, close by *Hildesheim.* The two first thrusts he parried, but then Stahl ran his sword under Tordenskjold's right arm, pulling it back in tierce. Tordenskjold, perceiving his death inevitable, calmly disposed himself to meet it with decency, and covering his wound with his handkerchief, resigned himself to his fate. As he expired from the loss of blood, he exclaimed: "God be merciful to me for the sake of my Redeemer." On hearing this sad event, king Frederic IV. shed tears, and ordered the corpse to be brought to Copenhagen and buried in the mariner's church, where Tordenskjold now rests in the same vault with *Otto Rud, Niels Juel, Cort Adeler, Raben, Sehested* and *Gabel*, who all so often had led the blood-red Danish flag from victory to victory on the Baltic ocean, the dark heaving wave.

Nov. 20, A. D., 1720.

By the peace of Fredericksborg, the duchy of Schleswig was once more reunited to the kingdom; but for the many centuries through which the counts of Holstein and the German-minded dukes of Gottorp had swayed the sceptre, the Danish nationality had had a difficult fight to wage. In the southern part of Schleswig the German language at length prevailed, while in the northern part the inhabitants were attached to their native tongue, and to the manners and habits inherited from their forefathers, although the dukes of Gottorp, by appointing German clergymen and introducing German schoolmasters and German legal procedure, sought to naturalize the German language, even in this part of the dukedom.

Notwithstanding Schleswig was now reunited to the kingdom and for all subsequent time governed by the Danish kings, that unnatural state of language, however, continued for more than one century, and first in modern times energetic regulations have been issued to

protect the Danish nationality in the northern part of Schleswig. But the reunion of Schleswig to the kingdom put Denmark, throughout a long series of years, to very much trouble and heavy expenses. The duke of Gottorp, *Charles Frederick*, making now the city of *Kiel* his residence, would neither subscribe to the resignation of Schleswig, nor come to any amicable agreement, and became a very dangerous enemy by marrying the Russian princess *Anna*, a daughter of Peter the Great. Frederick IV. had continually to keep fleets ready in the Baltic to secure Denmark against Russia, as Peter the Great, and his successor, the empress Catharina I., threatened to establish by force the claims of the duke. Certainly amicable terms were afterwards contracted with the court of St. Petersburg, but in course of time the strife was renewed in such a manner as to be very dangerous for Denmark. Frederick IV.
A. D. 1725. gained an accession of territory for the kingdom by laying hold on the fertile county of *Ranzau*, as the latter count had been killed, and his younger brother, on being brought to trial, found an accomplice in this crime.

During his whole reign, Frederick IV. was actuated by sincere and earnest motives to introduce useful institutions and remedy old mistakes. He deserved well of the Danish peasantry, by abrogating their slavish dependence on their masters. He enacted a law, that all peasants born after his accession to the throne should be free; concerning the others it was determined that they, on reasonable terms, could buy their freedom; the tenants should be permitted to keep their farms for life, and neither could they involuntarily be deprived of them, nor be forced, as before, to accept of desolate and barren farms; and on the whole this law contained very considerable mitigations of those feudal rights claimed by the noblemen over their peasants, which either were the most burdensome in their own nature, or had been made so by an abusive extension.

Already during the first war which Frederick IV. waged, his attention had been directed to several deficiencies in the military affairs, which he immediately tried to remedy; and after the treaty of peace (1700), he employed the interval of tranquillity in raising a militia of eighteen thousand men, in equipping a respectable fleet, and upon the whole, in paying close attention to the posture of defence. Besides this militia, there was kept a considerable army of levied soldiers; the cavalry was augmented by twelve regiments, each consisting of eight companies. He established two cadet schools in Copenhagen, to educate young men both for the fleet and the army; schools never organized before, and the want of which had been deeply felt. In order to protect the capital and the navy against the renewal of the dangers to which they had been exposed, when, in the year 1700, a Swedish, Dutch, and English fleet bombarded Copenhagen, he erected two sea-batteries, *Tre Kroner* (three crowns), and *Próvestenen* (touchstone). The navy was put in a good posture, and the number of marines was considerably increased. To augment the revenues of the kingdom, Frederick IV. had supplied Austria, England, and Holland, with twenty thousand men, who acquitted themselves with great courage in the war of the Spanish succession. Under the illustrious heroes, prince *Eugene*, of Savoy, and the duke of *Marlborough*, commander-in-chief of the forces of England, the Danish soldiers had shared the glory of the battles of *Hochstedt*, *Ramillies*, *Oudenarde*, and *Malplaquet*; and the Duke of Marlborough, upon whom now the emperor of Austria had conferred the dignity of a prince of the empire, wrote to king Frederick IV., that for the gaining of the victory in those celebrated battles he was mainly indebted to the lion-hearted bravery of the Danes, who likewise, under the great Eugene, fought gallantly in Hungary against the Turks.

Frederick IV. made many improvements in the regulation of the different colleges, and caused justice to be duly and quickly administered, and the laws carried into execution. He was very active himself, and sought to acquire a knowledge of all matters of consequence. To the administration of the finances he paid a strict attention, and kept the pecuniary affairs in an exemplary order. As economical as the king was in spending the public means, as particular was he in conferring titles and badges of honor. At his death the kingdom had incurred a debt of three millions of rix-dollars; which, however, when it is considered, that Frederick IV. waged expensive wars, and even after the peace, for many years, had to keep a standing army and fleet against Russia, and that many disasters visited the country, is only a trifle, and not to be laid to his charge.

An enemy more fatal than the swords of the Swedes, a frightful pestilence, raged from 1710 to 1712, in Copenhagen and on the island of Sjelland, with the most destructive effect, and took off great numbers; the North sea breaking through the dykes in the marshlands on the western coast of Schleswig, destroyed property to the amount of one million of rix-dollars, and Copenhagen was visited by a destructive fire, continuing for several days and consuming nearly two-thirds of the city; on which occasion science and the arts suffered a great loss, as a great deal of the large University library, with its many rare manuscripts, was destroyed. A. D., 1728.

Notwithstanding all these heavy losses, and his many great expenses, the king found, however, by his economy, means to erect the splendid palaces of *Fredensborg* and *Frederiksberg*, as also the spacious exchequer. Commerce and manufactures were vigorously promoted by Frederick IV. The trade with Greenland was renewed, and the East India Company, for a great while ruined altogether, was, at the close of his reign, again put in motion. The post-office department, having for a long time been entrusted to private men, was again administered at royal expense, the surplus being applied to pension civil and military officers, or their indigent widows. Previous, however, to giving an account of the private life and character of this excellent king, we must take a short connected view of the standing of school affairs and literature during his reign. The public instruction had, hitherto, almost entirely been neglected in Denmark, the commonalty growing up in the grossest mental darkness. But Frederick IV. merited highly the grateful thanks of the peasantry by erecting two hundred and forty brick school buildings, and assigning money to keep them in repair and pay the teachers. Amongst other charitable institutions, ought to be mentioned the founding of Vaisenhuset (the *Orphanotrophy*), for the education of orphan children, with which hospital an excellent school is connected.

In Greenland, Christianity was spread by the noble and pious *Hans Egede*, who left his pastorate in Norway, and went to Greenland with his wife, *Gertrude Rask*, a Christian heroine, "whose adorning did not consist in putting on of apparel, but in the hidden man of the heart, and in the ornament of a meek and quiet spirit, which is, in the sight of God, of great price." From 1721 to 1736, Hans Egede, enduring inexpressible privations, opened his mouth boldly, to make known the mystery of the Gospel amongst the heathenish and savage Greenlanders. His faithful wife, who had shared his hardships, died in Greenland; soon after which he went down to Denmark, where, on the fifth of November, 1758, he departed from life, aged seventy-three years, to receive the crown of righteousness, which the Lord shall give unto all them that have loved his glorious appearing. Pursuant to his proposal a Greenlandish seminary was established in Copenhagen, to educate missionaries, Egede himself teaching the Greenlandish language. His son, *Paul Egede*, continued for six years, with Christian fidelity, his father's missionary work in Greenland, to the great good and profit of many souls; and when he left them, his parting words were: "Preserve with meekness the ingrafted word, and grieve not the Holy Spirit of God, whereby you are sealed unto the day of redemption." Upon his arrival in Copenhagen, in 1742, Paul Egede was appointed minister of the Church of *Vartov* (the church of charity), where he, renouncing the vanities of all worldly pomp, showed himself an able minister of the New Testament, not of the letter, but of the spirit, whose praise is not of men, but of God. Besides discharging his pastoral duties, he translated the New Testament into the difficult language of the Greenlanders, and published other works of consequence for the Greenlandish mission.

For advancing learning and the arts, nothing of consequence was done during the reign of Frederick IV., as the king himself had not enjoyed any scientific education. Nevertheless there lived during his reign several men of letters: *Peter Hansen Resen*, who has distinguished himself by standard works on the Northern history and antiquities; *Thomas Bartholin* deserves particular regard for the universality of his genius, which embraced a wide circle of history, philosophy, and physic; *Niels Steno*, who, after having embraced the Catholic faith, passed the remainder of his days in foreign countries, acquired fame as an anatomist; the Icelander, *Torfæus*, who successfully applied the Icelandic sources to throw light on the history of the North, and preserved alive the embers of that literary spirit which already early had been stirring on that distant island, evinced a zeal for the cultivation of letters, which does him the highest honor; the Icelander, *Arne Magnusson*, deserved well of men of letters by collecting a great number of Icelandic manuscripts, and bequeathing the greatest part of his means to publishing them. *Thomas Kingo*, bishop of Fjunen, acquired the fame of being an unsurpassed hymnologist, his hymn book being in use for a long time.

Shortly after the death of his first queen, Louise, the king took in marriage *Anna Sophia*, a daughter of the deceased lord high chancellor, Count Conrad Reventlow. This marriage caused great disagreement in the royal family, particularly provoking the crown prince, Christian, because the king had cohabited with Anna Sophie, even while queen Louise was living.

Frederick IV., before his death, saw his kingdoms in

the possession of every happiness which could flow from economy, frugality, laboriousness, and from the salutary laws and institutions which he had established, when he died, aged fifty-nine years, after a glorious reign of thirty-one years. Whether we view him in his public or private character, he deserves to be esteemed as one of the most useful of the Danish kings. He united an enterprising spirit with the greatest prudence and moderation, the utmost vigor of authority with the most exemplary justice, and brought his kingdoms to a pitch of eminence and wealth which, till then, they had never attained. War was not his ruling passion, but he was able to meet it with firmness and valor. Nought but the memory of soldier-like bravery survives Charles XII., but Frederick IV. has left behind the memory of a life of restless activity, perpetually laboring for the improvement and prosperity of his countries; and while Charles left behind him nothing but ruins, Frederick IV. left two kingdoms in a flourishing condition, and with a well regulated administration. *A. D., 1730.*

But his admirable institutions were but partially and feebly enforced under his son and successor, *Christian VI.*, Denmark and Norway relapsing again into confusion and pauperism. No sooner had he obtained the sovereignty than he treated with great severity the queen-dowager, his stepmother, Anna Sophia, above mentioned, rightly accounted a stain on the royal family, removing her from the court to *Clausholm*, *A. D., 1730* a lonely manor in Jutland, and immediately dismissed a great number of the higher officers of state, who had enjoyed his father's confidence, entrusting the public affairs to the ministers of state, Baron *Ivar Rosenkranz*, the Counts *Louis Pless, Charles Pless, Schulin*, and *John Louis Holstein*, all of whom exercised a strong influence upon the government.

In the beginning, it was likely that the peasantry would flourish during the reign of this king, for he instantly abrogated the militia, above named, which on account of the feudal bondage therewith connected, had been greatly burdensome to the peasantry and permitted every countryman to settle wheresoever he might desire. By this change the peasantry got complete personal freedom, as well as the other orders; but, unfortunately, after a few months, he enacted a new law, forbidding, upon severe punishment, the country lads to abandon their native county, unless permitted by the noblemen concerned; and after a couple of years the militia was re-established, the time of military service being prolonged from six to eight, and thereafter to twelve years; and when a countryman, after his term of service had expired, would not receive whatsoever farm the nobleman might think proper to give him, he had to submit to military service for ten years more. The enrollment was extended to the fortieth year of age, and from his ninth year the country lad was bound to remain in his native county; thus again the liberal and salutary regulations of king Frederick IV. being annihilated, and the peasantry anew sinking under the domineering spirit of the aristocracy.

Several other regulations affected detrimentally the peasantry and the agriculture. Many noblemen, for instance, were permitted to break up the farms and unite the ground to their manors, the peasantry, of course, thereby decreasing, and the bond-service increasing. Such were the stipulations in favor of the higher orders of the state, which the king promoted to all offices of honor and emolument, and to which, from the very beginning of his reign, his partiality was abundantly conspicuous, while the peasantry was in the lowest stage of degradation.

Upon the whole, the government, under Christian VI., seems to have been extremely aristocratic. It was also of very detrimental consequences, that the king passed a law by which the merchants were restrained from importing grain into Denmark, the prices of corn thereby rising, and the progress in agriculture, of course, decreasing, as the greater certainty thereby produced for making a market, did not make it a matter of greater moment for the husbandmen to prepare the ground sufficiently for a rich crop, and could not fail to excite somewhat of a spirit of ease and inactivity.

But let us now observe some particulars of the religious life, perhaps worthy of more note than any other circumstances during the reign of Christian VI., since it will be found to have received a very great influence during the period under consideration. There are periods in which the human mind seems more than usually to turn strongly to religion and spiritual concerns, and to feel that the Heavenly Majesty must be worshiped in spirit and truth, and the flesh crucified, with the affections and lusts thereof, and such a period in Denmark was the reign of Christian VI.

In opposition to the unsubstantial trusting to the letter which had long prevailed, and to the exorbitant weight laid on the ecclesiastical formulas and symbols, all of which kill, while only the spirit gives life, there appeared in Denmark, as well as a little earlier in Germany, a revival, in general called the *pietistic* disposition of mind, which endeavored to remove that lukewarmness and stagnation, which undeniably in a great measure had long prevailed in the Lutheran churches. Great variances arose in the Church between the different parties, and separatistical conventicles were formed in many places. The king himself, being of a stern, religious mind, was highly in favor of the revival, which he regarded as a recovery from death to life, and tried in different ways to promote the religious spirit; but the means he used were almost altogether external, and not to the purpose at all, failing therefore entirely of the effect intended. The court chaplain, *Bluhme*, and the queen, *Sophie Magdalena*, exercised a great influence upon the foolish ordinances issued in reference to ecclesiastical matters

Going to church every Sabbath was peremptorily commanded by law, the withdrawal from which being in the cities punished by fines, and in the country by pillorying the peasants outside the church door. Dancing, masquerades, comedy, Christmas games, and like amusements, were forbidden, as hindering the attainment of spiritual and heavenly grace, and the alienation from selfishness and the world; the church discipline was vindicated by public penance and rebukes from the pulpits.

These ordinances very likely arose from the king's own unfeignedly religious mind; nevertheless, the happy mean was not found, and even his best advocates will find no apology for applying such compulsion in religious affairs, and cannot regard it as a commendable method of propagating the mild and pure religion of Christ, who will not have involuntary professors; and it was a matter of course, that instead of a real and pure fear of God, there appeared everywhere a feigned devoutness and a false piety, the people, to please the king, making use of the most melting religious terms of this valley of misery, of the heavenly Jerusalem, and the celestial Canaan, and so forth, to profit substantially by his grace; paying tithe, as Christ says, of mint, and anise, and cummin, but omitting the weightier matters of the law, judgment, mercy, and faith.

But, in spite of the many mistakes above mentioned, it is not to be denied that Christian VI., in many other respects, exercised a highly beneficial influence upon the spread of true Christianity, by introducing *the Act of Confirmation,* by which the young, after having attained to mature years, should confirm and ratify themselves the solemn promises made by others at their baptism; and by appointing a *Board of Inspectors*, which had to superintend the clergymen's and schoolmasters' administration of their offices, and to keep a watchful eye over their preaching the doctrines of the Church purely and genuinely, as also to ascertain that the books which were to be published were not of immoral or impure contents.

A. D., 1736.

The king also patronized highly the public instruction, by enacting a law, that public schools for the peasantry should be erected round about in the country, and by issuing useful rules for the method of teaching; a law, however, often meeting with great opposition, on account of the great expenses therewith connected; and although the king here ought to have made use of his absolute power to establish this important institution, the opposition, nevertheless, gained the victory, in many places no schools being erected.

The reign of Christian VI. may be considered as the epoch of the revival of literature in Denmark from that lethargy in which it had continued under Christian V. and Frederick IV., both of whom were not very much interested in literary affairs, and whose incessant wars diverted their attention from them. The University, which had suffered by the fire, (1728,) and was in a declining state, was restored; more professors were appointed, and given better salaries than before; the examinations were made more strict, and a new constitution was drawn up in writing, and published. An examination in law was for the first time instituted; and the science of law being considered the most important, next to that of theology, recovered a new life from the learned *Andreas Hóyer*, a man extensively versed in the European jurisprudence. The legal procedure was highly improved by a new regulation of the supreme court, and particular attention was given to the study of medicine, and its connection with the sciences of botany and human physiology; at the same time the subserviency of the studies to the practical uses of life being an object not to be neglected.

The Latin schools, of which there was one in each city, were diminished, some of them being changed into common schools, and the *Academy of Soró (Academia Sorana)*, which was founded by Christian IV. exclusively for young noblemen, but since the year 1665 had been out of use, was recalled to life and inaugurated a year after the death of Christian VI. A. D., 1747. To promote the fine arts the king erected the *Royal Academy* for painting and drawing, the Venetian and Flemish manner of tempering the colors with oil instead of water, being introduced, an invention which undeniably gave to painting a greater durability, as well as a warmth more approaching to nature.

During the reign of this king two learned societies were formed, the *Literary Society of Copenhagen*, and the *Society of the Danish Language and History*, from both of which excellent treatises have been and still are published.

Among literary men of this period deserve to be mentioned *Andreas Hóyer*, above named, distinguished both as jurisconsult and historian, and remarkable for his great judgment and perspicuity; *Erik Pontoppidan*, chancellor of the University, has composed, History of the Danish Church, History of Norway, Origines Hafnienses, and an Explanation of Luther's Catechism, all works classical in point of style, and to be depended on in point of facts; *John Gram*, royal Historiographer, possessed not alone of great philological erudition, but also of rare knowledge in the history of the North, on which he has composed many critical dissertations, all written with great judgment and impartiality; *Andreas Samsing*, for fifty years a faithful minister of the Gospel, has left behind him an excellent Latin translation of some of the best Danish hymns, of which I may be allowed to cite a proof:

"Tua, Jesu, mors cruenta et profunda vulnera,
Grata menti dant fomenta contra quævis tristia,
Si quid mali cogito, tua jubet passio,
Semper Tui recordari, et peccata detestari."

But all these authors wrote mostly either in German or Latin, thus exercising, properly speaking, no influ once upon the Scandinavian literature. We have, therefore, so much the more to pay attention to *Louis Holberg*, born in the city of Bergen, Norway, 1684, who has made a great epoch in the historical and dramatic literature of the Scandinavian countries, and not alone deserves, but will keep a lasting memorial. In the year 1718 he was appointed, first, Professor of Metaphysics, then Professor Eloquentiæ, and at length, Professor Historiarum et Geographiæ. During his professorship (1718–1747) he has influenced the Danish nation as hardly any one, either before or after him, partly by his historical, partly by his dramatical writings, being both original and the results of deep study. His Description of Denmark and Norway, his History of Norway, his History of the Church Universal, and his History of the Jews, are fruits of his indefatigable study and cultivated judgment, and of a purity and flexibility of language remarkable for the time in which he lived. His heroi-comic poems, Peter Paars and Niels Klim (the last written in Latin), in which he strikingly and wittily ridicules all that foolish pedantry, pertness, and vanity that prevailed amongst the higher classes of his time, and in which he sometimes soars to a pitch of the sublime equal to the finest flights of Homer and Virgil, whose kind of style he in a masterly manner has imitated, have the most captivating charms to all who are possessed of the smallest degree of genuine taste, and have, by an uncommon degree of candor, humor, and impartiality, preserved their value long after their immediate interest has ceased.

But the merit of the dramatic pieces of Louis Holberg is still much higher. Having taken the French comedian, Moliére, as his pattern, he ridicules, undeniably sometimes in too low a language, the fashionable women, who were overrun with a pedantic affectation of learning, and that arrogant and supercilious demeanor of the nobility, which demanded respect from the consideration of birth or fortune, without the possession of a single laudable or valuable quality. He certainly possessed that invention, which is the very first quality of a dramatic poet; he is never deficient in the expression of passion, and in his most laughable scenes we have to admire the art of the poet, and to participate in the delineation of his characters, every person of which is very often a highly-finished picture. Upon the whole, in most of his pieces we cannot but discern the marks of a great and comprehensive genius, an inexhaustible fund of imagination, the most astonishing ebullition of ridiculous representations, and an infinite knowledge of human nature; and when picturing the pedantry of the ladies, the pathetic style of ordinary writers, and the absurd pride of the ignorant nobility, he calls often to our memory, the words of Horace: "*Parturiunt montes, nascitur ridiculus mus.*"

In his youth he had visited four times the Universities of Oxford, Leyden, Paris, and Florence; he spoke fluently nearly all modern languages, not to mention that he, as every distinguished Scandinavian scholar, wrote and spoke Latin with the highest degree of correctness and volubility. After having been exalted to the rank of a baron, he repaired, because of physical infirmity, to his manor, *Terslóse*, on the island of Sjelland, where he died, unmarried, on the 27th of January, 1754, bequeathing his large real estates and extensive library to the Academy of Soró. His last words were: "I have always endeavored to be a useful citizen to my fatherland; now I am feeble and weak, and my only desire is to depart and be with Christ."

Christian VI. took a praiseworthy care of diffusing a spirit of commercial industry, and the prodigious increase of the commerce of Denmark is mainly to be ascribed to his reign. The trade of the East India Company was extended to *China*, and vigorously carried on; and that of the West India Company was considerably enlarged by buying the island of *St. Croix* of Louis XV. of France. A bank was founded in Copenhagen, exercising through a series of years a favorable influence upon trade and industry, and facilitating in a high degree the currency. The king put himself to great expenses in improving domestic manufactures. But although many manufacturers of cloth and silk were encouraged by the king's liberality, these efforts, however, fell short of success; their manufactures not being so cheap and good as to compete with the productions of foreign countries. Various expedients were thought of to obviate that rivalry, but for a long time without avail. Much money was also spent on foreign projectors, who, too willingly, were supported by the government, and became a very great drain to the wealth of the kingdoms. The navy has hardly ever been better administered than under Christian VI., by the talented *Frederick Danneskjold*, Count of Samsó. In the latter part of the reign of Frederick IV. the navy had been neglected, consisting, when Danneskjold undertook the management, only of seven men-of-war and two frigates, but numbering, when he left, thirty men-of-war and sixteen frigates. A *dry dock* was established, many new storehouses were erected, and important breakwaters reared to shelter the navy. Notwithstanding these expensive undertakings, the abilities of the good financier, Danneskjold, husbanded so well the amount of money he had to dispose of, that, on his leaving the administration, one million rixdollars was saved. Danneskjold, a man of great address and extensive knowledge, who had gained upon the favor of the king, also influenced other branches of the state concerns, and had the principal share in setting on foot the Bank of Copenhagen, above mentioned, and in granting protections to trade and industry; though he deserves highly to be blamed for his conduct toward two deserving naval officers, *Benstrup* and *Frederick Lütken*, with whom he had become at variance, and who, through his interference, suffered severe and inequitable treatment.

Although Denmark and Norway, during the reign of Christian VI., continued to enjoy the blessings of tranquillity, and their commerce grew with their navy, and Danneskjold labored with indefatigable industry in the finances the king, however, was in perpetual want of money, the kingdoms, at his death, being in debt for two and a half millions of rixdollars; about the same as during his predecessor, who had not reigned under so favorable conditions, but was involved in expensive wars. The reason was the king's boundless desire of raising new buildings and costly palaces, mainly to be ascribed to his ostentatious queen, *Sophie Magdalena* The palace of Copenhagen, which Frederick IV. with great expense had enlarged and repaired, was pulled down, a new one, called the palace of *Christiansburg*, being erected, and fitted up with such an excessive magnificence, that it rivaled the most splendid of Europe, and cost the kingdom the enormous sum of three millions of dollars. Furthermore, were built the palaces of *Fredericksruhe*, *Sophienberg*, *Eremitage*, and, twelve English miles from Copenhagen, the pompous palace of *Hirschholm*, erected on so miry a ground as soon after to be pulled down. Large amounts of money were also squandered away on relatives of the queen and other foreigners, who crowded into the country, and upon whom donations, pensions, and high offices were profusely bestowed. The German language prevailed again very much at the Danish court; Christian VI. himself spoke and wrote only German; nevertheless he was interested in the Danish literature, and took care to diffuse the Danish language in the northern part of Schleswig, while the queen professedly despised Danish.

Christian VI. had several difficulties with his neighbors. From his father he inherited a dispute with Hamburg, respecting an alteration made in the currency, and with Hanover a dispute arose as to the possession of the county of *Steinhorst*, in the duchy of Lauenburg, both of which, however, were composed. With *Charles Frederick*, the late duke of Gottorp, the king was continually on an unpeaceable footing, and although an alliance was made between Denmark, Russia, and Austria, which secured to Denmark the possession of the Gottorp part of Schleswig, and put an end to the dispute for a season, and Charles Frederick was offered a compensation of one million of rixdollars, he, nevertheless, obstinately rejected every proposal for an amicable agreement. Under his son and successor, *Charles Peter Ulrick*, these dissenting terms were about to turn highly dangerous for Denmark, as *Elizabeth*, the daughter of Peter the Great, was raised to the Russian throne, and now secured the inheritance of the imperial purple to her nephew, the above named Charles Peter Ulrik, and to the Swedish crown for her favorite, *Adolphus Frederick*, a prince of the younger line of the house of Gottorp, and through the Swedish king, Charles IX.'s daughter, Catharina, a

A. D., 1732.

A. D., 1743.

descendant from the warlike house of Vasa. The election of Adolphus Frederick to fill the throne of Sweden after the death of king Frederick of Hesse, came within a hair of occasioning a dangerous war between Denmark and Sweden, where a considerable part of the Swedish nobility, clergy, and peasantry, wished to secure the succession to the Swedish throne to the Danish crown prince, *Frederick*, of whose amiability, kind disposition, and popularity, favorable opinions were in vogue in Sweden. Particularly amongst the brave peasantry from the province of Dalecarlia a violent movement arose, five thousand of them advancing upon Stockholm, to force the election of the Danish crown prince. A most fearful and bloody conflict ensued within the city, and after several days of fighting, the undaunted peasants from the mountains of Dalecarlia were overmatched and compelled to submit. With a loss of two thousand five hundred men their military operations terminated, and Sweden, in order to please the Russian empress, and avoid hostilities, consented to elect Adolphus Frederick successor to the crown of Sweden, excluding the Danish crown prince. Dejected, melancholy, and even enraged at seeing his son's expectations frustrated, and yet cherishing a glimpse of hope of his success, Christian VI. equipped his army and fitted out his fleet, threatening to wage a sanguinary war; but Sweden making great preparations, and Russia promising to march twenty thousand auxiliary

A. D., 1743.

troops against Denmark, the Danish king deemed it unsafe to bid defiance to so mighty an alliance. The strife dropped fortunately, and amity was entertained with Russia during the reign of the empress Elizabeth, although Charles Peter Ulrick, the elected successor to the Russian throne, was highly exasperated at Denmark, and looked out for every opportunity to rekindle the flame of war.

Christian VI. was of a gentle, pious, and sincere disposition, and preferred and cherished the arts of peaceful industry to those of selfish and destructive war. He gained the affection and confidence of his subjects by many good institutions, tending to promote literature, public instruction, commerce, and naval affairs; and there is more pleasure in contemplating such a man's character, than that of a mad conqueror like Charles XII. of Sweden, the one producing happiness, and the other misery in the world. The king himself was of an unfeigned piety to God, and an exemplary Christian, and his mistakes in promoting a true religious life are more to be ascribed to the artful and hypocritical insinuations of his court chaplain, Bluhme, than to himself.

A. D., 1746. After a reign of sixteen years, he died in the vigor of his age.

No sooner had *Frederick V.* succeeded his father to
A. D., 1746. the throne of Denmark and Norway, than that seriousness and formality of manner which, during his father's reign, had prevailed at the Danish

court, was done away, and a more jovial life took place, comedies and concerts being again represented, and other public amusements permitted.

During the reign of Christian VI. there had been upheld a great distance between the people and the royal family, the members of which never appeared in public except when accompanied and attended by costly liveried servants and soldiers; the palace of Christiansberg, also, was surrounded by numerous sentinels; all of which ceased during Frederick V.'s reign, who regarded all stiffness and affected precision as not compatible with modern civilization, and married the jovial princess *Louise*, a daughter of George II. of England, both of whom, free from all pride and vain ambition, made themselves extremely beloved of their subjects. To see the royal couple making their appearance in the theatre, the celebrated Louis Holberg, before mentioned, called a fascinating sight. On the 10th of September, 1747, Frederick V. and his queen, Louise, were crowned and anointed in the palace of Fredericksborg, the bishop of Copenhagen, Dr. Hersleb, performing the solemn act. In the beginning, many tried to insinuate themselves into the queen's favor, thereby to obtain rank, dignities, and high offices, but she answered that she had come to Denmark to embellish the days of her royal consort, not to interfere in public affairs, which did not appertain to her sex. Count *Schulin*, one of the few able and skillful Germans who, during Christian VI.'s reign, had arrived in the country, and risen from a plain and poor student to the highest dignities, kept his situation under Frederick V.

After him the great politician and acute diplomate, *John Hartvig Ernst, Count of Bernstorf*, gained completely the confidence of his royal master, and signally displayed his splendid abilities, while, on the other hand, the highly deserving *Danneskjold*, above named, without any competent reason, was discharged. The financial affairs were excellently administered by the baron, *Otto Thott*. Also, the great favorite of the king, *Adam Gottlob Moltke*, later exalted to Count of *Bregentved*, a beautiful estate in the island of Sjelland, exercised a considerable influence upon the state affairs.

A. D., 1749. The dearly-beloved queen Louise became, on the 29th of January, mother to crown-prince Christian, afterwards king of both kingdoms by the name of Christian VII.; but two years after, the twin-kingdoms had to lament her death, shortly after her delivery of a still-born prince.

That spirit of disagreement which had so long existed between Denmark and Sweden, was done away with
A. D., 1750. by the wise diplomatic efforts of Schulin and Bernstorff, a treaty being concluded, by which *Adolphus Frederick*, the elected successor to the Swedish crown, and the head of the younger line of the dukes of Holstein, renounced his claims to Schleswig, and engaged himself to exchange the ducal part of

Holstein, when this soon, by inheritance, might devolve to his line, for the two counties, Oldenburg and Delmenhorst. The want of certain limits between Norway and Sweden, which long had caused violent disputes, was, in the following year, adjusted by plenipotentiaries from both kingdoms; and, to contract a yet firmer union between Denmark and Sweden, espousals were arranged between the Danish princess, *Sophie Magdalena*, and the Swedish crown-prince, *Gustavus*, a son of Adolphus Frederick, afterwards king of Sweden, by the name of Gustavus III. The wedding ceremony was, however, not performed till after the death of Frederick V.

At this time, nearly all Europe was involved in the devastating Prussian seven years war, which the talented warrior, *Frederick the Great*, waged triumphantly against Austria, Russia, France, Sweden and Poland, all regarding with jealousy the increase of the Prussian monarchy; and the empress Elizabeth of Russia entertaining a personal hatred to Frederick the Great, who had often made her the object of his political satires, and the empress of Austria, Maria Theresa, still being dissatisfied with the loss of Silesia by the peace of Dresden, 1745. A. D., 1756-63.

Although Denmark, through Bernstorff's wise diplomacy, was happy enough not to be involved in this destructive war, it was, nevertheless, the cause of heavy expenses, it being deemed necessary, to secure the frontiers, to keep a considerable standing army in Holstein.

Besides, an alliance was made between Denmark and Sweden, both joining together in having their fleets in the Baltic during the war, to protect the commerce of the North against the hostile privateers, all of which was a great drain on the public treasury.

The war, at length, approached to the Danish frontiers. A. D., 1757. The French troops had entered Hanover, where the French general, *D'Etrée*, defeated, near Hastenbek, an army of Prussians and Englishmen, commanded by the Duke of Cumberland; but Frederick V. of Denmark was happy enough, through the A. D., 1757. interference of Count *Lynar*, to effect the convention of *Zeven*, in Hanover, pursuant to which the allied army had to separate; a convention, however, neither ratified by the English nor the French king, and, therefore, of no long duration.

But it was the fate of Denmark soon to enter into a yet more critical situation. An unexpected event delivered the king of Prussia from the ruin, that seemed to threaten him at the close of his last campaign. Elizabeth, A. D., 1762. the empress of Russia, died, and was succeeded by her nephew, Charles Peter Ulrik, who now mounted the Russian throne by the name of *Peter III.*, and who entertained a romantic admiration of the Prussian king, but an unquenchable hatred against Denmark. He immediately re-demanded Schleswig, which Adolphus Frederick had renounced in 1750. Denmark peremptorily refusing his demand, Peter III.

marched an army to Germany to attack Denmark, and, as he declared, entirely to turn away the Danish royal family, against which he cherished the most inveterate hatred.

Meanwhile Denmark had made strenuous military preparations to meet the threatening tempest. Frederick V. launching his fleet in the Baltic, numbering thirty-six men-of-war excellently equipped, and marching to Mecklenburg, his army consisting of seventy-one thousand men, commanded by the French general, *St. Germain*, who, upon request of the Danish king, had undertaken to conduct the military operations. The Russian and Danish armies approaching each other in Mecklenburg, a bloody battle was impending, when the sudden intelligence was conveyed to the Danish court, that Peter III., who, by his imprudent reforms, had given offence to a great body of his subjects, had been dethroned, mainly by his wife, and killed in prison a few days after his deposition. A. D., 1763. It has, however, not been fully ascertained, whether he was the victim of disease or violence. Be it as it may, his death delivered Denmark from the imminent danger that threatened her, the more so as the empress, *Catharina II.*, who now usurped the Russian throne, renewed friendship and peace with Denmark, and resolved to observe a strict neutrality.

Nevertheless, it was easy to foresee that the peace with Russia was not to be trusted, as long as the disputable point concerning Schleswig was not settled. The celebrated Bernstorff, therefore, deserved highly of Denmark for getting this point satisfactorily determined. After long negotiations he was happy enough to adjust a treaty, by which the house of Holstein renounced all claims to the former Gottorp part of Schleswig, and Denmark obtained the ducal part of Holstein in exchange for the counties of Oldenburg and Delmenhorst, but had, at the same time, to pay the great debt of the house of Holstein, and to resign the diocese of Lübeck, which Frederick V., with great expense, had purchased for his younger son, the crook-backed prince, *Frederick*, whom the king had by his second queen, *Juliane Marie*, of Brunswick-Lüneburg-Wolfenbüttel, to whom he had been married on the eighth of July, 1752. This treaty being subscribed to a year after the death of Frederick V., was first ratified some years after, when the Russian crown-prince, *Paul*, in whose behalf his mother, Catharina II., had concluded it, was past minority. On the same occasion was *Hamburg*, after some controverted points were settled, unbound from her dependence on Holstein, and declared a *free imperial city*. Frederick V. bought that part of the island of Aró, which belonged to the duke of Glücksburg, with the proviso that he paid the debt contracted, amounting to about one million of rix-dollars.

During the reign of this king, as during that of his predecessor, large sums were spent in promoting domestic manufactures in Denmark; but however well-meaning these endeavors might be, particularly originating from the great Bernstorff, their consequences were not profitable nor permanent; the manufacturing of many things, as silks and other fine manufactures, with which many thousands in Copenhagen were occupied, was unnatural to Denmark and only brought to pass by large expenses, and by forbidding the import of foreign articles. These being cheaper, were, of course, imported into the country in great quantities, and greedily sought after, ignoring the severe punishments inflicted upon those who were found guilty of such importations.

Of greater use was the foundation of the armory near *Elsenore*, and of the cannon foundery and the powder mills near *Fredericksværk*, by which the army was provided with arms and ammunitions. In spite of the high tariff placed upon trade and other ways of living, in order to create for manufactures and home-bred commodities a home-market, nevertheless the great jurisconsult, *Henry Stampe*, who was attorney-general, and exercised a beneficial influence upon many branches of the state affairs, effected a modification of the pressing restrictions which, hitherto had been placed on commercial and mechanical corporations. Also *trade* and *navigation* were highly patronized under this king. Already Christian VI., towards the close of his reign, had contributed not a little to increase the Danish commerce in the Mediterranean, and in his name a treaty was concluded with Algiers, confirmed by Frederick V., who meantime had ascended the throne, and on the whole, continued his father's endeavors, concluding commercial treaties with *Morocco, Tunis, Tripoli, the Turkish Sultan*, Mustapha III., *Genoa* and *Naples*.

Hereby a foundation was laid for the important conveyance of freight, which Denmark had in the Mediterranean, but the immediate trade with Africa became of no consequence, though Denmark spent immense sums on equipping merchantmen for that purpose; while on the other hand the East and West Indian trade flourished, and, at length, was raised to a height hitherto unknown, and could not fail to be an inexhaustible source of wealth to the nation; and it can not be denied, that during the reign of Frederick V. a variety of excellent laws were enacted for the encouragement of trade.

But the *financial affairs* grew still worse during the reign of this king. In the first eight years the debt was reduced to one million of rix-dollars, but afterwards grew, year by year. The reason was, the great expenses in fitting out the army and the fleet on account of the Prussian seven years' war, and yet more, the necessary preparations for the war against Russia; finally the king's splendid court, as also the considerable amounts of money spent on supporting manufactures, mechanical occupations, and expensive commercial undertakings. Another hardy enterprise, on which was spent more than a million of rix-dollars, was the attempt at breaking and cultivating the vast heaths of Jutland by German colonists. The attempt, however, falling short of success, contributed, nevertheless, to make the cultivation of potatoes more known in Denmark, which now produces the finest kinds of this vegetable.

The public treasury was also very much incumbered by the purchase of the possessions which belonged to the duke of Plöen, and of the allodial estates of the duke of Glücksburg. To remedy the increasing scarcity of money, it was, therefore, resolved, upon the proposal of Count *Schimmelmann*, who, in the latter part of the reign of Frederick V., tried to put the finances upon a better footing, to dispose of the large estates which the crown possessed. These estates hitherto having only yielded very small revenues, were now sold with great profit, and amounted to considerable sums; moreover, an *extra tax* was imposed, which, to many, became very burdensome, every person, after having attained to the twelfth year of age, without respect of person, being forced to pay a tribute of one rix-dollar yearly.

But although this taxation was complied with, without the faintest murmur on the part of the people, and afforded the king the most abundant supplies for the accomplishment of all his designs, and for the enjoyment of the pleasures of his splendid court, the disorder of the finances was, nevertheless, so great, that at the expiration of the reign of Frederick V. the debt of the state had reached the immense amount of twenty millions of rix-dollars: a debt which ever since has been too heavy a burden for Denmark to get rid of, the king himself being most to blame in this matter, as his desire to imitate the luxurious court of Louis XV. of France, had highly contributed to exhaust the wealth of his kingdoms.

The severe restrictions placed on the peasantry by Christian VI. continued yet during the reign of Frederick V., and became yet severer than before, a law being enacted, that the country lad, from the very time he had filled his fourth year, should be bound to remain in his native county. The peasants groaned yet under all the miseries flowing from the despotic power of the nobility. The severe treatment to which they were exposed, occasioned many to concert measures for running from their native place and emigrating from the country, notwithstanding they, if apprehended, had to undergo the severest punishment. Many estates, therefore, were so deserted that the government found it necessary to permit the administrations of alms-houses and orphanotrophies to convey poor children to the noblemen to farm their estates.

The sale of the large estates belonging to the crown, also, had unfavorable consequences on the peasants, who in very few places were able to buy their farms themselves. Many new manors, therefore, were erected on the crown estates disposed of, and numerous farms pulled down, the peasants often, under these new masters not getting so good terms as during the royal administration.

But notwithstanding these encroachments so highly unfavorable to the peasantry, an active interest commenced just at this time to manifest itself for this class of society, and caused the attention of the government to be drawn to their pitiable condition, and to the gross deficiencies and abuses which prevailed among all the agricultural classes. The enlightened count, *A. G. Moltke*, before mentioned, was desirous of making the best possible improvements in agriculture, and prevailed upon the king to give the liberty of the press to such authors who published books on state affairs and agriculture; on which occasion several writings and treatises were issued, not only throwing light upon the bad condition of agriculture, but also proving this to be founded in the many restrictions and oppressions placed on the peasantry. A royal committee was appointed, which particularly had to attend to the economical part of agriculture, causing several laws to be enacted aiming at abrogating that hitherto existing community of ground, in so high a degree detrimental to agriculture.

The new spirit of liberty, which in view of the peasantry began to stir, did also appear in the efforts of several noble-minded lords to improve the economical situation of their peasants. Amongst these *Bernstorff*, minister of state, deserves to be mentioned, who, upon advice of his nephew, A. P. Bernstorff, parceled the grounds, and abrogated all community on his estates, and granted his peasants freedom from bond-service.

Frederick V., though not a man of letters himself, was nevertheless a munificent patron of science and the arts. The *Academy of Soró*, the re-establishment of which Christian VI. had prepared, was recalled to life and inaugurated. which is especially to be ascribed to *Holberg* bequeathing his immense riches of estate and money, and his large library, to this institution. There lived under Frederick V., and the following king, many celebrated men of learning, of whom I shall enumerate a few of the most eminent and remarkable.

A. D., 1747.

In the science of law *Kofod Ancher* and *Andreas Schytte* excelled, not to forget *Henrik Stampe*, before named, who all made an equally eminent figure in the political as in the literary world, their works being the fruit of mature study, and written in a refined and classical style. As historians, we have to mention the fundamental investigator, *Langebek*, who has gained a great reputation, both at home and abroad, by his work, *Scriptores rerum Danicarum Medii Ævi*, and *Peter Suhm*, whose favorite subject was the Northern mythology, on which he had published a work of deep erudition, which entitles him to the character of a thorough historian. *Erik Pontoppidan*, above named, continued to enrich the literature by eminent productions; for instance, his work, Exploits of the Danes abroad, written in Latin, acquired for him a great fame. Professor *Oeder* has, by his work, *Flora Danica*, distinguished himself as a great botanist. *Cramer* was a famous ecclesiastical orator—even known abroad. The German poet, *Klopstock*, who was supported by Frederick V., by his immortal works is known to the whole civilized world. In point of fancy and imagination hardly any poet has gone beyond him; and his poetry exhibits the most beautiful examples of the true pathetic. His lyric poem, *Messias*, has raised him an everlasting monument. The Danish poet, *John Herman Vessel*, born in Norway, 1742, died in Copenhagen, whose genius and humor are never to be forgotten, has delivered masterpieces in dramatic literature, all distinguished for a correctness of language, a harmony of numbers, and a brilliancy of metaphor hardly ever surpassed, not to mention the striking wit which he in a masterly manner knew how to apply.

A.D., 1785.

The great politicians, also, *Schlegel, Mallet, Roger*, and *Reverdil*, ought to be cited. Reverdil was appointed teacher in French to the young crown-prince, *Christian*, and afterwards availed himself of the great influence he exercised upon his pupil, to act in behalf of the oppressed peasantry; in which respect Oeder, also, the great botanist, merits an everlasting remembrance. The great statesman, *Bernstorff*, influenced the king to send the learned Professor *Niebuhr* to Arabia, whose researches have thrown a new light on mineralogy and oriental history. The celebrated Icelanders, *John Erichson*, *Skule Thorlacius*, *Grim Thorkelin*, and *Sandvig*, applied themselves diligently to examine the northern antiquities. Sandvig has made himself famous by his translation of the *Edda*, or sacred book of the Scandinavians, whose author, Snorro Sturleson, lived in the beginning of the thirteenth century, and was supreme judge of Iceland. Mallet, above named, has given an abridgment of this remarkable book, and shown that Snorro had composed it with the sole purpose of preserving the memory of the ancient Scandinavian poetry, and of the wild and massive mythology therewith inseparably connected.

During the reign of Frederick V., two important societies were formed in Copenhagen, and Throndhjem, Norway: *the Society of Belle Lettres*, and *the Literary Society of Norway*. Physics and cameralistics, for which Count A. G. Moltke had great affection, were vigorously pursued. Upon the proposal of Oeder, a *cabinet for natural curiosities* was erected in the palace of Charlottenborg, more professors being appointed to deliver lectures on the sciences of nature. Oeder laid the ground-plot of a *botanic garden*, and commenced to publish his famous work, *Flora Danica*, i. e., a description of Danish herbs. *Frederick's Hospital*, founded during the reign of Frederick V., was not only a highly beneficial institution, but also of great importance for the study of medicine. The fine arts were promoted by enlarging the school of painting and drawing, erected by Christian VI., and by changing it to an academy of sculpture, painting, and architecture, in which the immortal *Thorwaldsen*, who in sculpture stands unrivaled among the moderns, afterwards displayed his rare talents.

After a reign of twenty years, Frederick V. died on the 14th of January, 1766. Although not displaying any considerable degree of self-activity, he entirely possessed the affections of his subjects by his engaging affability, which in him deriving its origin from a native goodness of heart, was very different from that colored complaisance, the usual courtly engine for acquiring popularity, and which, therefore, was the subject of panegyric among his people, and has continued to be the object of honorable mention by posterity. He appeared just, liberal, and humane; and when a warrant for the execution of a criminal was brought to him to be signed, his courtiers often saw him walking long to and fro on the floor, before affixing his royal signature, entertaining a continual doubt of his right to take human life.

A.D., 1766.

Upon the occasion of his death a case happened which ought to be mentioned for the sake of its singularity. When the minister of the Church of the Mariners, of Copenhagen, pastor *Rothenburg*, who had got into the habit of drinking, next Sabbath after the death of the king, ascended the pulpit, he addressed the congregation in the following words: "Our most gracious king has exchanged his corruptible crown for the incorruptible; he was a mighty monarch, king of Denmark, Norway, Sweden, Russia, Prussia, Asia, Africa, America, and many other countries, which neither you nor I myself know." Of course, he was immediately deposed from his ministry.

II.

1766—1852.

Christian VII.—Alterations among the Higher Officers of State—Care for the Peasantry—The King's going abroad—Struensee and Brandt—Ove Guldberg, Minister of State—The Queen-dowager, Juliane Marie—Prince Frederick—Deed of Exchange with Russia—A. P. Bernstorff—The Armed Neutrality—The Finances—The Press—The Peasantry—Care for the Danish Language and Literature—The Charter of Naturalization—Crown Prince *Frederick*, afterwards *Frederick VI.*—A. P. Bernstorff—Henrik Stampe—Reventlow—C. Colbjórnson—Hostilities with Sweden—Neutrality during the French Revolutionary War—Independence of the United States acknowledged by Denmark—Tripoli—Hostilities with England—Renewal of the Armed Neutrality—Horrible Battle at Copenhagen—Copenhagen cruelly Bombarded, and the Fleet carried away—War with Sweden—Peace of Jónköping—Prince Christian August, of Augustenburg—His Death—War with Sweden, Russia, and Prussia—Alliance with France—Fierce Fight at Sehestedt—Peace of Kiel—Norway Lost—Emancipation of the Peasantry from Feudal Bondage—Other Important Alterations in Different Branches of the Government—Care of the King for Public Instruction—University and School Affairs—Literature—Pecuniary Affairs—Representative Council—*Christian VIII.*—School Affairs in Copenhagen and in the Country—Iceland—The Danish East India Possessions disposed of—Care for the Danish Language in the Northern part of Schleswig—Railroads—*Frederick VII.*—Horrible War with the Rebellious Duchies.

Christian VII., a son of Frederick V. and his first queen, Louise, succeeded his father to the throne of both kingdoms, in the seventeenth year of his age. Soon after his accession, Christian VII. married *Caroline Mathilde*, a sister of the magnanimous king of England, George III.; and the engaging manners of this young princess, only sixteen years of age when married to the king, won her the favor of the Danish king and people.

A. D., 1766.

Shortly after Christian VII. had mounted the throne several alterations amongst the higher officers were made. The well deserving Count *Danneskjold Samsó*, who, during the reign of Christian VI., had so gloriously managed the naval affairs, but under the whole royalty of Frederick V. had been removed from any share in the government, now regained the administration of the navy, and was again introduced into the privy council. Prompted by *Reverdil*, who was now appointed secretary of the cabinet council, the young king, by nature possessed of uncommon endowments of mind, took an energetic care of the peasantry, which be rightly regarded the majority of the nation. A committee, in which Reverdil and *Henrik Stampe* presided, was appointed to propose improvements in the condition of the peasants, who, in the whole county of Copenhagen, were emancipated from bond-service, and declared owners of their farms. Soon after, however, new alterations were made at the court. Reverdil was discharged, the deserving Danneskjold Samsó was suddenly, without any fault, deposed from all his offices, and banished from Copenhagen; likewise St. Germain, before mentioned, who for some years had commanded the land force, was dismissed. After Reverdil's discharge, Count *Holck* exercised a detrimental influence upon the morality of the young king, and led him into dissipated habits.

A. D., 1768. Soon after the king undertook a tour through Europe, for the purpose of acquiring more instruction and experience, and bringing back to his subjects the improvements of more refined nations. Having established a regency, to direct the government during his absence, he departed from his dominions in the train of his courtiers and numerous attendants. In Altona the young king contracted familiarity with the talented physician, *John Frederick Struensee*, who was appointed to accompany the king as physician in ordinary.

Shortly before the king left Denmark, his queen, Caroline Mathilde, had on the 28th of January, 1768, been delivered of the crown prince Frederick, afterwards king of Denmark and Norway, by the name of *Frederick VI*.

From Altona Christian VII. went to England, where he, by his handsome appearance, natural wit and engaging manners, won universal favor, the University of Oxford even conferring upon him the honorary diploma of *doctor juris*. On account of his talents and insinuating manners, and of his availing himself of every opportunity to please his royal master, Struensee became a great favorite with the king, and upon returning he monopolized the favor of the king and the queen to such a degree, that he was raised to the office of prime minister, or rather, sole ruler of Denmark and Norway, exalted to the rank of a count, and decorated with the order of the Elephant, exercising an omnipotent influence, and being able to undertake a complete revolution of the state affairs; the easier, as the king himself, by dissolute, licentious manners, had fallen into a temporary insanity. To accomplish his schemes, Struensee availed himself of his intimate friend, *Enevold Brandt*, who entertained the greatest familiarity with the king, had likewise been exalted to the rank of a count, and decorated with the order of the Elephant, and mastered Christian VII. so completely as to make him comply with his humor; Struensee and Brandt thus being the real rulers of the kingdom, the king himself only nominally. The old, generally-esteemed *Bernstorff*, being a stumbling-block to Struensee's carrying out his plans, was suddenly removed, through the interference of Count *Ranzau Ascheberg*, also striving for power and influence. The privy council was annulled, and its members, among whom was baron Thott and count A. G. Moltke, dismissed; a cabinet council being erected instead of it; which, however, signified nothing, Struensee himself deciding all matters of consequence, without any consultation either with the king or with the royal colleges, and soon gaining such an ascendency as to be authorized to pass com-

A. D., 1770.

A. D., 1771.

mands in his own name with the same validity as if they were subscribed by the king himself. Jealous of the unheard-of power and influence extended to Struensee and Brandt, count Ranzau Ascheberg soon became one of their most mortal enemies, and afterwards privy to the horrible conspiracy, which brought them to trial as criminals, and to suffer a dreadful death. Intoxicated with joy at the immense influence they exercised, they did not suspect that fearful event which was at hand.

Struensee's administration was vigorous, and, in many respects, very useful, many alterations which he made being highly laudable, while others were of doubtful utility, and some altogether injurious. One of the greatest benefits which the ministry of Struensee effected was *the liberty of the press.* Immediately after he had assumed his power, a royal rescript emanated, giving every individual right to express his opinion on the whole conduct of the government, without reserve, by word or writing; the press should be open to every thing, but after publication, such writings as offended in the particulars, should be subject to the penalties of the law; thus, at length, that tie was now untied, which for two centuries had retarded the free progress of literature and science, and furnished unjust officers with the most powerful impulse to every species of malversation.

A. D., 1770.

A better regulation of the finances was a main object

of his attention, and to accomplish his plans in this respect, he employed the skillful *Oeder*, and his efficient brother, *Peter Struensee*, counselor of state. A college of finances was erected to undertake the administration of all the revenues and expenses of both kingdoms, which formerly had been divided between different colleges; a more economical system was adopted and a fixed sum of money assigned for the expenses of the royal court.

As to the conferring of badges of honor and honorary titles, it was resolved henceforth to ascertain more minutely than before the worthiness of the persons on whom those titles were to be conferred, and no more to allow servants of the nobility offices in the kingdoms, the practice of which already long had intruded upon the patience of the people.

In reference to the magistrate of Copenhagen, important alterations took place, all the members of the magistracy being deposed and the council of the thirty-two men removed, after which the whole administration was regulated in a new and better way.

Of great importance was the erection of the *municipal court*, from which the defendant could appeal to the supreme court, if not content with the sentence of the municipal court. Formerly the law-suits in Copenhagen had been divided between many different tribunals: a great hindrance for quick and due procedure. It was also forbidden by law to put the criminals to the rack to compel them to confess their crimes.

Struensee was also highly desirous of improving the condition of the agricultural classes. In the beginning of the reign of Christian VII. something had been done for this purpose, but afterwards this important matter had again been dropped, only some few laws being passed as to improvements in agriculture, while the personal condition of the peasantry continued as before. But, prompted by Struensee, a new committee was appointed, in which Oeder, uniting a deep insight into agricultural affairs with ardent love of the peasantry, presided. Upon the recommendation of this committee a law was enacted, that the bond-service should be adjusted to their acres of land, as also other regulations favorable to the peasantry. Besides that, it was proposed by this committee, shortly before Struensee's declension, to emancipate the peasantry from all feudal bondage.

It also conduced to the advancement of manufactures in Denmark, that the Moravian brethren, distinguished for their industry, were permitted to settle in *Christiansfeldt*, in the duchy of Schleswig.

Struensee's attention was also directed to the many deficiencies in the regulation of the University, and to remedy them he called down from Norway the learned bishop *Gunnerus* of Trondhjem, who, with deep inspection, elaborated a proposal for a reformation of the University, which, however, at Struensee's declension, shortly subsequent, was laid aside.

But although these excellent improvements met with great approbation amongst the sensible and educated people, nevertheless, he incurred their displeasure and censure for having made them too precipitately, without preparation and assurance for the future. All eyes were bent jealously upon him, and misfortunes were accumulating fast upon his head. During the continuance of Struensee's useful designs, his friend, Count Enevold Brandt, a man of weak intellect, and without any vigor of mind, had plunged into the pleasures of the court, and in the midst of luxury and festivity indulged the king's passions, often taking advantage of his familiarity with him to forget the distance between himself and his royal master, while many looked jealously upon him, and he stood over a hidden volcano.

To return to Struensee; several of his institutions gave great offence to the manners and habits of his age; for instance, that he abrogated by law (26th of October, 1770) the following holy days: the third Christmas, Easter, and Pentecost days, the Epiphany, the Purification of St. Mary the Virgin, the Annunciation of the Blessed Virgin, St. John Baptist's day, and St. Michael's and All Angels, alleging that they were only used for idleness and vices, and not for true worship; that he annulled all difference between legitimate and illegitimate children, and finally commanded to bury all corpses early in the morning, aiming thereby, it should be observed, at diminishing that luxury and funeral pomp which long had taken place; all of which gave the more offense as Struensee was a known despiser of all religion and a man of immoral principles.

He is also blamed for having introduced the corrupting system of raising money by lotteries, and there soon appeared a general dissatisfaction with the reign of Struensee, the more as he was a professed despiser of the Danish language. The royal orders were issued in German, the royal colleges had to present their proposals in German, and applications and supplications from private people had to be written in German, if they might expect them to be taken notice of.

Struensee had formally monopolized the favor of the young queen; wheresoever she was, he accompanied her; he approached her without sufficient respect, and he was generally charged with having defiled the royal bed, which, however, never was clearly proved. Many officers had been despotically deposed from their offices, often without any pension; his haughtiness had given great offense to the Danish nobles, and the most influential families of the country had lost their influence. During some agitations arising from a few mariners and workmen, Struensee proved himself faint-hearted, which inspired his enemies with courage to precipitate him from his high place. His friend, Count Enevold Brandt, was charged with having taken advantage of the king's momentary insanity, even so far as to have beaten his majesty.

A conspiracy was formed against them, the principal leaders of which were the king's stepmother, the queen-dowager, *Juliane Marie*, and her son, the crook-backed prince, *Frederick*, both of whom, during the ministry of Struensee, had been neglected and stripped of all influence; *Ove Guldberg*, private secretary with Prince Frederick, whose teacher he had been; the two counts, *Ranzau Ascheberg* and *Osten*, Colonel *Köller*, General *Eichstädt* and Commissary-General *Beringskjold;* who all had before enjoyed the king's bounty, but by the influence of Struensee and Brandt had lost it.

It was resolved to involve the unfortunate young queen, Caroline Mathilde, in their fate, preparations being made to strike a decisive blow. The plot was laid with a depth equal to the atrociousness of the design. In the night, between the 16th and 17th of January, the infernal scheme was carried out. Soldiers appeared in the streets and round the royal palace of Christiansborg, barricades were erected, popular commotions took place in the capital, and the cry, "Down with the traitors!" resounded throughout Copenhagen. Struensee and his friend Enevold Brandt, not at all suspecting the peril to which they were exposed, were suddenly arrested at midnight, by virtue of an order which had been extorted from the imbecile king. While this was passing, Ranzau Ascheberg and Köller, guided by numerous soldiers, repaired to the royal palace, entered the queen's bed-chamber and dragged her

A.D., 1772.

naked out of her bed and commanded her to follow them. Pleading her complete innocence and appealing to her royal dignity, she cried: "I will speak with the king, my royal consort;" but they answered: "His majesty is asleep, we dare not awake him;" after which they placed her by force in a carriage, and sent her, a prisoner, to the fortress of *Kronborg*, near Elsenore, where she remained for six weeks. Dread of British vengeance saved her, perhaps, from personal violence. While a prisoner in Kronborg, she was, under the pretence of having committed adultery with Struensee, divorced, by a judicial sentence, from the imbecile king, Christian VII., and then permitted to retire to Hanover, where, from 1772 to 1775, in a small town called *Zelle*, the remainder of her life was spent in comparative obscurity, pious contemplations, and in the exercise of secret charity. She died at the age of twenty-four. Even when breathing her last she asserted her innocence of the crime with which she had been charged, declaring solemnly that she had been sacrificed by a base plot.

When she was carried away by force from Copenhagen, her little son, the crown-prince *Frederick*, afterwards king by the name of *Frederick VI.*, was only four years of age. She saw him no more. She is buried in a plain vault in the church of Zelle, with the laconic inscription on her coffin: "Carolina Mathilda, Regina Daniæ et Norvegiæ."

While this was passing with the young queen, Struensee and Brandt were sitting in their prisons, wrapped in gloomy thoughts and awaiting their horrible sentence of death, at the circumstances of which abominable tragedy we cannnot but shudder. They were insulted with the mockery of a trial, and their sentence was: " Struensee and Brandt have forfeited honor, life, and property; their right hands shall first be stricken off, then their heads; their bodies be divided into four parts and exposed on the wheel to public view;" to which cruel sentence the deranged king was easily brought to affix his signature.

Dr. Hee, minister of the church of the mariners, and Dr. Münter, minister of the German church, and father of the learned bishop of Copenhagen, Dr. Frederick Münter, were commanded to prepare the victims for death. On the 28th of April, the cruel sentence was literally carried into effect. A. D., 1772. Struensee, whose religious views had taken a happy change under his imprisonment, when ascending the scaffold, cried out: " The power of the blood of Christ speaks comfort to me."

This horrible scene excited horror and detestation in all the courts of Europe, calling it the Danish judiciary murder. The hard-hearted queen-dowager, Juliane Marie, who was seen looking from a window of her palace upon the dreadful spectacle, now usurped the royal authority for a long time, after having removed her rivals, and the young and talented nobleman, named *Bernstorff*, a nephew of the before mentioned count, was appointed minister of foreign affairs, which he conducted with excellent discretion.

Struensee thus removed, the former principles of government were introduced, the privy council was re-established by the name of council of state, the royal colleges were replaced on their old footing, most of Struensee's institutions being abrogated, the good as well as the bad, and nearly all the men whom he had employed in carrying out his reforms, deposed and removed, although many of them were highly efficient and deserving officers.

Besides the queen-dowager, Juliane Marie, baron *Otto Thott, Schack Rathlau,* and count *Schimmelmann,* exercised until 1784 the most important influence upon the government; while, on the other hand, Ranzau Ascheberg, and several others of the most efficient coadjutors in removing Struensee, were soon dismissed. Only *Ove Guldberg* was gradually raised to greater and greater dignity and influence, his authority becoming so considerable that this whole period has been called *the period of Guldberg. Andrew Peter Bernstorff*, a nephew of the elder Bernstorff, skillfully administered, (1773–1780,) as above mentioned, the foreign affairs, but afterwards laid down his office, not approving of the principles which Guldberg followed. But the administration of Bernstorff is remarkable for the fact that the treaty which his uncle, in 1767, had concluded with Russia, concerning the exchange of the ducal part of Holstein for Oldenburg and Delmenhorst, was now accomplished, the crown prince of Russia, *Paul Petrowitch*, now passing his minority. Denmark hereby coming into an undivided possession of Holstein, the motives for future disputes with Russia were removed; the more so, as the house of Holstein-Kiel renounced its claims to the duchy of Schleswig. The counties, Oldenburg and Delmenhorst, were, by Paul Petrowitch, resigned to the young *Frederick August*, a prince of the younger line of the house of Kiel, and on this occasion elevated to a grand duchy, by the title of the *Grand Duchy of Oldenburg*. A.D., 1773.

Six years after, also, the Glücksburg possessions, at the death of the last duke, by inheritance devolved to the Danish crown; all the small parcels which by earlier divisions had been separated from the crown were reunited to it, except the possessions of the duke of Augustenburg. A.D., 1779.

In 1775, twelve years from the peace of Paris, by which Nova Scotia, Canada, Cape Breton, and all other islands in the gulf and river St. Lawrence were ceded to the British crown, the American revolutionary war began, which, by the indefatigable efforts of the noble George Washington, and many other patriots, terminated in the final separation of the United States from the British empire. Several of the European maritime powers sharing in this memorable war, the Danish and Northern commerce was highly molested by the privateers of the belligerent powers, France, Spain, and especially England. To remedy this evil, *A. P. Bernstorff* labored energetically for effecting an alliance between Denmark, Sweden, and Russia, to protect the neutral commerce. His endeavors met, for a while, with difficulties, but at length a treaty was concluded, called the *Act of the Armed Neutrality*, by which these three maritime powers jointly engaged themselves in maintaining the axiom, that a free ship makes free cargo, or that all merchandise, when not contraband, freely and without any control, could be carried on neutral vessels, to and from the countries of the belligerent powers. This alliance, entered upon by several states, exercised a highly beneficial influence upon the Danish commerce, England now altering her policy in this respect, and France and Spain acknowledging the principles of the armed neutrality. Especially the lines of transportation in the Mediterranean and the West Indies were very flourishing, which latter was carried on to a great extent, and with considerable profit. For the advancement of the commerce, a channel was formed between the bay of Kiel and the Eider river, a conjunction being thereby effected between the Baltic and the North Sea. But, nevertheless, financial affairs grew still worse during this period. In the first years several considerable expenses occurred, which

A. D., 1780.

increased the debt, but even in the following years the debt was continually increasing, notwithstanding the sources of wealth were pouring in abundantly. In the year 1784 the debt, which from 1766–1772 had been reduced to sixteen millions, amounted to twenty-nine millions of rix-dollars. The government tried to remedy the scarcity of money by redeeming the private bank, which, during the reign of Christian VI., had been established, and changing it to a royal bank. This alteration, though undertaken diametrically opposite to the charter of the bank, and detrimental to the shareholders, made it possible for the government, when want of money might happen, to issue out bills without having a corresponding value of silver; which expedient, in the following time, was used to such an extent as to ruin altogether the pecuniary affairs of the country.

The *period of Guldberg* is distinguished by a great care for the Danish literature. Guldberg himself was a man of extensive learning, and an active promoter of scientific undertakings. The Danish language, which long had been neglected, and during the ministry of Struensee entirely trampled under foot, regained esteem. In the army the German drill words were exchanged for Danish; at the court the Danish language was spoken; the Latin schools were reorganized, on which occasion the mother tongue and history of Denmark were introduced as the objects of instruction. Also, the University was reformed, though not to that extent which bishop Gunnerus, during the ministry of Struensee, had in view. The *charter of naturalization*, issued during the period of Guldberg, bears a strong witness to the patriotic mind of the government. By this law, which the king enjoined his successors to regard as an unalterable radical law, it was determined, that only Danes, Norwegians and Holsteiners should have access to the offices of the state; such men, however, excepted, as by rare talents, uncommon knowledge, or great wealth, might be of great service to the kingdoms. Notwithstanding science and the arts being protected and promoted, the government, nevertheless, during the ministry of Guldberg, was very disaffected toward the liberty of the press. That liberty which, under Struensee, had been given to every individual to express his opinions without reserve, by word or writing, ceased unfortunately again altogether. A law was now enacted, forbidding to insert in the newspapers or periodicals anything concerning the government and public institutions, the mayor of Copenhagen being entitled to punish the violators of this law, either by fine or imprisonment, without allowing any appeal to the tribunals. Also, against larger works, a high degree of arbitrary power was exercised, the government encroaching upon them, either through immediate orders from the cabinet council, or in other ways preventing them from being published.

A. D., 1773.

In reference to the peasantry, also, during the ministry

of Guldberg, principles were established diametrically opposite to those of the former government. Guldberg himself was fully convinced, that the yoke of the peasantry could not be taken off without entirely subverting the state. The committee which, under Struensee, had been appointed to propose improvements in the condition of the peasantry, was dissolved, professor *Oeder*, its most active and skillful member, being discharged, with the notification, that he had forfeited the king's favor. The law concerning the bond-service, so favorable to the peasants, which had been enacted during the ministry of Struensee, was annulled, the bond-service again being made indefinite, and replaced on its old despotic footing. The pressure on the peasantry also grew still worse by the erection of many new manors, which came up by continually disposing of the crown estates. Nevertheless, after count *Joachim Gotshe Moltke* had been appointed president of the exchequer, a law for the abrogation of the community of ground was enacted, highly important and beneficial for the agricultural classes.

The revolutionary war in America, of seven years' duration, had been waged vigorously, and successfully in its results to the cause of freedom. Misfortunes seemed to attend almost every scheme undertaken by England for coercing the Americans into obedience. The great continental powers, jealous of the maritime and commercial prosperity of England, and dissatisfied with her policy, ardently desired her humiliation, and rejoiced heartily at every misfortune that befel her, and the northern kingdoms shared in the universal joy, and mentioned Washington's name with respect and admiration; and when the proclamation of the cessation of hostilities was made to the army, on the 19th of April, 1783, Sweden had already, by virtue of the articles of peace, signed on the 30th of November, 1782, acknowledged, 5th of February, 1783, the independence of the United States; whereupon *Christian VII.*, on the 25th of February, 1783, for Denmark and Norway, subscribed to the independence of this great Union. Already, the year before, Holland had, 19th of April, 1782, acknowledged said independence. The expenditure of blood and money which this war had cost England was enormous. Of course, also, the United States had suffered during the war; the trade and the commerce of the country were almost destroyed, and agriculture was greatly interrupted and depressed, and the great Union was burdened with an immense debt, from which they, however, soon recovered, by maintaining a strict neutrality, and engaging themselves in an extensive and profitable carrying trade.

Crown-prince *Frederick*, son of Christian VII. and the unfortunate queen Caroline Mathilde, had now
A. D.. grown up and been confirmed by the court chap-
1784. lain, Dr. Bastholm, whereupon he conducted the reign; his father, Christian VII., being so mentally

deranged as not to be able to rule the kingdoms. A few days after his confirmation, the crown-prince removed Ove Guldberg, whose ministry ceased pursuant to an order in writing, signed by the imbecile king and the crown-prince, who now created a new ministry of state, into which were admitted the great and liberal jurisconsult, *Henry Stampe,* and the celebrated diplomate, *Andreas Peter Bernstorff,* who, after an absence of four years, returned to Denmark to conduct again the foreign affairs.

The peaceable terms on which Denmark was with Sweden, were for a little while interrupted, Sweden having attacked Russia, which Denmark, according to an earlier alliance, had to assist. Consequently a Danish army made from Norway an inroad into Sweden, and, commanded by crown-prince Frederick, advanced briskly into the Swedish frontier-provinces, which were unable to make any resistance, the Swedish troops having pitched their camp in Finland, in order to attack the Russians. A victory was obtained over the Swedes at *Qvistrum Bridge,* by the Danes, who advanced upon Gothenburg; but England interfering, and threatening Denmark with war, the hostilities soon ceased. This short campaign, however, had cost Denmark the considerable sum of seven millions of rix dollars. Shortly after, the unfortunate Louis XVI. of France was guillotined in Paris, and the democratic spirit, which had called forth the revo-

A.D. 1788.

Jan. 21, A.D., 1793.

lutionary war of America, was borne back to France by her chivalrous sons, who, in aiding the oppressed Americans, had imbibed their principles. The ancient constitution of France was overthrown, and the French Revolution was hurried forward, involving most European powers in a sanguinary war. But Denmark, through A. P. Bernstorff's wise diplomacy, being happy enough to maintain an unshaken neutrality, abundantly enjoyed the blessings of peace, carrying on the most flourishing commerce. The East India and China trade was so profitable, that for many years merchandise was yearly brought to Copenhagen, to the amount of five millions of rix-dollars; and the carrying trade in the Mediterranean, together with the North American and West Indian commerce, was likewise pursued with great profit. The trade, however, in the Mediterranean, was for a long time greatly molested by the Dey of Tripoli violently outraging the Danish merchantmen. But, notwithstanding peace having long reigned, the Danes had not degenerated from the ancient Northern bravery. The undaunted Admiral, *Steen Bille*, gained a complete victory over a superior Tripolitan fleet, and compelled the Dey to pay respect to the Danish flag, thus securing to the Danish trade in the Mediterranean due freedom and progress. The victory gained, the Dey presented Steen Bille, to show him his esteem, with a costly sabre.

A.D., 1797.

But, in the course of the French revolutionary war,

Denmark had a difficult game to play, frequent collisions occurring with the belligerent powers, especially with England, who despotically treated the neutral merchantmen. England now extending the list of contraband goods, by which before only munitions of war were meant, to meal, grain, and other bread-stuffs, and claiming the right of searching neutral ships for contraband articles, and of seizing vessels not laden with exceptionable cargoes, attempted to forbid Denmark to enjoy free navigation from one port to another, and to bring meal and grain, her most important articles of exportation, to France or other countries, which were waging war with England. Nevertheless, the wise Bernstorff succeeded in getting it determined, that all effects conveyed by Danish merchantmen, excepting only warlike stores, should be free, and in maintaining the peace and dignity of Denmark and Norway. A. D., But, unfortunately, Bernstorff died amidst these 1793. critical circumstances.

To protect the merchantmen against future outrage, Denmark now commenced to convoy them by ships of war; but England stubbornly claimed the right of searching even such merchantmen as were convoyed. Mutual recriminations were, therefore, almost constantly passing between the Danish and the English governments, the former complaining, that great numbers of Danish vessels, not laden with contraband goods, had been seized and carried into the ports of England; the latter accusing the former of supplying the enemies of England with naval and military stores. A slight collision in the English Channel, between *Freia*, a Danish man-of-war, and a superior English vessel, which, after a brave resistance, at last captured her, together with the merchantmen sailing under her convoy, increased the hostile feelings of the two nations; a war being about to break out, when fortunately a *Convention* was concluded, pursuant to which England returned the captured vessels, and Denmark promised not to convoy her merchantmen by ships of war until the matter in question was settled.

In the meantime, Napoleon, since the 10th of November, 1799, seated on the consular throne of France, was successfully planning a union of the northern powers against England, and on the 16th of December, a Maritime Confederacy was signed by Russia, Sweden, Denmark, and soon after by Prussia, on principles similar to the Armed Neutrality of 1780, and its effect would have been, if fully carried out, to deprive England of her naval superiority. Denmark having lately concluded a convention with England, was not inclined to accede to this new confederacy, but gave way, however, to the wish of the Russian emperor, Paul, who was highly exasperated at England; the Danish government now ordering her armed vessels to resist the search of the British cruisers, and the Russian emperor issuing an embargo on all the British ships in his harbors.

Still, England maintained her superiority at sea, and, determined to anticipate her enemies, despatched, as soon as possible, a powerful fleet to the Baltic, A. D., under the command of Sir *Hyde Parker* and 1801. *Nelson.* Passing through the sound at Elsenore under a tremendous fire from the Danish batteries, on the 30th of March, the English fleet, numbering fifty-one men-of-war, came to anchor opposite the harbor of Copenhagen, which was protected by an imposing array of forts and floating batteries; but the Danish men-of-war were old and almost unmanageable, commanded by admiral *Olfert Fisher.*

It is an interesting fact, that Charles G. Sommers, a Baptist minister in the city of New-York, still living, was in Copenhagen on the eventful day of the 2d of April, 1801. I cannot refrain from quoting the following graphic words from the "American Pulpit," published by Henry Fowler, Professor of the University of Rochester, N. Y.:

"Within two miles from Copenhagen the British fleet came to anchor, in the evening of the first of April. Here these mighty battle-ships lay all night, in a foreboding silence, broken only by the dash of waves against their huge black sides, or by sound of revelry, and low murmur of preparation, which ever and anon issued from the open port-holes. In the British fleet it was a night of wild joy and hope, and glorious anticipation of the morrow's victory, with the thrilling excitement which nerves the arm and steels the heart of soldier and seaman in the prospect of desolating contest. But the gloom of night, which settled over the doomed city of Copenhagen, was but a faint image of the forebodings shutting down so darkly on the hearts of all its desperate defenders. About ten o'clock on the following morning (Good Friday), Lord Nelson's ships had taken their allotted places, and at the signal opened their tremendous fire on the Danish armament. *April 2, A.D., 1801.* It was returned by the shot of one thousand guns, which spoke in terms not to be misunderstood, of the desperate bravery with which the Danes would defend their native land, and of the terrible destruction through which the British flag must pass, ere it waved in triumph over the citadel of Copenhagen. For more than five hours did these two mighty combatants, the flower of the English navy, and the concentrated strength of Denmark, wage upon each other a warfare of magnificent bravery, but of awful carnage. It was one of the hardest fought battles that humanity ever has been called to mourn over. Young Sommers was witness of it all, in its terribleness, its havoc, and its magnificence. When Nelson came on shore, Sommers had a good sight of him. *Villemoes*, too, he often saw, and describes him as of a very modest and retiring appearance, of whom the following is told A Danish youth of seventeen, named Villemoes, particularly distinguished himself on this memorable day.

He had volunteered to take the command of a floating battery, which was a raft, consisting merely of a number of beams nailed together, with a flooring to support the guns; it was square, with a breastwork full of port-holes, and without masts, carrying twenty-four guns and one hundred and twenty men. With this he got under the stern of the Elephant, below the reach of the stern-chasers, and, under a heavy fire of small arms from the marines, fought his raft till the truce was announced, with such skill and bravery as to excite Nelson's warmest admiration. Nelson requested of the crown-prince of Denmark, that Villemoes might be introduced to him; and shaking hands with this young northern hero, told the prince, that Villemoes ought to be made an admiral. The prince replied: 'If, my Lord, I am to make all my brave officers admirals, I should have no captains or lieutenants in my service.'"

After a continued fight of five hours the Danish fleet was almost altogether destroyed, but Nelson had undergone so great a loss as not to be able to continue the battle, his largest men-of-war being in a dangerous situation. The formidable fire from the Danish batteries being silenced, Nelson sent a white flag ashore, and negotiations were transacted. Nevertheless, it is not to be denied, that the victory in this horrible engagement rested with the English, but the Danes had fought with such courage and obstinacy as to procure them everlasting honor, to which Nelson's words to the crown prince bear witness: "Your royal highness! I have been in one hundred and five engagements, but that of Copenhagen was the most terrible of them all." Six thousand of Denmark's bravest sons were taken from her; the English loss was two thousand two hundred men, but many of their men-of-war had blown up. Against each other were arrayed men who knew no inspiration equal to that of their country's call, and paid no heed to personal safety, when her safety was endangered.

Nelson, a man of refinement of manners, humanity, and with studied courtesies of polished life, was, after the battle, cordially received in Copenhagen; and as an instance of his courtesy, it is related, that in the very midst of the battle, when the work of carnage and destruction was the hottest around him, and he judged it expedient to propose a cessation of hostilities, a wafer being brought to him to seal his communication to the Danish authorities, he rejected it, directing the wax and a taper to be brought, saying: "What! shall I send my own spittle to the crown-prince?"

An armistice was now concluded for fourteen weeks, during which time Denmark abdicated active participation in the Armed Neutrality. This armistice soon led to a complete peace, when the Russian emperor, *Paul*, the founder and head of the Northern Confederacy, who had provoked the indignation of the nobles and the people, was murdered by a party of

June 24, A.D., 1801.

conspirators, who placed upon the throne his son, *Alexander I.*, who immediately resolved to abandon the armed neutrality, and to cultivate the friendship of Great Britain. Sweden, Denmark, and Prussia followed his example, and thus was dissolved the League of the North, the most formidable confederacy ever arrayed against the maritime power of England.

Denmark soon retrieved the consequences of this war, and her commerce continued to flourish as before; but the incessant wars in the north of Germany occasioned immense expenses, Denmark deeming it necessary to keep her army in Holstein to protect the frontiers. Meanwhile Napoleon had rapidly extended his supremacy over the continent of Europe, and when the German empire was dissolved, and fourteen princes of the south and west of Germany were induced to form the Confederation of the Rhine, and place themselves under the protection of France, that feudal obligation in which Holstein had been to the German emperor ceased, and Holstein was now incorporated as an inseparable part of the Danish monarchy. A. D., 1806.

Denmark having hitherto sought, as far as possible, to keep out of the terrible war in which the French Revolution had involved most of the other states of Europe, was suddenly thrown into the middle of the great movements, which then shook Europe; and the blessed peace which Denmark, except a few short interruptions, had enjoyed since the year 1720, was now exchanged for a seven years' war of the most lamentable consequences.

It was generally believed that Napoleon intended to blockade all the harbors of the continent against Great Britain, and that he would compel Denmark to give up her neutrality, and probably avail himself of the Danish navy to execute his old project of an invasion. To prevent such an enterprise England sent, without any previous declaration of war, a powerful armament against Denmark, under the command of admiral *Gambier* and general *Cathcart*. An imperious demand for the instant surrender of the Danish fleet and naval stores, to be retained as a deposit by the English until the conclusion of the war, being peremptorily rejected, the Danes were briskly attacked by land and sea; but as their army was in Holstein to protect the frontiers, and was prevented by English men-of-war, cruising round in the Belts, from coming to the assistance of the capital, they could only make a very weak resistance.

Sept. 2-5, A. D., 1807. After Copenhagen had been furiously bombarded for three days, general *Peymann* was constrained to submit to the demands of the British, and the Danish fleet was, six weeks after, removed, while the indignant people could scarcely be prevented from avenging the national insult, even by the presence of a superior force. A militia, consisting principally of men who had never stood under fire, commanded by general *Castenskjold*, tried at *Kjöge*, four Danish miles from Copenhagen, to make head against the British troops, but were immediately routed. The enemy carried away thirty-three men-of-war and several frigates, besides a great store of ammunition.

Here I may quote the following graphic account from the *American Pulpit:* " It was six years after the horrible battle of 1801, that a British fleet suddenly appeared off Elsenore, the toll-gate city of Denmark. It amounted to nearly a score of line ships, a large number of frigates and gun-boats, with transports carrying some twenty thousand men. As they swept into the straits under a light wind, with all sails spread, flags, pennants, and streamers flying from mastheads, bows, and sterns, every yard throughout the whole fleet manned with seamen, Mr. Sommers describes it a magnificent sight. And when the bands of eleven regiments struck up the national air : ' Rule, Britannia, Britannia rule the Waves,' the effect was thrilling. With his usual enterprise in search of incident or information, Sommers jumped into a skiff with a companion, and pulled off for the Prince of Wales, a ninety-eight gun ship. Going on board, he was most kindly received, and invited below to a repast with the officers. He frankly inquired where they were going with such a fleet. An officer replied: " We do not know; sealed orders have been given us, which will be opened this afternoon; and we *hope* it is not to Copenhagen." But alas, it was. That afternoon the fleet weighed anchor for that unfortunate capital, and the next morning the booming of cannon was heard at Elsenore, twenty-four English miles distant, and Copenhagen was bombarded.

"This attack was made under the command of Lord Gambier. It was done for the purpose of getting possession of the Danish fleet, which lay dismantled in its harbor. This fleet the English government was informed by their active minister abroad, Jackson, was to come into possession of the French, which John Bull could not, and would not allow. The fleet was captured; English sailors swarmed on board of the stripped vessels, rigged them, fitted them for sea, and the two fleets passed over to England. In this engagement, the enthusiasm of young Sommers would not allow him merely to sit quietly on the end of a ship-crane. but he must assist in the defence of Denmark, his adopted country. So he joined the company which manned the old fort of Kronborg, the guns of which swept the straits, and there played away at the ships as they passed."

This act of violence against Denmark, called so by the whole of Europe, furnished the Russian emperor with a pretext for breaking off his connection with Great Britain. He complained, in strong language, of the disregard which England had ever shown for the rights of neutral powers, and the unscrupulous use that had been made of her naval supremacy, and many of the maritime states seconded his remonstrances. Denmark, though deprived of her navy, resented the blow inflicted on her by England, by throwing herself without reserve into the arms of France. Shortly after, A. D., 1808. Denmark declared war against Sweden, whose king, *Gustavus IV.*, a son of the celebrated Gustavus III., who, in 1792, at a masked-ball, had been murdered by Captain John Jacob Ankarström, was in the closest connection with England, and strove for the possession of Norway. A few days after the breaking out of the war with Sweden, the imbecile Christian VII. died in Rendsburg, Holstein, and his A. D., 1808. son, who, since 1784, had ruled Denmark and Norway as crown-prince, ascended the throne of both kingdoms by the name of *Frederick VI.*

The kingdoms were, at that time, in a very critical situation, involved in a double war, and on account of the loss of the fleet not able to undertake anything of consequence against England, their most dangerous enemy; their commerce was weakened by England's capturing many hundred merchantmen, and their agriculture was greatly interrupted and depressed. The capital had suffered greatly by the English bombardment; and some years before, 1794, it had been greatly injured by a fire, which even consumed the splendid palace of Christiansborg, considered one of the most costly and beautiful in Europe.

French reinforcements arrived in Denmark under the

command of *Charles John Bernadotte*, prince of Pontecorvo, one of Napoleon's most celebrated marshals, and preparations were made to make a descent upon Skane in Sweden. The reinforcements consisted mostly of Spanish soldiers, who mutinied, and the expedition was abandoned. But on the Norwegian frontier, the war was waged very successfully by the skillful, talented, and generally beloved prince, *Christian August*, of Augustenburg.

Meanwhile the eccentric *Gustavus Adolphus IV.*, who, by his imprudent reign, had brought Sweden into the most miserable condition, had been deposed on the 13th of March, 1809, and his uncle, *Charles XIII.*, raised to the Swedish throne. After his accession to

A. D., 1809. the crown of Sweden, peace was concluded with Denmark, in Jónkóping, by which everything remained as before the war, and with Russia the same year, in *Frederikshamn*, by which peace Sweden lost *Finland*, which for six hundred and fifty years had belonged to Sweden—the most unfortunate peace Sweden has ever concluded.

Charles XIII. being old and childless, the Swedes

A. D., 1810. elected prince Christian August, of Augustenburg, successor to the throne. By the name of Charles August he arrived in Sweden, where he, by his mild and unaffected deportment, made himself highly beloved; but while he was reviewing a regiment of hussars in Skane, at Quidinge Heath, he died suddenly, not without some suspicion of poison. Count *Axel Fersen*, suspected of having poisoned him, was, when the body of the dearly beloved crown-prince was escorted to the tomb, cut to pieces by the mob of Stockholm. The Swedish senate feeling convinced that a tried warrior was, under the sad circumstances, necessary for Sweden, tendered the succession to Charles John Bernadotte, who had won their favor by the leniency and prudence he had displayed some years before in the North of Germany. Bernadotte, willingly accepting the glorious offer, to the secret annoyance of Napoleon, who had long been jealous of his military fame and independent spirit, arrived in Sweden in October, 1810, by the name of Charles John.

A.D., 1810.

To return to Denmark: against England the war could only be waged very weakly, Denmark being deprived of her fleet; and the few men-of-war which had escaped the attention of the English in 1807, were successively captured, amongst others, the *Prince Christian*, which, after a most heroic resistance under admiral *Jessen*, was entirely cut up on the northern coast of Sjelland. But, notwithstanding Denmark had nothing but a few small vessels and gun-boats, which had been built by patriotic private people, to oppose the English men-of-war cruising all the time round in the Danish sounds and belts, the Danish sea-warriors often battled bravely against the enemy, and caused him, in the course of the war, many severe losses. But an attempt made by the Danes to recover the island of *Anholt*, in the Cattegat, was defeated by the English garrison; a great loss to the international commerce.

Sweden could scarcely be said to be at war with Great Britain. Bernadotte soon discovered that subserviency to France was inconsistent with the interests of his adopted country, and he secretly entered into negotiations with the Russian emperor for restoring their mutual independence.

In the year 1812 the situation of Denmark became yet more critical. On the 24th of June, 1812, Napoleon crossed the Niemen at the head of "*the Grand Army*," and entered upon his ever-memorable Russian campaign. On the morning of the 7th of September the great battle was fought at the small village of *Borodino*, seventy miles from Moscow, where neither side gained a decisive victory. Napoleon now approached Moscow, the ancient capital of the Czars, revered by the Russians as Jerusalem by the Jews. The citizens resolved not only to abandon their beloved metropolis, but to consign it to the flames; and Napoleon, not able to check the conflagration, had to undertake his perilous retreat.

Exasperated at Napoleon, and to acquire assistance against this his enemy, and, if possible, to break him entirely, the Russian emperor, Alexander, although there was at that time peace and amity between Denmark and Russia, offered Sweden his aid in depriving Denmark of Norway. The following year Den-

A. D., 1813.

mark was summoned to share in the war against Napoleon, and *resign Norway to Sweden*. This iniquitous request left nothing to Denmark but to take a yet closer part with France, whereby all the powers which were allied against France now became Denmark's enemies; and after Napoleon, on the 18th of October, 1813, had been signally defeated at Leipsic, an immense army of Swedish, Prussian, and Russian troops, commanded by the elected crown-prince of Sweden, Prince of Pontecorvo, now called Charles John, rushed upon the frontiers of Denmark. The Danish army, which had pitched its camp in Holstein, had to retreat, but fought bravely against superior numbers. A division of the army had on its retreat been cut off from the fortress of *Rendsburg*, but, after an honorable and obstinate battle at *Sehestedt*, won the field. A. D., 1813.

Denmark having now, through seven years, endured a desolating war, could no longer afford to continue the contest, and Frederick VI. submitted to conclude the peace of *Kiel*, by which Denmark resigned Norway to Sweden. Thus the close union which, for four hundred and thirty-four years, had existed between Denmark and Norway, was dissolved, and Denmark lost a large kingdom, the inhabitants of which had always obeyed the Danish kings with love and loyalty; and the allies have incurred just censure for aiding in this forcible annexation of Norway to Sweden, against the earnest remonstrances of the inhabitants As a sort of compensation for the loss of Norway, Denmark obtained *Swedish Pomerania*, which was afterwards exchanged with Prussia for the duchy of Laüenburg and a sum of money. Peace was also concluded with England at Kiel, by which Denmark had to concede Helgoland, a rocky island in the North Sea, to Great Britain.

Nevertheless the Norwegians tried to defend their independence under the Danish hereditary prince, *Christian Frederick*, who gave Norway a free constitution, and was proclaimed king, but never acknowledged by any European state. The Swedish crown-prince, Charles John (Bernadotte), now marched his victorious army into Norway, and the Swedish fleet conquered Frederickstad. The fortress of Frederickshald was besieged, and the Swedish army advanced upon Christiania, the capital of Norway. The superiority being too large, the Norwegians hastened to secure their persons and property by a capitulation in *Moss*, upon condition that Norway should belong to Sweden, and Christian Frederick immediately leave Norway; the Swedish king, however, confirming that free constitution which Christian Frederick had given to Norway.

August, A. D., 1814.

Although Norway is now under the same crown with Sweden, it is in reality little connected with the latter country. Its democratic assembly, called *the Storthing*, meets for three months once in three years, by its own right, and not by any writ from the king. If a bill passes both divisions of this assembly in three successive Storthings, it becomes a law of the land without the royal assent; a right which no other monarchico-legislative assembly in Europe possesses.

In the meantime the fate of France was decided; Napoleon was, on the 2d of April, formally deposed, and, by a treaty between him and the allies, promised the sovereignty of the island of Elba and a pension. But when he suddenly landed at Frejus, (March 1, 1815), and soon again found himself at the summit of power, and re-ascended the throne of France, Denmark took part with the other European powers in fighting against him; and after having lost the memorable battle of Waterloo, nine miles south of Brussels (18th of June, 1815), Napoleon a second time abdicated the throne of France, and was banished by the allies to St. Helena, where he died on the 5th of May, 1821. A. D., 1814.

At the general congress of the allied powers, which assembled at Vienna, the Danish king, Frederick VI., was present, and subscribed to the incorporation of the duchy of Holstein into the Germanic Confederation. Of Schleswig not a word was spoken, it being considered an inseparable part of the Danish body. Since that time the peace of Denmark has not been interrupted until 1848, when the rebellious duchies tried to shake off the Danish yoke, and erect themselves into independent states, and waged a sanguinary three years' war against the Danish king, being assisted by more than twenty thousand Prussians and Hanoverians A. D., 1815.

Of the favorable period previous to the breaking out of the war, the government had availed itself, to make important improvements in agriculture and in other matters. When crown-prince Frederick, in the year 1784, during his father's imbecility, assumed the reins of government, the peasantry was in a most lamentable condition, and agriculture very defective. Community of ground still prevailed in most places, although in 1781 a strict law had been enacted against it, but on account of prevailing prejudices, it had been very difficult to carry this law into execution. Not less detrimental for the advancement of agriculture was the bond-service, with a few exceptions, yet in use. The number of owners of farms decreased more and more, and the tenants were in most places impoverished and oppressed. Many sorts of grain were not cultivated at all, and when sterile years happened, the country could not supply itself with provisions. Public instruction was yet at a very low ebb, though Frederick IV. and Christian VI. had made active efforts for improving it. As far as the personal relation to the nobility was concerned, the tenants were subject to the greatest despotism. When the nobleman was just and well-minded, the tenants did tolerably well; but if he would intrude upon them, it was difficult for the peasants to be protected against oppression and injustice. After military service of many years, the country lad was obliged to return to that estate from which he was enlisted, and then to take what farm soever the nobleman might please to give him, and on whatsoever terms. The bond-service being indefinite, the nobleman exercised the most unlimited power over the tenants' time and labor, and was authorized to lash them and punish them with the wooden horse and jail; a right which the nobility often exercised in its full extent, and occasionally with circumstances of peculiar atrocity.

But the crown-prince, a warm and munificent patron of the peasantry, appointed (1784) a committee, consisting of *Christian Frederick Ditlev Reventlov*, *Andrew Peter Bernstorff*, and *Chr. Colbjórnsen*, who, by their skill and activity in improving the condition of the agricultural classes, have acquired an immortal name. The beginning was made in the counties of Kronborg and Fredericksborg, near Copenhagen; the ground was parceled, bond-service abrogated, the tithes changed to a money tribute, and the farms were given to the peasants as property.

As the result of this reform, a general improvement took place among the peasantry. Next year a law was immediately enacted, which forbade the nobility to exercise any despotism over them, their mutual rights and duties being exactly fixed. The noblemen were now forbidden to inflict punishment upon the peasants, either by stripes or imprisonment, and it was decided that the farms, previous to being given to the peasants, should be examined by umpires;

A. D., 1785

controversies respecting the farming out should be decided upon by the magistracy, and no longer left to the sentence of the despotic nobleman.

Yet more important was the *emancipation of the peasantry from feudal bondage*. A law was enacted enfranchising all the peasantry who were under fourteen or above thirty-six years of age, and all others from the first of January, 1800. This memorable law restored personal liberty to the Danish peasantry, and made the peasant a free citizen of the state, as well as the other inhabitants of the country. The government also extended its care to the peasantry of the duchies, where an abominable slavery resting upon the peasantry, and depriving not only the males but also the females of personal liberty, was entirely abolished.

June 20, A. D., 1788.

All these thorough reformations in the condition of the agricultural classes, met, however, with great opposition from a great part of the nobility, an application signed by one hundred and two noblemen being tendered to the crown-prince, to repeal the new laws, which they particularized as detrimental to the country, and repugnant to their own privileges; but, fortunately, the crown-prince had firmness enough to answer in the negative, and the government continued to follow the humane principles it had adopted. Those inequalities in burdens and privileges among the citizens of the state, which through centuries had been kept up, were now successively diminished. The great privilege which the nobility had of appointing clergymen and judges on their estates, gave no assurance that these important offices would be filled by qualified persons, and had often occasioned the grossest abuses. No sooner, therefore, had the crown-prince ascended the throne, than he changed this detrimental privilege to a right of nominating (*jus proponendi*), upon the practice of which, moreover, many restrictions were placed. A. D., 1809.

The Jews, in Denmark as well as in most other states, deprived of all civil privileges, and excluded from exercising any profession and filling any offices, were now placed nearly on equal terms with the other inhabitants, and Frederick VI. already, when crown-prince, testified to his humane and philanthropic principles, by putting a stop to the slave-trade in the Danish West Indies; and it is remarkable that Denmark and the United States preceded England in declaring the slave-trade unlawful. But the example thus set forth has afterwards been followed by all the great maritime countries of Europe and America. At length, in the year 1807, under the Grenville administration, an act for the abolition of the slave-trade passed the British legislature, to which the impulse was given in the year 1784, when Dr. Peckard, vice-chancellor of the University of Cambridge, proposed as the subject of a Latin essay, for which a gold medal was to be given, an answer to the question: *Anne liceat invitos in servitutem* A. D., 1782.

dare? or, "Is it right to make slaves of others against their will?" But, although both the king and the people of Denmark have manifested the strongest repugnance to the traffic in human beings, this trade lingered in her colonies in the west for years after it had been declared illegal. So difficult is it to enforce just laws in distant possessions, demoralized by a vicious and criminal system.

Besides the institutions above mentioned, Frederick VI. made, in other respects, many important improvements. The criminal code was highly improved by a new law on theft. The tribunal of inquisition, also called the sharp examination, the branding, and the barbarous running the gantlet, were abrogated. Of great importance for commerce was the new tariff, which regulated the commercial affairs according to sounder principles than before. Useful alterations were also made in the organization of the army; the enrollment of foreign soldiers was abrogated, the army now consisting exclusively of the native subjects, while formerly German soldiers comprised a considerable part of the Danish army. The military officers' higher scientific education was provided for by the erection of a *Military Academy*, where the young engineers learn mathematics, and to unite mobility of manœuvre with rapidity of fire and precision of aim.

That the peasantry might enjoy the right fruit of the many improvements which had been made for their advancement, Frederick VI. deemed it necessary thoroughly to organize and ameliorate the public instruction. To train up qualified teachers for the peasantry, *normal schools* (seminaries) were established in various sections of the country; many new schools were built, and money was assigned for the salaries of the teachers. A new school-law was enacted, and every peasant was enjoined to send his children to school for instruction.

The *Polytechnic School*, founded upon the recommendation of the celebrated natural philosopher, *Hans Christian Oersted*, has exercised a considerable influence in promoting the study of the science of nature, and spreading useful knowledge and greater skill amongst mechanics. The University and the learned schools were thoroughly reorganized, mainly to be ascribed to the active and skillful Frederick Christian, duke of Augustenburg, who, in the beginning of the present century, was appointed patron of the University. The examinations were made more strict, and a special examination was enjoined upon those, who intended to be teachers in the learned schools, called *Examen philologicum*. The Academy of Sorö, consumed by fire in 1813, was rebuilt and recalled to life in 1822, and solemnly inaugurated in 1827. It deserves also to be remarked, that Frederick VI. founded the University of Christiania, in Norway, which the Norwegians, therefore, call *the Frederick's University*. [Sept. 2, A. D., 1811.]

Although Frederick VI. had not himself had the benefit of a thorough education, we have to observe how much literature was indebted to him for its advancement and dissemination in Denmark. Classical learning, the art of criticism, poetry, and history, began from his time to make a rapid progress. The two learned bishops of Copenhagen, *Frederick Münter* and *Peter Erasmus Möller*, enriched the historical, antiquarian, and theological literature with invaluable treasures. Münter is also celebrated for his extensive knowledge in the oriental languages. *Malte Conrad Bruun*, who, for having by his writings offended the government, was banished, acquired in Paris an immortal name as the greatest geographer of the world. *Rask* is celebrated as a great linguist. *Bróndsted* has immortalized himself by deeply searching into the curiosities of the Greek antiquities. *Finn Magnusson* and *C. Rafn*, both yet living, unite deep knowledge in the antiquities of the North, with perspicuity of narration and force of language. The study of jurisprudence was vigorously promoted by Kongslev, E. Colbjórnson and F. Schlegel; that of medicine by Tode, Saxtorph, F. L. Bang, Winslów, and Herholdt. *H. C. Oersted* is known over the whole civilized world, for his deep knowledge, and discoveries in physics. *Tetens, Bugge*, and *Degen* have signalized themselves as great mathematicians, and *Abildgaard* and *Viborg*, as superior veterinarians.

Bertel Thorvaldsen has placed himself at the head

of all the sculptors that ever the world produced. *Oehlenschlæger* has won a great name as a poet, and the strict unity of his pieces demonstrates a thorough acquaintance with the rules of the classic tragedy. His genius was original, and he disdained to imitate. Coeval with Oehlenschlæger was his friend, the illustrious theologian and poet of Sweden, bishop *Esajas Tegner*. He was born on the 13th of November, 1782. In the year 1824 he was appointed bishop of Vexó, and justified this promotion by the most zealous guardianship of the educational institutions of his large diocese. His spirited speeches on public occasions often excited an extraordinary sensation, and his eloquent address to the assembly of the Swedish clergy, in Vexó, in 1836, has not been confined within the limits of his diocese, but convinced all classes, that he no less deserved consideration as a deep and fearless theologian, than as an accomplished and nearly unequaled poet. In his charming poem, *Frithiof's Saga*, he has bequeathed a poetic inheritance to posterity, never to be lost, in which he, in a masterly manner, resolved the epic form into free lyric romances. The noble, the high-minded, the bold, the great features of all heroism, are not wanting there. His is, therefore, a perpetual glory, "*cui neque profuit quisquam laudando, neque vituperando quisquam nocuit.*"

Hans Christian Andersen has, by his poems and novels, made an agreeable impression upon his readers, d has acquired a great name in Europe and even now in the United States. His productions are not the fruit of deep study or learning, but of native talent; and it is to be observed to his honor, that in all his works, goodness and virtue are inculcated, as he himself is the impersonation of goodness and morality. This characteristic distinguishes him from the many worthless novelists, who, in a variety of licentious novels, have prostituted excellent talents in the service of vice.

As Latinist, *J. N. Madvig* stands nearly unsurpassed, and has acquired such a renown, that the great German philologers, when uncertain how to interpret a difficult passage in the Latin classics, write: "*Consulamus juniorem Madvigium Daniæ.*" Dr. *Jacob Peter Mynster*, bishop of Sjelland (*ob.* 1854), has, as a learned linguist, theologian, and talented pulpit-orator, gained a name never to be forgotten. The truth of Christianity, which he, after a deep philosophic searching, had embraced with all his heart, appears eloquently and powerfully embodied in his edifying sermons and theological writings, in the clear reflections of which a rich fullness of sublime thoughts and a deep insight into the human heart are manifest. The strength of his pious and devout feelings warmed his audience; a mild, but ministerial earnestness gave his words dignity, and in short, he had a strong and vigorous intellect, rendered, by scientific culture, capable of clear discrimination, correct analysis, and happy combinations. His views of the Christian doctrines were clear and decided;

he received the great system of evangelical truth in its simplicity, and he defended that truth with modesty and gentleness. In all his preparations for the pulpit, his great and leading desire and purpose were to set forth Christ, the great high-priest of our profession. When he departed this life, the great theologians of Germany wrote: "Who can predict the day when Mynster's name shall be forgotten?"

Nicolai Frederick Severin Grundtvig, still living, equally remarkable as a pulpit-orator, poet, and deep historian, has exercised a mighty influence upon the religious and literary life, and in his learned explanations of the massive Northern mythology, he is generally considered unrivalled. As elegant and thorough historians, *L. Englestoft*, *E. Werlauf* and *C. Molbeck* in Denmark, and *Geyer* in Sweden, deserve to be mentioned, who all have sought to inspire their readers with esteem for history, to warm their hearts and strengthen their moral power.

But I shall not close this hasty sketch of Scandinavian literature, without mentioning *Henry Nicolai Clausen*, supreme theological professor at the University of Copenhagen. Richly endowed with gifts and graces, he has published, both in Latin and Danish, many learned works, which have gained him a great number of disciples and admirers, both at home and abroad. He ascended, in early youth, to the post of a theological professor, and there he has stood, from week to week, during a period of nearly thirty-two years, reflecting from his own clear and polished mind the light of divine truth, and communicating it to his numerous disciples, who, after having sat at the feet of this approved master in Israel, have come forth from his instruction able ministers of the New Testament. Besides his theological erudition he has excited admiration by managing the Latin language with an uncommon degree of volubility and genius, and, on the whole, I can convey but a faint idea of that portraiture of the Christian and the learned professor, which his life has exhibited. There have rarely been combined such simplicity and spirituality, such youthful elasticity and manly vigor, such gentleness of manners and decision of character, as are seen in him.

The seven years' unfortunate war, terminating in so heavy losses, had excessively enervated the state. Agriculture was in a most lamentable condition, commerce almost annihilated, industry was stagnant and money matters deranged. The interest of the public debt remained unpaid, the certificates of it depreciated every day, and many, who held them, were obliged to sell them for almost nothing. To remedy these evils, A. D., the surplus revenue from the duties on imports, 1818. and the change of the royal bank to a national bank, administered without the control of the government, were appropriated. This measure immediately restored public credit, certificates of public debt rose to par, and those who had purchased low realized immense fortunes. Business of all kinds revived, and the country entered upon a career of prosperous activity and enterprise. Nevertheless, the national debt yet amounted, in 1847, to one hundred and six millions of rix-dollars.

Sweden having also suffered very severely by her war with Russia and Denmark, was, however, this year, happy enough to get rid of her inefficient and demoralized king, Charles XIII., who expired in February, 1818, and *John Baptista Julius Bernadotte*, prince of Pontecorvo, who already (21st of August, 1810,) had been elected Swedish crown-prince, ascended now the throne of Sweden and Norway, and was solemnly crowned on the 11th of May, 1818. His personal influence, due alike to his diplomatic wisdom, his virtues, and his eminent military talents acquired in Napoleon's school, became of the utmost importance to Sweden. During the twenty-six years of his wise administration, all differences with foreign nations had been settled; public and private credit was restored, and ample provision made for the payment of the public debt. When ascending the throne, he assumed the motto: "The love of my people is my reward," and he fully realized it. This celebrated monarch, to whom Sweden is indebted for her present influence and temporal happiness, was born on the 26th of January, 1764, in the city of Pau in the southern part of France, and married to Eugenia Bernhárdina Desideria, daughter of a rich merchant in

Marseilles, by whom he only had one son, prince Oscar, afterwards the talented and highly beloved king of Sweden and Norway, by the name of *Oscar I.*

Although, as above mentioned, the kingdom of Denmark had commenced to enter upon a career of activity and enterprise, its rapid thriving was highly retarded by a series of unfavorable years, through which the grain prices were so low, that the king had to lighten the taxes for the peasants. The flourishing commerce which Copenhagen had carried on with China, America, and the East and West Indies, and which had been a rich source of wealth for the whole kingdom, had, during the war, been utterly ruined, and since that time the commerce of Copenhagen has not been of any consequence. Only in the last decennary of the reign of Frederick VI., the country recovered a little strength, the commerce of the cities increased, and on account of the improvements which had been made in agriculture and in the condition of the peasantry, the productions of the country increased to such a degree that the exports almost doubled; even in industry and home-trade a brisker life began to stir up.

But the very last part of the reign of Frederick VI. has been remarkable for an institution which became of great influence upon Denmark's felicity and advancement. Since the introduction of the absolute power, 1660, the people had been deprived of all influence upon the legislation and the rule of the state; this was altered by the introduction of a *council representative of the people* Already, in the year 1720, Sweden, under Frederick of Hesse Cassel, had become a hereditary monarchy, with a representative Diet consisting of four chambers, formed respectively of deputies from the nobility, clergy, burghers, and peasants, and in a great part of Europe the people had obtained either a deciding or an advising influence upon the government; and the Danish people, influenced by the European culture and by the increasing enlightenment, had gradually come to such a maturity as to make its co-operation in the government highly desirable. Frederick VI., though as fond of his sovereignty as a baby of his puppet, resolved, nevertheless, to meet the demand of the time by the introduction, both for Denmark and the Duchies, of a *council representative of the people*; a resolution [May 28, A.D., 1831.] received with every demonstration of joyous enthusiasm throughout the whole kingdom. All measures respecting government, all questions regarding public affairs. all propositions for the public good, might take their rise indifferently in this council and be discussed there, and then presented to the king's consideration. But being only a *deliberative* assembly, the king was not compelled to admit the proposals of the council, but had promised to take all proposals, which had taken their rise from this council, into serious consideration, and make them laws, if *his wisdom* thought it proper or prudent to do so. This inestimable privilege of the Danish subjects was productive of very much good, and made Frederick VI. yet more beloved and popular than he already, by his unassuming manners, his national and sincere mind, had been, when, at the age of seventy-two, and after a remarkable reign of fifty-five years, first twenty-four years as crown-prince, then thirty-one years as king, the Lord removed him from this scene of trial to inherit life everlasting. His people mourned for him, but offered thanksgiving to God that he had raised up for them so good and so faithful a steward, who had always been found willing to share their hardships. Twelve peasants from the county of Copenhagen asked permission to bear the royal coffin, on which was written " The memory of the just is blessed." *Prov.* x. 7. His queen was the virtuous and intelligent *Marie Sophie Fredericka*, a princess of Hesse Cassel, who survived him thirteen years. Having no sons by her, he was succeeded in the reign by his cousin, Christian Frederick, ascending the throne by the name of *Christian VIII.* Enriched by nature and cultivation, he was, when assuming the reins of government, considered one of the most enlightened monarchs of Europe; and added to this his prepossessing appearance and engaging manners, and that, from his shoulders and upward he was, like Saul, higher than any of the people, he was received everywhere with the greatest enthusiasm and veneration, Denmark flattering herself with the prospect of enjoying golden days under his sway, and of profiting by the liberal spirit to which he, twenty-five years ago, had testified in Norway. Puffed up, as we have noticed before, by a transient gleam of prosperity, he had in Norway, 1814, assumed the title of king, but was after a little while, by Bernadotte, whose star was then on the ascendant, compelled to resign the crown of Norway. But, however short his reign was in Norway, he has left behind him an undying monument in the hearts of the Norwegians, by giving them the free Constitution above mentioned, by which he sowed the seeds of freedom, and produced a rich harvest in the blessings of independence, which spread quickly over the whole kingdom.

The Danish people, on good grounds expecting that the new king, Christian VIII., would bless them with a like freedom, were nevertheless highly deceived in their expectations, as the king, having confined all his ideas to the power, dignity, and splendor of the crown, decidedly declined giving a free constitution, asserting that the people had not yet attained to such a degree of intellectual maturity as to be capable of duly enjoying the blessings of freedom. A spirit of opposition, which confined itself to complaints under this reign, began in the next to break out into active efforts. But, although declining to bless Denmark with the privilege of liberty, and unwilling to renounce even the smallest particle of the royal prerogatives, he was in many other respects a useful ruler. He reformed the laws, encouraged commerce; and science and the arts, which the king himself loved dearly, were munificently patronized by him.

During his reign Dr. *Hans Larsen Martensen*, now bishop of Sjelland, commenced to draw the attention of the learned of Europe to his brilliant talents. After having, in the year 1832, passed his theological examination at the University of Copenhagen, to the greatest satisfaction and admiration of his examiners and the faculty, he went to Berlin, where he deeply profited by the instruction of the great theologians and philosophers, Neander, Marheinecke, Schelling, and Twesten, and joined their scientific debates. Upon his returning, Christian VIII. appointed him theological professor at the University, where Martensen, to the most crowded and refined audience, delivered his spirited lectures on the strict conjunction of the scientific theology with philosophy, and on the exegesis of the New Testament. His brilliant gifts as a public orator induced the king to appoint him court chaplain, expecting in him an able champion and defender of the Christian faith. The king was not disappointed in his expectations. In the king's chapel he mounted the pulpit, where he did not shun to declare the whole counsel of God, proclaiming His severity in due conjunction with His loving-kindness. Peculiarly skilled in setting forth the awfulness of Sinai, and in launching forth the terrors of the law, he never fails in the tender presentation of the great sufferings and love of our Saviour, and of the attractions of his cross to dying men. In the year 1846 he published his *Dogmatics*, a clear and learned work, which immediately was translated into German, and received with great applause among the learned theologians of Germany.

Christian VIII. not only patronized literary men, but also directed his royal attention to other branches of his kingdom's welfare and advancement. Railroads were laid down in Holstein and Sjelland, the Sound Dues at Elsenore were reduced, the public and learned schools were re-organized, a new seminary (normal school) was erected in Jutland, Iceland was given a council representative of the people, and the East India possessions no longer being of any pecuniary profit to Denmark, were disposed of to England. Many circumstances had long contributed to check the prosperity of the Danish East India Company, but none more than the pertinacious jealousy of the Dutch, who excluded them from the most profitable branches of trade; and Christian VIII., therefore, did well in selling them. But, although the kings of Denmark were not successful in carrying out any considerable commerce there, they have honorably distinguished themselves by their zeal for the propagation of the Gospel; and, notwithstanding their limited means they have diffused the principles of true religion through a considerable portion of the south of India and of the east of Africa.

In North Schleswig, where the Danish language was used in divine service and school-teaching, Christian

VIII. commanded it to be used also in lawsuits and public affairs, instead of the German language, before used, as he also in other ways has promoted the interest of the mother-tongue. During his reign the neighboring kingdom, Sweden, lost, on the 8th of March, 1844, her great and talented king, Charles John XIV., once, as we know, Napoleon's celebrated marshal. He was succeeded in the Swedish throne by his son, *Oscar I.*, born on the 4th of July, 1799, and married to *Josephine Maximiliane Eugenie*, princess of Leuchtenberg, daughter of Napoleon's step-son, prince Eugene. By her King Oscar has four sons and one daughter. Sweden thus now ruled by French blood, and no more by the descendants of the celebrated house of Vasa, has, nevertheless, not had any reason of complaining over it, Charles John XIV. being an excellent king, and his son, Oscar I., having wielded the sceptre with clemency, wisdom, and justice.

In the year 1859, Sweden and Norway had to mourn for the loss of this high-minded and accomplished monarch. His son, the crown prince Carl Eugene, then ascended the throne of the twin-kingdoms, on the 8th of July, of the same year, under the name of Carl the Fifteenth, whose genius and talent for government, combined with knowledge of the eminent masters of antiquity, will enable him to redeem the expectations of his dear Swedish and Norwegian subjects.

Christian VIII., although declining to give Denmark a free constitution, thought, however, at the close of his life, of meeting the demand of the time, and had himself, delineated such a one, when, in an earlier hour than he and his people expected it, death claimed him. *Jan. 20, A D., 1848.* He was married to *Caroline Amalie,* a princess of Augustenburg, and sister to the rebellious duke who mainly involved Denmark in the horrible war with the Duchies. She is still living, and has, loving her God and her Redeemer, done, and is doing, very much to promote a true religious life. After the death of Christian VIII., the crown was placed on the head of his only son, *Frederick VII.,* born on the 6th of October, 1808. No sooner had he ascended the throne, than he yielded to the clamors of his subjects, dismissed his father's old aristocratic ministry, appointed a new one, and gave Denmark the long desiderated *free constitution,* which made him very popular and beloved, Denmark now being no more an absolute, but a constitutional monarchy. The Constitution, freed from all those despotic restraints with which it had been fettered by the Act of Sovereignty in 1660, was now fixed on a basis more favorable to the people's liberties than had ever been known in the annals of the nation. Undeniably, a few men, who had put this important wheel in motion, had made patriotism a cloak for their views of private interest, and made a great harvest; but, be it as it may, it is sufficient to say, that, under the influence of this Constitution, of which Denmark now, together with the United States and Norway, has to boast, the condition of society, whatever fluctuations it must, from the constitution of our frail human nature, be liable to, has been such as to answer all the wishes of the good, the virtuous, and the industrious part of the community, and its restraints have proved grievous to the overweening nobility alone, on whom restraint was necessary.

Frederick VII. mounted the throne under critical circumstances, but before entering on the abominable war with the Duchies, wrought by the treacherous policy of the rebellious duke of Augustenburg, it will be necessary to cast a brief glance at the affairs of Europe.

A revolutionary spirit pervaded, in the year 1848, nearly all Europe, like an epidemic fever. Louis Philippe, of France, having acquired a high reputation for wisdom and firmness, was, however, far from finding his throne a bed of roses. In the beginning of his reign, zealously supported by the middle classes, who looked upon him as their guarantee for constitutional freedom, he soon lost their favor, as they believed themselves deceived in their expectations, and an all-pervading feeling of discontent taking place, led to the Revolution of February, 1848. On the 23d of February, crowds appeared in the streets of the capital, barricades were erected, and the cry: "To arms! Down with Louis Philippe! Down with the Bourbons!" resounded throughout Paris. The troops allowed themselves to be disarmed by the mob, who then demanded the abdication of the king, who, with his queen, escaped to St. Cloud, and thence, in disguise, to England. Royalty had vanished, and France was again a Republic. No sooner had the accounts of the affairs in Paris reached Germany, than popular commotions took place, and the people demanded a political constitution, that should give them a share in legislation, establish the liberty of the press, and otherwise secure them their rights. The grand-duke of Baden had to yield to the demands of his people, and appoint a ministry from the popular party. The king of Saxony was compelled to grant the requests of his subjects. At Munich, the capital of Bavaria, the people stormed the arsenal, and forced from the king the concessions in question. The elector of Hesse-Cassel yielded, after a severe conflict. The king of Hanover also yielded, when he saw that resistance would have cost him his throne. Frederick William IV., of Prussia, vainly and foolishly resisted a popular revolution in Berlin. In Vienna, the capital of Austria, the citizens, headed by the students of the University, sympathized with the Parisians, and expressing themselves openly upon the great subject of reform, presented their petition for a constitutional government, a responsible ministry, liberty of the press, and religious freedom. After a formidable struggle in Vienna, during which many victims fell, the Emperor was compelled, on the 15th of March, to comply with the demands of the people. Also, the subjects of Ferdinand II., king of Naples and Sicily, had revolted early in 1848, and their request for a constitution was granted. That victory which had followed the popular commotions of France and Germany, was an inducement for the two southern duchies of Denmark, *Schleswig* and *Holstein*, to revolt. The duke of Augustenburg had already long, through speeches and periodicals, sown that seed of resistance and discord which now commenced to break out into acts of violence. The two Duchies, long, without any reason, dissatisfied with the Danish rule, and irritated by the refusal of the king to accede to any of their imperious demands, declared the new ministry appointed by Frederick VII. hostile to their privileges and themselves independent of Denmark. On the 24th of March, 1848, a message was written from Rendsburg to Copenhagen: "Schleswig-Holstein twenty-four hours ago became an independent state, shook off the Danish yoke, and appointed a provisional government." On the 25th of March, the duke of Augustenburg arrived in Rendsburg, where the provisional government resided, and the insurgents assembled under the command of his brother, Prince Frederick. On the 26th of March, there was written: "The king of Prussia has ordered his army to check the Danish troops, if they make their appearance."

The king of Denmark, Frederick VII., of course not

evincing any inclination to abate his pretensions to the Duchies, guaranteed him by England and France, and decidedly declining the admission of Schleswig into the Germanic Confederation, to which it had never belonged, marched his army into Schleswig, where it arrived between the 28th and 29th of March, under the command of the generals *Hedemann* and *Meza*. Meanwhile German volunteers, amongst whom were many enthusiastic young students, resorted now from all parts of Germany to assist the rebellious Duchies, whose interest they joined. The first battle between the Danes and the Schleswig-Holsteiners was fought at Bau, near to Flensburg, on the 9th of April, 1848. The battle was brief, but for its duration sanguinary enough; the insurrectional troops were entirely routed, and eight hundred prisoners of war carried to Copenhagen. From Prussia numerous troops now arrived, under the command of General Bonin, declaring that any attack of the Danish army on the Schleswig-Holsteiners would be regarded a declaration of war against Prussia. Easter Day, 23d of April, 1848, eleven thousand Danes, while preparing to attend divine service, were unexpectedly attacked by nineteen thousand Prussians, close by the city of Schleswig. The combat was very obstinate; the Danes, although fighting as madmen, and with the greatest contempt of death, were defeated, and General Hedemann had to yield to superior numbers; but, as the Roman senate formerly thanked Varro, *quia*

A.D., 1848.

A.D., 1848.

de republica non desperasset, so Frederick VII. rendered thanks to his soldiers for that bravery they had displayed at Schleswig—a good omen of future success.

Norway and Sweden now sided with the Danes, and two thousand Norwegians and Swedish volunteers arrived in Schleswig, to join the Danish army. Shortly after the unfortunate battle of Easter Day, the Danes gained a glorious victory at Düppel, 28th of May, A.D., 1848. over the Prussian general, Wrangel, though having a difficult game to play—twelve thousand Danes against sixteen thousand Prussians. Proposals of mediation were now made by Russia, which sided with Denmark, and on the 26th of August an armistice was agreed on. A.D., 1848. The insurgents, nevertheless, continuing to cherish a revolutionary spirit, and the partisans of anarchy taking advantage of the popular excitement, the king of Denmark declared, 26th A.D., 1849. of March, the armistice invalid, ordered the fortress of Fredericia to be more strongly fortified, and his army to enforce the royal authority, and prepared to strike a decisive blow against the insurgents, who at first gained some advantages at the towns of Ulderup and Kolding, and threw a strong garrison into Fredericia, which they seized. The Danes, seeing that no moment was to be lost, determined to defy the whole strength of the insurgents, and on the 6th of July A.D., 1849. the Danish army attacked the Schleswig-Holsteiners at Fredericia. The garrison was numerous, the resistance obstinate, and the insurgents fought as lions; but the Danish artillery made so dreadful a havoc in the hostile line, that after a most sanguinary combat, of more than eight hours' duration, the insurrectionary army was irretrievably ruined; six hundred of their best troops were left dead on the field, and two thousand were taken prisoners. The Danes lost three hundred men, and sixteen hundred severely wounded, but had to mourn over the loss of Olaf Rye, a native of Norway, one of their most gallant officers

Prussia having more seemingly than sincerely assisted the Schleswig-Holsteiners, now settled (10th of July) the preliminaries to a peace with Denmark, A.D. 1849. and a convention of truce, pursuant to which the king of Prussia promised to withdraw his forces, and no more to act in concert with the insurgents, whose affairs seemed to be more and more on the decline. Their chief leaders, the Duke of Augustenburg, and his brother, Prince Frederick of Nóer, to the latter of whom the insurgents had committed the command of their army, had, in a military point of view, accomplished very little, Prince Frederick being a wretch without spirit, courage, or tactical ability, who, after the lost battle of Bau, fled into the city of Flensburg, narrowly escaping being made prisoner; and the duke, for his personal safety, selecting the securer occupation to travel round to fan the flame of insurrection. The revolutionary spirit continued, and Schleswig-Holstein was in a ferment.

Through immense exertions the insurgents raised an army of thirty thousand men and eighty-two field-pieces, under the command of General Willison, and formed a bold plan for carrying on the war against Denmark; but the end of the mighty power, which the rebellious Duchies had tried to wield, was fast approaching.

As it was impossible, save in blood, to quench the revolutionary spirit, and compel the Duchies into subjection to their hereditary monarch, Frederick VII. ordered an army of thirty-eight thousand men and ninety-six great guns, to march out of the camp under the command of the noble and undaunted warrior, General *Krogh*, and the brave Assistant-General, *Schleppegrel*. On the 13th of July, 1850, the rebel troops crossed the Eider river, frequently skirmishing with the Danes, until, on the 24th of July, the royal army gained, at the town of *Idsted*, the most brilliant victory that had been obtained during the war, over the united forces of the Schleswig-Holsteiners. This dreadful battle, lasting two days without intermission, and attended with a most cruel carnage, cost Denmark three thousand six hundred and fifty-seven men and one hundred and forty officers; amongst whom were the magnanimous General Schleppegrel, and the skillful tactician, Colonel Læssóe.

The insurgents were, however, not yet tranquilized, but, to the inexpressible astonishment of every one, formed a new plan for the destruction of the Danes. On

A.D., the 29th of September, 1850, they laid a terrible
1850. siege to the city of *Frederickstad*, situated on the Eider. Through five days they showered fire-balls upon the unfortunate town, and vast clouds of smoke arose in awful sublimity over the bloody scene, until the Danish artillery, commanded by the courageous Norwegian, General *Helgesen*, after having made a most dreadful havoc amongst the insurgents, compelled them
A. D., to raise the siege and order a retreat. Finally,
1851. next year, on the 1st of February, 1851, after almost one continued battle of three years, the insurrection ceased, the royal authority and the whole state thus again being considered re-established.

But the turmoil of the war had not diverted the new ministry's attention from the internal affairs of the country. The free constitution, which the king had promised his subjects, had been elaborated and finished, to which, on the 5th of June, 1849, the royal signature was affixed; and the same year the possessions on the coast of Guinea, proving unprofitable to Denmark, were disposed of to England for the amount of ten thousand pounds sterling.

Frederick VII. having, when crown-prince, been twice married—first to the Danish princess, Wilhelmine, daughter of king Frederick VI., and then to princess Caroline Charlotte Mariane, daughter of the grand duke of Mecklenburg-Strelitz, but on account of domestic disagreement, divorced from both of them—was, 7th of

August, 1850, by the bishop, Dr. Mynster, solemnly joined in a morganatic marriage to Louise Christine, Countess of Danner, *née* Miss Rasmussen. She had, for some years back, kept a millinery shop in Copenhagen. Although thus not of royal blood, and, therefore, now and then overlooked by the aristocracy, she has, nevertheless, by her cultivated understanding and refinement of manners, exercised, and is still exercising, a very beneficial influence upon the king; and by her indefatigable munificence, she has gained the favor of the mass of the people, who have more and more reconciled themselves with the idea of their king's connecting himself with one of plebeian blood.

The insurrection having been crushed (1st of February, 1851), the cessation of hostilities taken place, and the king of Denmark thus having regained his authority over the Duchies, a treaty was concluded in London, on the 8th of May, 1852, between *Denmark, Sweden, Norway, England, Austria, France, Russia,* and *Prussia,* which yet more firmly than before by the peace of Fredericksborg in 1720, guaranteed the integrity of the Danish monarchy. Though a hollow reconciliation is thus established, the revolutionary spirit is still fermenting in the minds of the Schleswig-Holsteiners, waiting only for a favorable opportunity to break out into a new rebellion. The perfidious duke of Augustenburg, of course, deprived of his ducal possessions, and now an exile traveling round in Europe with the stigma of Judas Iscariot on his forehead, is still fanning the flame of rebellion; and what the future conceals in its bosom, He only knows, who, as David sings: "Shall strike through kings in the day of his wrath, and turn their hearts whithersoever he will."

"The gracious God," once said, metaphorically, the great *Talleyrand*, "has always a miracle in his pocket to save the little Denmark." Acquiescing in this conviction, I look safely forward to the fate of Denmark, my dearest native country, where my cradle was rocked, where I received blessings upon blessings, and the ingrafted word of God, which is able to save souls.

Thus have been sketched the leading events, political and civil, of the Scandinavian kingdoms, especially of Denmark, from her first feeble and scattered establishments to her formation into a prosperous and now highly enlightened nation. It depends, of course, upon the religion and morality of the people, these indispensable supports of political prosperity, whether the great problem of the possibility of a permanent and well-ordered constitutional monarchy shall be solved as the sincere friends of free institutions desire.

I conclude by commending the welfare of the three Scandinavian countries to the protection of the Almighty, entreating for them, and for their rulers, *Frederick the Seventh* and *Carl the Fifteenth*, His heavenly guidance and blessing.

THE END.